THE MICRO-POLITICS
OF CAPITAL

THE MICRO-POLITICS OF CAPITAL

Marx and the Prehistory of the Present

JASON READ

State University of New York Press

Cover art: "Rapture," by Jon Read.

Published by
State University of New York Press, Albany

For information, address State University of New York Press,
90 State Street, Suite 700, Albany, NY 12207

Production by Kelli Williams
Marketing by Patrick Durocher

Library of Congress Cataloging-in-Publication Data

Read, Jason.
  The micro-politics of capital : Marx and the prehistory of the present /
Jason Read.
    p. cm.
  Includes bibliographical references and index.
  ISBN 0-7914-5843-1 (alk. paper) — ISBN 0-7914-5844-X (pbk. : alk. paper)
    1. Marxian economics.   2. Philosophy, Marxist.   3. Economics—
Philosophy.   4. Capitalism—Political aspects.   5. Intellectual capital.
  6. Production (Economic theory).   7. Post-communism.
  8. Postmodernism.   9. Subjectivity.   10. Marx, Karl, 1818–1883.
  11. Althusser, Louis.   I. Title.

HB97.5.R42 2003
335.4'12—dc21

                                                                    2003050530

10 9 8 7 6 5 4 3 2 1

To my parents,
Robert Read and Deborah C. Arntz,
for their constant support.

CONTENTS

Introduction: There Is No Time Like the Present   1

1. The Use and Disadvantage of Prehistory for Life: Marx's "Pre-Capitalist
      Economic Formations" and the Constitution of the Subject of Labor

    Primitive Accumulation   19
    Immanent Causality   26
    The Prehistory of Capitalism   37
    Production   48
    Antagonistic Logic (Part One)   56

2. What Is Living and What is Dead in the Philosophy of Karl Marx:
      The Politics and Ontology of Living Labor

    Abstract Labor   61
    Living Labor   76
    Disciplinary Power   83
    Antagonistic Logic (Part Two)   90
    The Production of Subjectivity   98

3. The Real Subsumption of Subjectivity by Capital

    Real Subsumption   103
    The Fragment on Machines   114
    Immaterial Labor   122
    Subjectivity: From Reproduction to Production   135
    The Common   149

Conclusion   153

Notes   163

Bibliography   199

Index   209

ACKNOWLEDGMENTS

I thank Meredith Michaels and Bill Haver for helping me develop my questions and research at an early stage and, more important, for giving me at least the image of what it might mean to live a life dedicated to the practice of interrogation and reflection. I thank explicitly all of those who read and reread sections of this project in its many guises—from dissertation and manuscript to book—and provided criticism, commentary, and suggestions: Kira Brunner, Christopher Fynsk, Bill Haver, Michael Hardt, Lily Jacobs, Fouad Kalouche, Warren Montag, Robert Read, Stephen David Ross, and Hasana Sharp. I thank Ophelia Selam for helping me with my forays into the world of translation; "The Materialist Workshop" at State University of New York–Binghamton and all of the people who have been associated with that infamous title at one time or another (Peter Carlo, Alejandro de Acosta, Mark Frezzo, Pete Morse, Diana Taylor, Chad Wilson, Soenke Zehle, to name but a few), for providing fertile soil for the development of many of these ideas; Stefano Harney, Bill Martin, Gabrielle Soldatenko, Paul Zarembka, Laurie Ousley, The Brecht Forum, and The Graduate Group for Marxist Studies at the University of Buffalo for inviting me to present parts of my research. A special thank you to the students in my course on Marxism at the University of Southern Maine for their excitement, energy, and curiosity. Carol Varney provided a great deal of support, encouragement, and advice during the final days of preparing the manuscript, and I am eternally grateful for all of her help. Finally, I am very grateful for the patience and support of Jane Bunker and Kelli Williams at State University of New York Press.

INTRODUCTION

THERE IS NO TIME LIKE THE PRESENT

Marxist theory can fall behind history, and even behind itself, if it ever believes that it has arrived.

—Louis Althusser, "Is it simple to be a Marxist in Philosophy?"

The twentieth century really is incomprehensible. We could say, perhaps, that it does not exist, that it is merely a numerical abbreviation, an empty series, or a nominal expression. To a certain extent it is a repetition of the ideologies, hopes, and mystifications for which the nineteenth century is well known. However, the repetition of these elements has taken place at a faster pace and pushed them to their limit, in a word, made them extreme. Hence, such repetition represents a "temporal exasperation" that has launched us into the twenty-first century without having first let us emerge from the nineteenth.

—Antonio Negri, *The Politics of Subversion*

At the exact moment in time in which capitalism, as ideology, practice, and economy, has penetrated all dimensions of social life, announcing its victory on newsstands and broadcasts across the globe, the critique of capital, of political economy, has for the most part disappeared. The terms *class, class struggle, commodification, and exploitation* seem to ring hollow, as if they belonged solely to other places and times. This disappearance is readily explained by the voices of celebration; there was, after all, nothing to critique. The market is, and always was, synonymous with freedom. Rather than deal directly with such arguments and apologetics here, I would like to suggest another fundamentally different explanation for the paradoxical conjunction of the expansion of capital and the exhaustion of any critical vocabulary with which to confront it.

Capitalist production has undergone a profound mutation in the past thirty or so years. Stated briefly, it is no longer possible to separate capital, as the producer of goods and commodities, from what used to be called the superstructure: the production of ideas, beliefs, perceptions, and tastes. Capitalist production today has either directly appropriated the production of culture, beliefs, and desires or it has indirectly linked them to the production and circulation of commodities. It is difficult perhaps to think of any commodity that can be separated from its attendant "lifestyle" or subculture. In the advertisements and images of today's mass media it is not only the production process that has vanished, moved offshore, but it is also often difficult to find the commodities themselves: magazine ads instead illustrate a lifestyle, an image of cool, and it is that image that we are supposed to buy. This transformation also entails a fundamental mutation of labor: It is no longer simply physical labor power that is put to work but knowledges, affects, and desires. In short, capitalist production has taken on a dimension that could be described as "micro-political," inserting itself into the texture of day-to-day social existence and, ultimately, subjectivity itself. The old terms ring hollow because they are not yet attuned to the fact that not only has their object changed—we are no longer living in the nineteenth century—but the very terms of critique have changed as well. It is no longer possible to critique capital according to the grand schemes of universal history or to oppose it from the last vestiges of values and desires kept isolated from its sweeping mutations. Critique must become attuned to the micro-political dimension of capital, it must become what Michel Foucault called "a critical ontology of ourselves."

It remains unclear, however, on what level critical thinking should confront this reality. At first glance the focus on a transformation of the productive process would appear to lend itself to a sociological or economic discussion. In which case the transformation I have alluded to would lend itself to an empirically verifiable, or contestable, discussion regarding the status of the "new economy"; that is, the dominance of communication, information, and services over other types of production within the economy. At the same time, it would seem that in suggesting that this transformation is a mutation of the relationship between "subjectivity" and "production"—one that affects the fundamental human activities of perception, thinking, and acting—it extends beyond a simple alteration of tasks and priorities within something identified as the "economy"—a matter of how many people are employed producing goods, or services—to a fundamental transformation of the very structure, or basis, of human existence itself. Thus, in stating that critical thinking must confront this transformation, it would already seem that there is a deficiency at work within the very categories and divisions that pre-exist any such critical project. In other words, the very division between an economic analysis, which works with a determinate and demarcated area of existence—the economy as the sphere in which goods and services are produced and circulated— and a philosophical analysis—which deals with human perception, desires, and knowledge on the assumption that such are, at least implicitly, ahistorical—would act as a fundamental barrier to grasping the transformations of the present.

Perhaps it is this very division between the historically shifting realm of production and the timeless sphere of cultural values that Karl Marx sought to overcome with the term *mode of production*. Such a citation and suggestion that there is something useful, perhaps even indispensable, in Marx's concept or problem of the mode of production will no doubt seem anachronistic at best in the contemporary philosophical and theoretical climate. Anachronistic, not because it suggests the return to the mode of production debates of the 1960s and 1970s, themselves no doubt forgotten, but for the more fundamental reason that it suggests a continued philosophical, rather than simply sociological or economic, relevance for Marx's writing.

It is far beyond the scope of this book to take stock of the various declarations of the "Death of Marxism" and their histories, but it is worth noting, if only in passing, that one thing unifying the various positions on this debate is the assumption that Marx's thought leaves nothing for philosophy. Even for those in philosophy who remain sympathetic to some version of the Marxist political project, the name Marx stands either for an unthematized ethical complaint against the reality of exploitation or for the basic tools of a purely economic analysis. Beyond this, Marx's philosophy is limited to the earlier works on alienation, which reveal themselves to be nothing more than a spirited yet immature assault on G. W. F. Hegel. In fact much of "post-Marxism," specifically that of Ernesto Laclau, Chantal Mouffee, and Judith Butler, has remained relatively silent on what, if anything, Marx's later writings, *Capital* and the *Grundrisse*, offer for contemporary philosophical and political practice. Instead, post-Marxism takes its bearings from a history of political practice, most notably Antonio Gramsci's practice of hegemony; and it is more or less assumed that any engagement with Marx's writings, the analysis of the contradictory tendencies of the capitalist mode of production, can only result in the most reprehensible political and intellectual results.[1] It is assumed that if one reads Marx philosophically, all one will find is Hegel's subject of history rewritten for the revolutionary proletariat. It is not my intent to deal directly with the arguments of post-Marxism here, rather my goal is to produce a fundamentally different understanding of Marx.

This quiet omission of the philosophical arguments of Marx's texts cannot simply be attributed to a change in the philosophical climate, rather it relates to the problem I stated previously regarding the relationship between economic and philosophic critical inquiry. As I have stated, this division is perhaps detrimental to understanding changes in contemporary culture, politics, and ultimately existence, in which it becomes more and more difficult to maintain the categories of culture and the economy in some sort of hermetic isolation from each other. As much as such divisions, insofar as they are not subject to scrutiny and interrogation, prove to be liabilities in relation to understanding the world around us, they also stand in the way of grasping just what might be at stake in Marx's writing. Marx famously wrote in the eleventh thesis on Ludwig Feuerbach, "The philosophers have only interpreted the world in various ways; the point, however, is to change it." For many this statement would also constitute Marx's definitive condemnation of, and departure from, philosophy. Marx's later writings would then be understood as works in political economy, history, and political analysis. It was in part against this idea, which located Marx's philosophy solely in the early writings of the 1840s, that Louis Althusser developed his controversial thesis of Marx's "epistemological break," a fundamental change of orientation separating the young from the old Marx, the merit of which ultimately was to draw attention to the philosophical problems underlying such works as *Capital*.

If Althusser was right in underscoring the novel philosophical problems underlying Marx's later critique of political economy, then it must also be acknowledged that the philosophical problems are indissociable from a novel mode of exposition. In *Capital* and the *Grundrisse*, elements of philosophical speculation, of a philosophical anthropology and philosophy of history, intersect with concrete analyses of machinery, factory legislation, and political struggles. The latter are not merely illustrations or examples of the former but, fundamentally, alter the more general and perhaps properly philosophical statements.[2] This confrontation of philosophical speculation with the "facts" of various dimensions of existence is materialism in practice, a reflection of philosophy's demarcated place within a particular social situation, and at the same time it poses a particular challenge and difficulty for interpretation. In the words of Étienne Balibar, Marx's writing simultaneously "goes beyond philosophy," exposing the universal claims of philosophical knowledge to its particular historical and material conditions, and "falls short of philosophy," presenting statements regarding the nature of knowledge, and existence as seemingly arbitrary theses.[3]

It is at this point that we can turn to Marx's concept or problem of the mode of production and begin to understand it as a philosophical problem and not just as another name for economy or society. Marx used the term and concept "mode of production" to conceptualize the historically variable relation between a particular production of material existence, and a particular social order, including forms of consciousness. As Marx writes in a passage, which gives the most expansive presentation of this concept:

> In the social production of their existence, men inevitably enter into definite relations, which are independent of their will, namely *relations of production* appropriate to a given stage in the development of the material *forces of production*. The totality of these relations of production constitutes the economic structure of a society, the real foundation [*Basis*], on which arises a legal and political superstructure [*Überbau*] and to which correspond definite forms of social consciousness.[4]

This famous, or infamous figure of the edifice of base and superstructure establishes the centrality of the mode of production for Marx's thought of social relations, although it does so with some degree of ambiguity, or at least this ambiguity has been produced after the fact, so to speak, by the various interpretations of Marx's work. If one wanted to read this passage for a definition of the mode of production, then it is unclear if mode of production designates simply relations of production or the effects of these relations (and forces) of production on a political and legal superstructure and the corresponding forms of consciousness. The mode of production is at one and the same time a limited concept, referring to the relations of the economy, and an expansive concept, referring to the totality of the social.[5] In each case the position of consciousness or subjectivity is ambiguous: In the first, limited understanding it is not clear whether subjectivity can itself be included within the relations of production, while in the second, forms of consciousness arise from the base. The foundational role of the mode of production in Marx's thought is well documented, from the polemics against left Hegelianism which introduced the concept in *The German Ideology* to Marx's statements stressing the priority of the mode of production over class struggle (or the dependence of class struggle on a determinate phase mode of production). I could add, albeit a bit crudely, that without a thought of the mode of production as the material and historical ground of practice (including theoretical practice), Marx's philosophy and political work collapses into moralism (capitalism is bad) and (incorrect) prophecy. Despite, or perhaps because of, the centrality of the mode of production in Marx's thought, it cannot be reduced to a simple definition, its status in Marx's writing is more of a problem, or in Althusser's terms, a problematic: an apparatus for posing questions.

The problematic of the mode of production can at least be provisionally identified through four separate but interrelated elements: (1) The relation between consciousness (which may or may not be translated into more contemporary terms as either sociality or subjectivity) and production; (2) the relations between the different forms of "social practice": economic, legal, technological, and political, this "element" would necessarily include the actual and possible effects that these "practices" would have on each other; (3) a periodization of history into the different modes of production: communal, Asiatic, ancient, feudal, and capitalist, and the transitions, or revolutions, between these "modes"; (4) historicity, or, the tension of "reproduction" (or determination) and "dissolution" (or underdetermination) in every mode of production, and the coexistence of different modes at any point in history.

I should add that this list is perhaps drawn a bit too hastily. First, the neat numbered organization of the list overlooks the "uneven," "incomplete," and even conjunctural status of Marx's writing. These different elements are developed to different degrees at different points in Marx's writing in relation to different exigencies. For example, the problem of consciousness and its material production is not explicitly developed in much of Marx's writing, beyond the early texts such as *The German Ideology* which are concerned with the critique of philosophy, while the third and fourth elements of the problematic make up the bulk of *Capital*, which is concerned with the historicization and transformation of (or the rise and fall of) the capitalist mode of production. Second, such a list in its linear presentation eclipses the fact that there may be an implicit tension between these different elements. To return to and expand the example given: Beyond *The German*

Ideology, Marx's texts arguably do not offer much in terms of a theoretical inter-section of the production of consciousness and the transformation of the mode of production. The absence of such a relation in later texts, such as *Capital* which focus on the history and the historicity of the capitalist mode of production, would begin to suggest a possible tension between these two elements of the prob-lematic. The materialist production of ideas and subjectivity would then have a primarily didactic role, appearing primarily in Marx's conflict with German Ideal-ism, and is glaringly absent from the examination of the formation and conflicts of the capitalist mode of production. Thus the analysis of the production of con-sciousness, or subjectivity, would appear to be most absent where the current con-juncture would require it the most: in the interworkings of the capitalist mode of production.

Framed in such a way, as a series of problems, the mode of production takes its place in relation to a group of philosophers identified by the term *post-structuralism*—most notably Michel Foucault, Gilles Deleuze, and Félix Guattari (and to a lesser extent Jacques Derrida). In each of these writers one can find concepts such as 'ap-paratuses,' 'social machines,' and 'abstract machines,' which answer to the above set of problems: specifically the relationship between "consciousness," now called sub-jectivity, and its material conditions, and the articulation of the relation between different practices (political, economic, legal, and so on).

This similarity is perhaps the strongest in the case of Foucault, who has not only offered competing periodizations based on fundamental changes of power, rather than production (from the sovereign power of kings to the disciplinary powers of surveillance and control characteristic of modern states), but also shares something of a methodological similarity with Marx. Like Marx, Foucault was trained in philosophy but carried out his critique of contemporary society through the writing of histories, or genealogies, of the present. As Foucault writes, describ-ing his own intellectual project: "My books aren't treatises in philosophy or stud-ies of history; at most, they are philosophical fragments put to work in a historical field of problems."[6] Even though such a description may not correspond with the official version of Marxism, generally understood as the last philosophy *of* history, the explanation of all of history under the overarching logic of the "class struggle," such an idea of a philosophy *in* history, the working out of philosophical problems against concrete historical moments, could be productively used to understand Marx's own philosophical production. All of Marx's major concepts—'ideology,' 'commodity fetishism,' and 'mode of production'—as well as the fundamental in-terrupted status of his writing—the drafts left to the "gnawing criticism of mice" and the incomplete volumes of *Capital*—could perhaps be understood as reflec-tions of this fundamentally situated and conjunctural mode of thinking.

I do not want to suggest that this book has as its primary concern an attempt to adjudicate between Marxism and post-structuralism as methods or antagonistic camps within academia. It is, of course, quite possible that the vague similarity al-luded to above is nothing other than the fact that they are situated on the same ter-rain: the intimacy of adversaries. This book has a relation to a different provocation and a different sense of conjuncture, and it is against this conjuncture as backdrop that these various researches and provocations both take their bearing and measure their effectivity. It is quite possible that the question of the ultimate relationship between Marx and Foucault (or Deleuze, or Derrida, or Guattari) is unsolvable, but it is more than likely that framed in such a way, as a question of the relationship between Marx and this or that thinker or intellectual movement, the answer to such a question would have little bearing beyond the reconciliation of some academic debates and hostility.

What interests me are not the differences between post-structuralism and Marxism in themselves but the way in which their differences point to a lacunae that it is imperative to address today. On one side, stemming from Marx, there are the tools for an examination of the transformations and development of the capitalist mode of production in which subjectivity remains an afterthought or consequence, while on another side, stemming from Foucault and post-structuralist thinkers, there is an examination of the production of subjectivity as a "relation to self," which is examined apart from the transformation of capitalist valorization.[7] Thus despite the break with all previous methods and prejudices that are presumed to be involved with post-structuralism, we find ourselves in the grip of the division between the economy and culture. In the current conjuncture we find ourselves stranded between these two lines of investigation, unable to grasp the transformations of politics, culture, and the economy by new intersections of production and the production of subjectivity.

This book works in two simultaneous directions. The first is a reading of Marx for a theory of the production of subjectivity, a theory that exceeds any citation of the conceptual figures of forces and relations or base and superstructure. It might be more accurate to call this a "thought," or a "problem," of the production of subjectivity because Marx does not explicitly develop this theory; rather, it exists in the interstices and the points of tension and contact of his concepts. Thus, such an examination entails reading Marx "against the grain." Perhaps less against the grain of Marx than against much of the work on Marxism that finds in the early works an appeal to a humanist conception of subjectivity (necessarily preexisting its later alienation in an original fullness) and in the later works nothing but a purely economistic exposition of the laws of capitalist development. This reading against the grain is made possible by several texts that constitute provocations of sorts, including Foucault and other post-structuralists I mentioned previously and also the so-called structural Marxism of Althusser, Balibar, and Jacques Rancière; the "autonomist Marxism" of Antonio Negri, Mario Tronti, Leopoldina Fortunati, Maurizio Lazzarato, and Paolo Virno; as well as other writings in critical theory and feminist philosophy. These texts make possible the reading of Marx carried out here and, in turn, constitute virtual points of extension of concepts and problems drawn out from Marx's text.

The point, however, is not to distinguish between proper and improper interpretations of Marx, nor is it simply to chart out a history of interpretations as a history of truth and error ending with this book. Thus, the second dimension of the project extends this nascent theory of the production of subjectivity into a relation with contemporary interpretations of Marx and competing theories of the production of subjectivity. The point is to extend this reading of Marx into contact with the demands of the current conjuncture. The above statement regarding a "philosophy in history" functions not just as a description of Marx's method but as something of an ideal to which this project aspires: not to have the last word on the intellectual legacy of Marx's project but to read Marx, and Marxism, in such a way as to produce an understanding of the contradictory tendencies inhabiting the present.

The charge will perhaps be leveled that I have turned Marx into something of a post-Marxist, or post-structuralist *avant la lettre*; finding structures, aporias, and textual tensions where we know that one should find class struggle, contradiction, and actual history. Alternatively, others will argue that I have reduced Foucault, Deleuze, and others to nothing other than "crypto-Marxists" finding the stable presence of materialism and capital beneath the agonistic struggle of power and desire. Ideally, these two criticisms would cancel each other out, or at least turn back on themselves, revealing as much about the limitations and reified nature of academic categories as they indicate the limitations of this project. Beyond this there are two ways to answer these charges: First is to make sure that all of the philosophers involved (Marx, Foucault, and others), have said exactly what I have attributed to them. This book is marked by an almost obsessive attentiveness to the actual writing, and arguments, of Marx. It is important to actually read Marx, especially the unguarded Marx of the drafts of *Capital* and the *Grundrisse*, to get beyond the stale formulas of official and academic Marxism.

Second, this project constructs an intellectual history, or at least lineage. I have already stated that there is something of a shared intellectual legacy between Marx and post-structuralism, marked by a refusal of any appeal to transcendence (or an affirmation of immanence) and an attentiveness to the contingent historical production of supposedly ahistorical entities (such as the subject). More important, this general intellectual similarity, which will be expounded upon in the following pages, is itself a reflection of transformations in the history of the nineteenth and twentieth centuries, which is to say the history of capital. The transition from an examination of the mode of production to the production of subjectivity is itself a response to changes in capital itself: As capital moved deeper into the social networks that produce and reproduce life, critical thinking in part followed this migration, turning its attention to the production and reproduction of subjectivity. It is for this reason that Althusser's structuralist Marxism functions prominently in this book. Althusser's immense philosophical production functions as a "vanishing mediator" between the supposedly antagonistic camps of Marxism and post-structuralism.

A case in point, Althusser's most provocative philosophical concept 'structural, or immanent, causality,' a concept from which his later researches into "overdetermination" and the materiality of ideology follow, can be situated at the level of both a historical juncture, charting the development of contemporary capitalism, and a philosophical juncture, opening up later researches into "immanence" and the contradictory logics of Marx's text.[8] Althusser argued that *Capital* entailed a radical rethinking of causality, what he called structural or immanent causality. Rather than divide between a cause and its effects, a division which always posits effects as merely appearances of an underlying essence, immanent causality posits a cause that exists nowhere outside of its effects, which is another way of saying that all effects are equally and at the same time causes.

> This implies therefore that the effects are not outside the structure, are not a pre-existing object, element or space in which the structure arrives to *imprint its mark:* on the contrary, it implies that the structure is immanent in its effects, a cause immanent in its effects in the Spinozist sense of the term, that *the whole existence of the structure consists of its effects,* in short that the structure, which is merely a specific combination of its peculiar elements, is nothing outside its effects.[9]

Such a theory of causality destroys some of the most rigid hierarchies underlying most official "Marxist" ideas about the mode of production. If everything is immanent, both cause and effect, then it is no longer possible to understand the superstructure, the ideas and production of consciousness, as simple effects emanating from, or reflecting, the conflict between forces and relations of production. They must be understood as causes as well, as the constitutive conditions of the reproduction and the dissolution of a particular economy, or mode of production. There is no pure and simple economy that is transformed and altered by different cultures and belief systems; there exists only a mode of production, which is always already conditioned and undermined by a particular production of subjectivity. Immanent causality ultimately entails a reexamination of the materiality of subjectivity itself, the materiality of a "mode of subjection" existing alongside (and within) the mode of production. As Balibar writes, in a provocative formulation that offers an extreme illustration of the difference between immanent causality and the traditional Marxist schema:

> I even think that we can describe what such a schema would ideally consist of. It would not be the sum of a "base" and a "superstructure," working like complement or supplement of historicity, but rather the combination of two "bases" of explanation or two determinations both incompatible and indissociable: the *mode of subjection* and the *mode of production* (or, more generally, the ideological mode and the generalized economic mode). Both are material, although in the opposite sense. To name these different sense of the materiality of subjection and production, the traditional terms *imaginary* and *reality* suggest themselves. One can adopt them, provided that one keep in mind that in any historical conjuncture, the effects of the imaginary can only appear through and by means of the real, and the effects of the real through and by means of the imaginary; in other words, the structural law of the causality of history is the *detour through and by means of the other scene.* Let us say, parodying Marx, that economy has no more a "history of its own" than does ideology, since each has its history only through the other that is the efficient cause of its own effects.[10]

Thus, it is possible to recognize in immanent causality not only the precursor to Althusser's later investigation into the "materiality of ideology" but also something of the later importance of the problem of immanence and the production of subjectivity in contemporary post-structuralism. If immanent causality is founded on the rigorously materialist idea that materialism exceeds the production of things and includes the production and productivity of ideas, relations, and desires, then its necessary correlate is the assertion that "matter is discussed in many senses."[11] The materiality of subjectivity is not said in the same sense as the materiality of production, of machinery and relations of power, and this difference is not historically static. Immanent causality opens up the question of the materiality, or effectivity, of the different dimensions of society.

Extending the concept of immanent causality into the problem of the production of subjectivity entails going beyond Althusser's development of the concept; however, this "going beyond Althusser" works in two directions at once: via an examination of those who Althusser influenced (notably Balibar, but less famously Deleuze and Guattari) while at the same time returning, as it were, to the scene of the crime—to Marx's original texts. As I argue in the following chapters it is possible to reinterpret Marx's epochal distinction between precapitalism and capitalism, as well as his distinction between formal subsumption of capital and the complete, or real, subsumption, in light of the fundamental difference of the "effectivity" of subjectivity.

In precapitalist modes of production, productive activity is subordinated to the reproduction of a particular form of life, and particular structures of subjectivity. As Marx argues, in the ancient world new developments of production are subordinated to the demand to produce and reproduce "citizens." In the capitalist mode of production, production is no longer fettered to the reproduction of any particular structure of belief, desire, or tradition. As Marx famously wrote in the *Communist Manifesto*, with capital "all that is solid melts into air," all of the traditions and mystifications of previous modes of production are destroyed by the cash nexus, by the fact that everything has its price. The capitalist mode of production is itself founded on an "abstract subjective potential," the capacity to do any work whatsoever, which it must simultaneously develop, through discipline and cooperation, and contain, through discipline and various techniques of subjectification. At least, I will argue, this general schema remains true for what Marx calls "formal subsumption," the earliest form of capitalism made possible by the imposition of the wage on preexisting social and technological structures. As for real subsumption, or what Marx sometimes calls the "specifically capitalist mode of production," subjectivity is not reproduced but is made directly productive, not in the form of an abstract potentiality but in the form of knowledge, desires, and affects. It is this concept of Marx that comes closest to at least opening up some of the questions of the present. However, my point here is not to provide a complete summation of the following research, just to indicate that the immanence of subjectivity to the mode of production is not a simple fact, stated once and for all, but a problem that opens up an examination of the differential relation of subjectivity and production within the different modes of production.

The differential analysis of the relation between the mode of subjection and the mode of production, to follow Balibar's terms, is not to be confused with a functionalist understanding of society. It is not simply that capital, or any other mode of production, produces the sort of subjects it needs in an infinite act of self-production. In such a view every difference, all antagonism, would only serve to reproduce the system; a point of view that has become more and more popular in these pessimistic times. Rather, such an understanding, the recognition of subjectivity as simultaneously effect and cause, makes possible an understanding of the nonidentity of effect and cause.[12] As I will argue in the following chapters, the production of subjectivity always simultaneously exceeds and falls short of the demands of the specific: in this case, capitalist mode of production. The recognition of the multiple effects of the mode of production as causes implied by the very idea of immanent causality does not finalize the idea of functionalism but explodes it, making possible multiple examinations into the historicity and contingency of any mode of production.

The general recognition of the fact that the most ephemeral and fleeting dimensions of existence, the desires and beliefs that constitute subjectivity, are the material conditions of transformations in production is itself occasioned by the transformation of capital itself: the commodification of knowledge, desire, and sexuality. The opposition that is assumed to exist between these two camps only exists if one excludes not only Althusser's writings, and the writings of his circle, but the history that is traversed in this writing.[13] If one wanted to continue with such an intellectual history, starting from Althusser's writing on immanent causality in the 1960s, then it is possible to trace a history of the problem of immanence continuing through continental philosophy and post-structuralism throughout the end of the last century.[14] Deleuze and Guattari's formulation regarding the immanence of desire to all social relations, or Foucault's assertion regarding the immanence of power to subjectivity and knowledge, can be understood as not only inheriting Althusser's intellectual legacy, but as inheriting the same problem as well: thinking resistance when, as Fredric Jameson argued, those last reservoirs of transcendence, nature and the unconscious, have been thoroughly commodified and exploited.[15]

Moreover, in the former authors, the rejection of a traditional Marxist enquiry into the exploitation of labor takes the form of the redefinition of an expansive sense of production: the production of desire or the productivity of power relations. There is a critique of the idea of production, or labor, as an anthropological constant that opens up the possibility of an exploration of the "productivity" and materiality of multiple dimensions of human existence.[16] The rejection of an anthropological and instrumental "schema" of labor, a subject working on an object through the use of an instrument, would historically coincide with the rise of a "services-" and "knowledge-" based economy in which labor has expanded to include the production of subjectivity (tastes, desires, concepts) by subjectivity. From the perspective of an intellectual history such an overlap is perhaps more than a coincidence. However, I am not primarily concerned with the construction of such an intellectual history; rather, I am concerned with how situating the work of Althusser, Foucault, Deleuze, and Guattari in relation to Marx's concept, or problem, of the mode of production overcomes the theoretical impasse I have introduced.

The concept of immanent causality does not simply introduce a general continuity between seemingly opposed modes of inquiry (a continuity that is obviously more complex and vexed than I have suggested here). To produce this concept Althusser must apply a particular strategy of reading to Marx's writing based on Marx's own engagements with the texts of political economy. Marx was not content to simply correct the errors and argue with the assertions of bourgeois political economy; instead, he critically excavated the unconscious theoretical presuppositions of political economy: its anthropology and philosophy of history. Althusser named this mode of reading for the unstated presuppositions and limitations of a particular text "symptomatic reading" *(lecture symptomale)*. He applied this method to Marx's own works, primarily *Capital*, works which were seen by many to be works of political economy and thus entirely outside of philosophy, to produce immanent causality as a concept of the articulation of social relations. A symptomatic reading produces the concept of immanent causality through attentiveness to the unstated presuppositions and problematics of Marx's own thought. Marx never approaches the concept or term immanent causality, rather, it is written between the lines of the various philosophical statements and concrete investigations, from an anthropology of labor to historical documents on the struggle over the working day, that comprise the text of *Capital*.

By focusing on the overall articulation of Marx's thought, Althusser (along with such fellow travelers as Balibar, Rancière, and Pierre Macherey) definitively broke with some of the more intellectually impoverished hermeneutic strategies that have constituted the history of Marxism; strategies that cite one or two of the bolder statements from such texts as the "Manifesto" as "decoders" for the entire corpus. More important, in later works Althusser (and Balibar) expanded this attentiveness to the "logic" of Marx's writing to an examination of the tension between the different philosophical, political, and historical exigencies at work within it. Whereas Althusser's earlier works attempted to construct the unity of Marx's thought against the deviations of Marxism, both Soviet and Western, the latter strategy attempted to recognize that these so-called deviations (namely, "economism" and "humanism") were possibilities produced by Marx's own writing. The attentiveness to the overall logic or articulation of Marx's writing, which produced the concept immanent causality, then produces the possibility of a recognition of the multiple logics in Marx's writing and the tensions between them. This is not necessarily a limitation, nor is it the condition of only a perpetual gesture of theoretical humility, rather, it is the condition of a reading of Marx that can be innovative: the absence of doctrine makes possible a reading that is *productive* (of concepts, problems, questions) rather than *reproductive* (of doctrine). Once the question of a definitive interpretation is dropped (as well as the related question of establishing a truly Marxist pedigree), it becomes possible to read Marx to produce concepts in light of the demands of the present.

The autonomist Marxism (or *Operaismo*) of Tronti, Negri, Virno, and Mariarosa Dalla Costa also plays a fundamental role in developing this book. Like the so-called structural Marxism of Althusser and Balibar, autonomist Marxism brings a novel hermeneutic and ontological perspective to Marx's texts, and like structural Marxism such a perspective works to unravel the division between the base, understood as the production of things, and the superstructure, understood as the production of subjectivity or consciousness. However, it is not possible to extend this symmetry to argue for a "genealogical" position as an overlooked point of transition within current intellectual history. For the most part post-structuralism and post-Marxism have completely overlooked autonomist Marxism, the only significant exception being Deleuze and Guattari who draw from Tronti and Negri in significant ways.[17]

In Althusser and Balibar the point of convergence between the hermeneutic and the ontological, or between an interpretive strategy and a fundamental redefinition of materiality, was immanent causality, while in Tronti and Negri a similar point of convergence has been named the "autonomist hypothesis." Basically stated the autonomist hypothesis is the assertion that resistance, the resistance of the working class, precedes and prefigures the transformations and development of the capitalist mode of production.[18] In this view it is not capital itself that is revolutionary, transforming the technical and social dimensions of its mode of production and moving to cover the world, rather, it is forced to change and transform itself by its antagonistic confrontation with subjective labor power.

The clearest example of the way in which such antagonisms ultimately transform the capitalist mode of production is Marx's documentation of the struggle over the length of the working day and the resulting legislation (discussed in chapter 2). The assembling of a group of worker's on the space of a factory floor brings together a network of cooperation that, although put to work for capital, is not reducible to such an effect. This "cooperative subjectivity" puts its powers and energies to work struggling against the length of the working day. The successful legislation of a shortened working day leads to a reorganization of the capitalist mode of production: It is the passage from a regime of extensive exploitation to a regime of intensive exploitation, labor is made more productive in a shorter time through the use of machinery, and so forth. What is important about this example, an example which I argue illustrates and animates much of Marx's thought of resistance, is not the irony of history nor the cunning of reason but the relationship between antagonism and the constitution of the capitalist mode of production. The shortened working day does not resolve the issue but makes possible new conflicts, new antagonisms, over such things as the technological transformations of the workspace with their accompanying transformations of the pace and structure of work. As Negri writes, "Every constitution of a new structure is the constitution of antagonism."[19]

The autonomist hypothesis expands and deepens what is traditionally gestured at through the class struggle: the antagonism constituent of the capitalist mode of production. It converts what sometimes risks becoming a simple metaphor—of two great classes locked on the field of battle—to a concrete analysis of the interlocking tactics of resistance and exploitation. These tactics are located on the "micro" scale of the factory and shop floors, where a variety of technologies and techniques are employed to convert the heterogeneous bodies, hands, and minds assembled there into a calculable commodity called "labor power." Thus, there is a point of critical comparison between an understanding of the "antagonistic" dimension of capital and Foucault's analytics of power. The current opposition between an analysis that focuses on power and an analysis of the capitalist mode of production (generally understood to be the current restaging of the longstanding conflict between Marx and Max Weber or Marx and Friedrich Nietzsche) proves to be itself the byproduct of contemporary prejudices and distinctions, rather than unavoidably inscribed in the world itself. At the same time an understanding of the antagonistic constitution of capital is not simply limited to the factory floor, a site that risks becoming a dangerous fetish in an age in which capital has extended well beyond the walls of the factory to encompass all of social space.

According to the autonomist hypothesis the transformation of capital, its extension into new spaces and technologies, is the effect and displacement of prior conflicts. The modern high-tech productive processes conceal and maintain the traces of past struggles. The capitalist mode of production is transformed by these struggles, and as it changes the very terms of conflict change as well. Thus, as I will argue in the following chapters, the autonomist hypothesis makes it possible to extend and transform the antiquated schema of class struggle into the contemporary networks and relations of twenty-first-century capital. As with the example of the struggle of the working day, these contemporary struggles increasingly involve contestations over subjectivity, over how the knowledges, desires, and relations of labor are to be utilized or exploited. As I argue in the final chapter, antagonism "against capital" nowadays is often framed around the expropriation and exploitation of social activity at its most basic level: of knowledge, desire, and communication.

If the autonomist hypothesis seems too difficult to reconcile with much of what has been written under the official name of Marxism, a discourse that despite its (over)stated intention to overthrow capitalism seems to almost masochistically delight in the image of the pervasive power of capital, it is because excavating this perspective requires a critical strategy of reading. It requires a sort of symptomatic reading that can extract the figure and force of antagonism in such passages as the pages Marx devotes to "primitive accumulation" (the violence necessary to destroy precapitalist social relations), the struggle over the length of the working day, and the conflict over machinery. In these passages, which constitute something of a minor logic of Marx's writing, there is an analysis of the manner in which the subjectivity of the working class, the demands and desires of what Marx at times calls "living labor," functions as both the condition and limit to the development of the capitalist mode of production. (This symptomatic reading extends beyond the completed volume of *Capital* to include the notes and drafts compiled in the *Grundrisse,* drafts which are more attentive to the disruptive power of living labor power.) As with immanent causality the autonomist hypothesis challenges the very idea of capitalism as functioning like an economy, a self-sufficient series of market relations that function as "natural laws" of society, by exposing the antagonistic and overdetermined historicity of the formation and development of capitalism.

However, there would appear to be a significant difference between the two interpretive strategies, which will be negotiated in the following pages. To state this difference crudely, whereas immanent causality ultimately demonstrates that the mode of production itself depends on the production of subjectivity, on the production of a subject that in Marx's terms regards the requirements of the capitalist mode of production as "self-evident natural laws," the autonomist hypothesis posits the massive productive power of subjectivity, of living labor, underlying and making possible the immense production of wealth in capitalism. These two different strategies can be understood to relate to two different senses of the genitive. On the one hand, there is a line of thought, stemming from Althusser, that focuses on how subjectivity is produced by the multiple strategies, ideologies, and technologies of capital, while on the other hand, there is a tradition of thought extending through Tronti and Negri that focuses on the immense productive power of subjectivity underlying capital. Although it could be possible to oppose these two perspectives as two different theoretical points of view, corresponding to pessimism and optimism, alternatively, it is ultimately more productive to trace them through a critical reading of Marx's texts. It is only through this reading that it is possible to arrive at an understanding of the current conjuncture in which it is more and more clear that the world is made and transformed by the immense powers of labor, which produce not only the wealth of objects but also the knowledge, affects, and desires that constitute the lived world, and yet capital's domination of the productive power seems to me more and more entrenched. To think and engage with this contradictory identity of "subjection" and "subjectification," which would seem to characterize the present, it is necessary to bring these strategies and perspectives together.

My point, here in the introduction, is first to demonstrate that the various intersections between Marx, Althusser, Negri, Tronti, Foucault, Deleuze, and others explored in the following chapters is not just the byproduct of a sort of theoretical eclecticism; rather, there are strong philosophical undercurrents and conflicts linking these various perspectives. That these conceptual undercurrents are eclipsed by the contemporary categories, and intellectual shorthand used to make sense of the present, does not mean that they do not exist. More important than any such intersections is that these intersections point to a problem that I argue is essential for any attempt to philosophically grasp the present: the production of subjectivity. Thus at the same time that I have sketched out a dim outline of the intellectual histories and trajectories underlying this book, I have stressed that I am not interested in simply producing the sort of intellectual "counter-history" that breaks apart the oppositions of the present. The problem and hypothesis that I am developing here—that capitalism as a mode of production cannot be critically grasped except as a production of subjectivity—will ultimately have to be judged on its own merits, as an interpretive strategy for approaching Marx, for understanding the political and philosophical exigencies underlying much of contemporary philosophy (what used to be called "theory"), and for understanding the present itself. That is, the production of subjectivity will have to be understood according to its "use value," for the possibilities it opens in the present.

OUTLINE OF THE CHAPTERS

The first chapter lays out both the general strategy of reading and argumentation used throughout the book and introduces the intersecting problems of the mode of production and subjectivity. It does so, however, not through a general discussion or overview of Marx's writing but through a reading of two texts: the chapters on primitive accumulation in *Capital* and the notebooks entitled "Pre-Capitalist Economic Formations" in the *Grundrisse.* The selection of these texts serves to illustrate the tension between different logics in Marx's writing. Second, these texts pose, in a unique way, the problem of the relationship between the mode of production and subjectivity. The chapters on primitive accumulation do so primarily in a negative way; that is, insofar as these chapters are poised critically against the myth of "so-called primitive accumulation" underlying classical political economy, they criticize not only the overt ideology of this myth but also its implicit anthropology. Central to this anthropology, which argues that capitalism is founded on the thrift of the first proto-capitalist, is the underlying idea of a subject that acts on history insofar as he or she is posited outside of history. Marx's account of primitive accumulation overturns not only the image of the idyllic origins of capitalism but also, in stressing the complex and overdetermined conditions of the emergence of capitalism, posits another theory of the relationship between subjectivity and history. In these chapters Marx breaks with both the implicit idea of a transcendental subject underlying classical political economy (of course this idea extends far beyond political economy) and any conception of a subject of history to stress the material constitution of subjectivity. At the origin of the capitalist mode of production Marx does not find the intentions of a subject producing history, the myth of the first capitalist, but rather the complex history that expropriated peasants and transformed them into the first subjects of labor.

Marx's theory of primitive accumulation moves in a primarily negative direction, critiquing the idea of subjectivity underlying not only classical political economy but ultimately much of official Marxism as well. In these chapters we see how subjectivity, the laboring subject necessary for capitalist accumulation, is constituted through the violence of history but not how it is constitutive; it is viewed as effect but not as cause. The notebooks on "Pre-Capitalist Economic Formations" move in a primarily affirmative manner, sketching out the outlines of a relation between the mode of production and subjectivity, in which the latter is not simply an effect of the former but is itself fully implicated within the generation and corruption of the mode of production. The various precapitalist modes of production are founded on the reproduction of a particular form of sociality. They are threatened as much by the breakdown of the subjective conditions of reproduction as they are by the objective conditions of production. In other words, a collapse in the structures of belief and desire—for example, the belief in the power of despot—is just as threatening to the reproduction of the precapitalist modes of production as a transformation of the economic relations. Marx's notebooks on "Pre-Capitalist Economic Formations" assert in an uncompromising way the materiality of subjectivity.

Chapter 2 takes its general bearing from the problem elaborated in chapter 1, the relations between the mode of production and the modality of subjection, at the same time articulating the relation between this general problem and the transition that Marx's "Pre-Capitalist Economic Formations" foregrounds: the transition from precapitalist to the capitalist modes of production. As Marx argues in "Pre-Capitalist Economic Formations" the precondition of the capitalist mode of production is the "dissolution" of the previous mode of production, most importantly the dissolution of any relation (property or community) that would connect the worker with the conditions of production. Thus the task of this chapter is to continue to develop the concept of the materiality of subjectivity developed in the reading of Marx's texts on precapitalist economic formations, while at the same time investigating the fundamental transformation that capitalism is in the production of subjectivity.

The capitalist mode of production is founded on an abstract subjective potential, the indifferent capacity to do work, and it is this capacity that must be simultaneously produced and contained. Capitalism must simultaneously develop the flexibility, cooperative networks, and potentiality of the subjectivity of labor while at the same time reducing the possibility for conflict and antagonism. Marx develops an understanding of this contradictory tendency through the concepts of 'abstract labor' and 'living labor.' I argue that a close reading of the intersections and contradictions of these concepts, a reading which interprets *Capital* against the backdrop of the *Grundrisse*, makes possible an examination of what I call the "antagonistic logic of capital." In the first instance this antagonist logic gives a certain primacy to struggle and conflict, not as events framed against the indifferent backdrop of the development of the capitalist mode of production but as constitutive of the capitalist mode of production. Second, this antagonistic logic is riddled with detours and unintended effects, for example, the struggle over the working day produces as unintended consequences the social and technological "fine-tuning" of the capitalist mode of production. Through the antagonistic logic of capital it is possible to read the development of the capitalist mode of production as something other than its continual self-perfection; that is, it is possible to read it as produced from intersecting and antagonistic tendencies. More important, these tendencies increasingly intersect with the production of subjectivity, in both senses of the term. Thus, it is possible to see in the history and historicity of the capitalist mode of production not the inevitable progression of the laws of the economy but the deepening conflict over the subjectivity and sociality of labor.

If, as I argue in the second chapter, the capitalist mode of production is constituted by antagonistic strategies, then this must necessarily alter how one views the concept of the 'real subsumption' of society by capital. Marx used this concept to name the end point of the tendency of the capitalist mode of production: the point at which capital no longer simply subjects a preexisting social and technical order of production to the formal conditions of the wage and commodity production but, rather, creates its own technological and social conditions. Viewed from the perspective of the antagonistic logic of capital, from the massive subjective potential that subtends the capitalist mode of production, it becomes necessary to produce the other, antagonistic side of the concept. I argue that this "other side" can best be examined through the position of subjectivity in real subsumption. In real subsumption, subjectivity is paradoxically placed in a position of both maximum power, as capital depends more and more on the cooperative networks of living labor, and maximum subjection, as this cooperative power is continually seen as the power of capital.

Unpacking, or moving beyond, this paradox of power and subjection entails reworking Marx's concepts of 'production,' 'fixed capital,' and 'consumption.' This reworking is necessary to chart the fundamental transformation of labor in real subsumption. Labor is no longer isolated in the factory or in other spaces but is extended across the social fabric to include the productive powers of knowledge, desire, and communication. Thus it is necessary to wrest Marx's concepts from the model of the factory, and of factory production, which silently holds sway over them. It is a matter of understanding the predominance of immaterial labor, or what could be called the "production of subjectivity by subjectivity." Ultimately it is a matter of rethinking the place of subjectivity in the mode of production. In real subsumption, subjectivity (in the sense of specific modes of subjection) is no longer reproductive for capital but rather becomes directly productive. What capital puts to work are the lifestyles, desires, and knowledges that are formed outside of it.

In this chapter, it is much less a question of tracing a logic of antagonism, since that requires a retrospective position on the manner in which certain tendencies have run their course, but of engaging with the difference of real subsumption. It is a matter of charting the possibilities, the fault lines, and the spaces and stakes of new struggles.

One

The Use and Disadvantage of Prehistory for Life

Marx's "Pre-Capitalist Economic Formations" and the Constitution of the Subject of Labor

---

In every moment of the development of the capitalist mode of production, capital has always proposed the form of cooperation. This form had to be functional with the form of exploitation when it did not actually inhere within it. It was only on this basis that labor became productive. Likewise, in the period of primitive accumulation, when capital enveloped and constricted pre-existent labor forms to its own valorization, it was capital which posed the form of cooperation—and this consisted in the emptying of the pre-constituted connections of the traditional laboring subjects.

—Antonio Negri, *Twenty Theses on Marx*

PRIMITIVE ACCUMULATION

It is a matter of common knowledge that Karl Marx presents the difference between his analysis and all previous (bourgeois) understandings of political economy as a historical versus an ahistorical conception of capitalism. What is considerably less certain is how Marx, or those who came after him, understood this disparity; that is, What are its theoretical grounds and what were or could be its effects in the realm of philosophy, historical understanding, and political practice? There have been many interpretations of this difference; in this day and age this difference is often represented as either an incorrect prophecy (capitalism will collapse) or a contribution to a vague and inconsequential awareness of history (something, some economy existed before capitalism). If it is possible today to propose another thought of the distinction between Marx and political economy, or to attempt to reanimate the question, problem, and lines of investigation from behind this accepted bit of academic common sense, I would suggest that for Marx this difference, the difference history makes, has entirely different grounds, and different effects, than mere prophesy, transforming what is understood by society, materiality, power, and subjectivity.

To begin to grasp this difference it is necessary to pose the question of what is at stake in what Marx called the "mode of production." The mode of production, specifically the capitalist mode of production, was the name that Marx gave his particular object, and it is from this object that Marx proposes an understanding of history, politics, and the possibility of political practice. Furthermore, it is through a definition of this particular "theoretical object" that Marx develops a critique of the objects of idealist philosophy and bourgeois political economy, objects conventionally known as "society" and the "economy."[1] This critique is most overtly aimed at the political motivations at work in the manner in which the bourgeoisie understood its object (it almost goes without saying that the bourgeoisie had an interest in understanding capitalism as eternal) or what is commonly referred to as "ideology critique" in its most banal and basic sense. However, Marx's criticism goes beyond the simple investigation of political interest to indicate the unexamined presuppositions of the objects of bourgeois economics and philosophy. One such presupposition was the understanding of human nature that silently supported the theoretical space of classical bourgeois political economy. "Human nature" here is intended in a broad sense to include not only the particular philosophical anthropology that provides classical political economy with its alibis and justifications but also the more practical problem of the place of human desires, motivations, and beliefs (or subjectivity) in history: their conditions, limitations, and effects.

Marx's critique of the conceptions of human nature and subjectivity supporting bourgeois political economy, as well as his development, albeit partial and often incomplete, of a radically different thought of the historicity and materiality of subjectivity, are perhaps nowhere more forcefully developed than in the points where Marx presents his account of the formation of the capitalist mode of production and its radical difference from all prior modes of production. I am referring here to the final chapters of the first volume of *Capital* and the notebooks entitled "Pre-Capitalist Economic Formations" in the *Grundrisse* and suggesting that these texts be read as something more than elements of a world history or speculative anthropology; that is, as contributions to an understanding of the materiality of social relations and subjectivity and, ultimately, despite appearances, to an understanding of the capitalist mode of production itself.

This intersection of historical formation and contemporary existence is underscored continually throughout Marx's critique of so-called primitive accumulation [*sogenannte ursprünglichen Akkumulation*]. So-called primitive accumulation, which is sometimes called "previous or original accumulation," is the answer posed by political economy to a seemingly irresolvable problem: The fact that capitalist production would continually presuppose itself, it presupposes wealth in the hands of capitalists as well as a population of those who have nothing but their labor power to sell. These elements, capital and workers, are the preconditions of any capitalist production, yet they cannot be explained from it. Capitalist accumulation would seem to be something of an infinite regress, always presupposing its own conditions. To accumulate capital it is necessary to possess capital. There must then be an original or previous accumulation, one that is not the result of the capitalist mode of production but rather its point of departure and that constitutes the originary differentiation between capital and workers. This foundational distinction has generally been understood by political economy as a moral difference. As Marx writes:

> This primitive accumulation plays approximately the same role in political economy as original sin does in theology. Adam bit the apple, and thereupon sin fell on the human race. Its origin is supposed to be explained when it is told as an anecdote about the past. Long, long ago there were two sorts of people; one the diligent, intelligent, and above all frugal elite; the other lazy rascals, spending their substance, and more, in riotous living. The legend of theological original sin tells us certainly how man came to be condemned to eat his bread in the sweat of his brow; but the history of economic original sin reveals to us that there are people to whom this is by no means essential. Never mind! Thus it came to pass that the former sort accumulated wealth, and the latter sort finally had nothing to sell except their own skins.[2]

Thus, as much as so-called primitive accumulation posits a theory of the formation of the capitalist mode of production, albeit one predicated on a presupposed division between the diligent and the lazy, it turns this explanation toward the present in the form of a moral tale. The origin provides the present with a moral alibi, dividing the capitalist and the worker along the lines of the good and the bad.

Not only does the theory of so-called primitive accumulation function in the present, aiming for the present or a particular moral characterization of the present, it never leaves the present even as it offers itself as history. So-called primitive accumulation takes the idealized memory of an individual capitalist's accumulation—saving money, which itself is a morally coded, or best case (ideological), presentation of accumulation within capital—and turns it into the conditions of capitalist accumulation in general. It mistakes this memory for history, the conditions *within* capitalist accumulation for the conditions *of* capitalist accumulation. Étienne Balibar asserts that, "The analysis of primitive accumulation thus brings us into the presence of the radical *absence of memory* which characterizes history (memory being only the reflection of history in certain predetermined sites—ideology or even law—and as such, anything but a faithful reflection)."[3] As a theory of the capitalist mode of production, so-called primitive accumulation constitutes a failure to think different conditions, limitations, and effects in history, or to think history as difference—a failure that is perhaps not entirely explained by self-interest. So-called primitive accumulation can only extend the conditions of the capitalist mode of production infinitely backward in time: Capitalism was (and always will be) possible; to become real, it only required the industriousness and intelligence of the first capitalist.

The fantasy of the thrifty proto-capitalist, whatever its function as nursery tale may be within the schoolbooks and ideologies of capital, is wholly inadequate to the task of accounting for the formation of the capitalist mode of production. The accumulation of money without the conditions to transform it into capital, such as workers or those who have only their labor power to sell, is not capitalist accumulation but "hoarding" [*Shatzbildung*] (CI 227/144). For Marx hoarding is a subjective disposition toward money, and in part produced by money, prior to capital; that is, prior to the possibility of investment or surplus value. Hoarding as a disposition is constituted by money and its particular character of being qualitatively without limits—it has the power to stand in for any other commodity, for anything desired—and quantitatively limited, one always has a particular finite amount of money.

What is interesting for our purpose here is that Marx's deduction of the affective comportment of hoarding from the money form as an unstable combination of work, thrift, and greed reproduces at least a certain presupposition or assumption of the theory of so-called primitive accumulation—that desire and will are themselves sufficient to generate history—but it does so parodically as farce. Without the proper historical conditions the "miser's" desire for accumulation is destined only to collide into certain structural limits. As Marx states, "This contradiction between the quantitative limitation and the qualitative lack of limitation of money keeps driving the hoarder back to his Sisyphean task: accumulation. He is in the same situation as a world conqueror, who discovers a new boundary with each country he annexes" (CI 230/146). Assuming that hoarding or the desire for wealth is in some sense contemporary with the money form, and thus preexists capital, it is possible to invert Marx's formula and argue that farce comes before tragedy.[4] (The comic image of the miser with his bags of money comes before the tragedy of capitalist accumulation and massive expropriation.) The questions then become: Under what conditions, and through what other causes, is this desire actualized? How does accumulation cease to be the dream of the hoarder and become an effective practice, one that constitutes an entire mode of production?[5]

For money to constitute capital and for the desire to hoard to constitute capitalist accumulation, there must be the conditions for its investment; that is, the capitalist must be able to purchase both the means of production and labor. These elements must be dissociated from any form of property or social relation that would leave the means of production, tools, or the land in the hands of the producers. Thus, there are at least two conditions of the formation of the capitalist mode of production. As Marx writes, in a deceptively simple and frequently repeated formula:

In themselves, money and commodities are no more capital than the means of production and subsistence are. They need to be transformed into capital. But this
transformation can itself only take place under particular circumstances [*bestimmten
Umständen*], which meet together at this point: the confrontation of, and the contact between, two very different kinds of commodity owners; on the one hand, the
owners of money, means of production means of subsistence, who are eager to val-
orize the sum of values they have appropriated by buying the labor-power of others;
on the other hand, free workers, the sellers of their own labor-power, and therefore
the sellers of labor. (CI 874/742).

The capitalist mode of production, the definition of which we are approaching
through this seemingly simple fact, are formed by the conjunction of possessors of
money and those who have only their labor power to sell. Marx calls this second
group free or "bird-free" [*vogelfrei*], meaning at one and the same time, that while
they are not property (as slaves) they are themselves without property and cast out of
the human community, as a community of property owners—uprooted (or deterritorialized). The conjunction of these two elements, as the necessary or minimal constitution of capitalist accumulation, indicate that the capitalist mode of production
cannot, in either its constitution or definition, be considered as a simple effect of one
term or element—it is a relation, or an ensemble of relations.[6]

To argue that the capitalist mode of production ought to be grasped as an "ensemble of relations" is in a primary and almost entirely negative (or critical) sense
to separate a thought of the capitalist mode of production from a thought of
"human nature." The capitalist mode of production cannot be understood as a
simple expression or deviation of human nature: It is neither the realization of a
fundamental and originary selfishness nor the suppression of an ancient communal essence.[7] In the *Theses on Feuerbach*, Marx uses the term *ensemble of human relations* to displace the question of the human essence. Marx argues against Ludwig
Feuerbach's concept of the 'abstract human essence' and its alienation in religion:
"But the human essence is no abstraction inherent in each single individual. In its
reality (*in seiner Wirklichkeit*) it is the ensemble of the social relations (*das Ensemble der gesellshaftlichen Verhältnisse*)."[8] Marx's statement "displaces" the question of
the human essence in that it does not argue against essence in general but rather
proposes that such an essence does not exist in an idea but rather exists, or effectively exists, in the multiple and active relations that individuals establish with
each other.[9] What human individuals have "in common" is not some abstract idea
of humanity but their specific relations, which are constituted each moment in
multiple forms. There is an affirmative aspect of this concept of an 'ensemble' that
follows this displacement: Just because capital cannot be related back to some abstract essence of humanity does not mean that it is separable from human desires,
human intention, or human subjectivity, altogether, but rather these desires must
be considered from the particular relations and the history of these relations. Or
put otherwise, the formation of the capitalist mode of production is not reducible

to the simple desire to accumulate on the part of the capitalist, nor to the simple moral difference between capital and worker, although it involves and implicates desire as well an entire moral discourse on the values of saving and spending as its component elements.[10] However, these elements or relations do not have as their causes some abstract nature of humanity, but rather their causes are other relations, which coexist and precede this particular ensemble of relations. For Marx the relations that form the capitalist mode of production are "the product of many economic revolutions, of the extinction of a whole series of older formations of social production," the most direct and immediate extinction being the breakdown of the feudal mode of production (CI 273/183).

The "extinction" of the feudal mode of production encompasses multiple elements and trajectories. It includes the dissolution of the regime of the guilds, the breakdown of the system of peasant landownership, and the massive disintegration of existing structures of wealth and prestige through merchant capital and usury.[11] These elements of dissolution are not the effects of a single strategy or aspects of a single process, rather they are entirely disparate. Balibar explains that "the elements combined by the capitalist mode of production have different and independent origins."[12] These elements of dissolution such as usury often stem from the margins and "pores" of the old society and only begin to occupy center stage in terms of their effects, the effects of constituting a new economy and a new mode of production. Whatever intelligibility or unity they have is produced after the fact when they retroactively become the conditions of the capitalist mode of production.

Where the theory of so-called primitive accumulation imagines a vague identity of past and present, unified by a particular memory and morality, Marx finds the intersection of disparate historical trajectories and itineraries that only come together in the common space that they mutually create. For example, the laws and acts that turned common lands into pasture and forced the peasantry off the land did not have as their goal the creation of the proletariat as a propertyless working class; rather, this was an unintended effect that was later seized by other agents and actors (CI 885/752).[13] To continue the comparison between so-called primitive accumulation and primitive accumulation, we could add that where the theorists, or apologists, of political economy find an idyllic and moralizing transformation Marx finds violence and bloodshed. This violent transformation has two acts: First, as I have noted, there are multiple conditions of expropriation, including usury, which quite literally tear the producers from their means of production, most importantly the land. Expropriation in itself does not produce "free workers," however, only disenfranchised peasants and artisans who are just as likely to resort to begging or crime as they are to show up at the doors of the factories and mills of the newly emergent capitalist class looking for work. As Marx writes in the *Grundrisse:* "The propertyless are more inclined to become vagabonds and robbers and beggars than workers."[14] The period of expropriation is followed by the period of "bloody legislation": laws are drawn up and regimes of penalization and torture are enacted to curtail criminality and control the new class of criminals.

Hence at the end of the fifteenth and during the whole of the sixteenth centuries, a bloody legislation against vagabondage was enforced throughout Western Europe. The fathers of the present working class were chastised for their enforced transformation into vagabonds and paupers. Legislation treated them as "voluntary" criminals, and assumed that it was entirely within their powers to go on working under the old conditions which in fact no longer existed. (CI 896/762)

Although such laws are founded on the fantasy that it is possible to go on being a peasant after feudalism, their secondary, and perhaps unintended, effect is the control and containment of a working class, of those who have only their labor power to sell. Those "freed" from previous forms of labor and existence must be violently coerced into and contained in the new structures of labor and existence. The transition from feudalism to capitalism is neither smooth nor easy, and it requires the necessary intervention of law, the state, and new forms of police to transform disenfranchised peasants and artisans into subjects of labor.[15] As Marx argues, the state, and particularly its powers of police and violence, are then a contingent, but necessary constitution of the capitalist mode of production (CI 899/764).

Is the question of primitive accumulation simply a matter of two different origins and two different moralities, the first of which locates the good on this side of the proto-capitalist for his or her thrift and industriousness and the bad on the side of the proto-laborer for his or her waste, while the second morality locates the bad on the side of the proto-capitalist for his or her violent aggressions, and the good on the side of the proto-laborer for his or her romanticized innocence? Or is something other than a competing history, or mythology, at stake here? As I have suggested, it is through the critique of so-called primitive accumulation that the elements of the historical definition of the capitalist mode of production are given. So far these elements are perhaps only given in a dim outline through the points of contrast with the moralists of so-called primitive accumulation. First, a mode of production is irreducible to, and in excess of, the intentions of an individual subject. Even though the "fairy tale" of primitive accumulation founds the possibility of historical transformation and capitalist accumulation on individual intent and the morality of those that save rather than squander, Marx argues through the character of the miser not only that intentions in general cannot be actualized without their material conditions, but that these conditions are constitutive of intentions. Subjectivity is inseparable from the ensemble of relations that makes it possible.

There is perhaps a second, albeit more oblique, element to this materialist critique of intentionality. Marx's account of the disparate conditions of primitive accumulation would separate this thought of the mode of production from a subject of history. It is not the same subject that dissolves the old mode of production and produces the new one.[16] At the most basic level this means that Marx's thought of a mode of production is distinguished from any attempt to write a "great man" philosophy of history, in which history is nothing more than the realization of ideas and intentions within the tabula rasa of history. More important, Marx's history is not the simple intention or progression of a single class or even of the struggle between two classes. Classes and subjectivities do not preexist their particular material conditions. Finally, Marx's critique of so-called primitive accumulation begins to point to a specific problem within the mode of production: the manner in which a mode of production is constitutive and constituted by desires, forms of living, and intentions: subjectivity.

IMMANENT CAUSALITY

Although Marx's critique of so-called primitive accumulation is perhaps a condition for a theorization of the conditions of the capitalist mode of production, as well as some of the general elements of a concept of a mode of production, it is a paradoxical point from which to begin to elucidate a consideration of the capitalist mode of production. This is paradoxical because it is unclear where or within what mode of production the conditions of primitive accumulation are to be located according to a historical periodization: They could be placed within the feudal mode of production, from whose dissolution they stem, or within the capitalist mode of production, whose birth it constitutes. Primitive accumulation is situated between two types of violence and two types of power relations: between the feudal forms of servitude that it destroys and the capitalist forms of exploitation that it renders possible. Thus primitive accumulation would seem to exceed any strict periodization, or division of history, into a succession of modes of production (Asiatic, ancient, feudal, capitalist, and communist); it is rather a point of passage and transition.

It is unclear, however, whether primitive accumulation simply can be relegated to the past or to the simple prehistory of the capitalist mode of production as a moment of transition. As a process of accumulation it would appear to encompass both the conditions for the historical formation of capital and its extension into other spaces and other modes of production. As Marx writes in a passage illustrating the overdetermined historical appearance of capital:

> The discovery of gold and silver in America, the extirpation, enslavement and entombment in mines of [the] indigenous population of that continent, the beginnings of the conquest and plunder of India, and the conversion of Africa into a preserve for the commercial hunting of blackskins, are all things which characterize the dawn of early capitalist production. . . . These different moments are systematically combined together [*systematisch zusammengefßt*] at the end of the seventeenth century in England; the combination embraces the colonies the national debt, the modern tax system, and the system of protection. These methods depend on brute force [*brutalser Gewalt*], for instance the colonial system. But they all employ the power of the state, the concentrated and organized force of society [*Gewalt der Gesellschaft*], to hasten, as in a hothouse, the process of transformation of the feudal mode of production into the capitalist mode, and to shorten the transition. Force is the midwife of every old society which is pregnant with a new one. It is itself an economic power [*ökonomische Potenz*]. (CI 915/779)

As this passage indicates, primitive accumulation is situated both at the historical formation of the capitalist mode of production and at the point of its extension into other modes of production through the forceful violence of colonization.

Primitive accumulation serves as the name not only for an event but also for a process: the expropriation and legislation necessary to destroy other economic and social relations to make them productive for capital. Primitive accumulation is the process of the separation of labor from the means of production and reproduction of its existence.[17] Thus primitive accumulation becomes not only a cause of the capitalist mode of production but also its effect.[18] The two essential results of primitive accumulation—workers with only their labor power to sell and capital free to invest anywhere—are also effects of the capitalist mode of production's encounter not only with other modes and economies but also with the remnants of noncommodity production internal to capitalist societies. Primitive accumulation can be said to take place at every point where something in common is converted into private property (e.g., from the land used to gather firewood to the genetic code of indigenous crops) or where the conditions for the production and reproduction of existence are converted into commodities (e.g., the transition from home garden plots to fast food).[19] It is thus possible to talk about an endo-colonization (the colonization of the remainders of noncommodified or nonexploited dimensions of existence internal to capitalist societies) alongside exo-colonization (the extension of capital to other spaces). As much as these concepts make it possible to extend the idea of primitive accumulation beyond that dark night when capitalism was born, they do so as moments of transition. The transition is extended beyond a singular point in time to become a process, but the definition of primitive accumulation remains exterior to the definition of the capitalist mode of production.

The previous passage also begins to indicate a second sense in which primitive accumulation is irreducible to a simple moment of transition. We can approach this second sense by posing the following questions, When does the moment of primitive accumulation end? And How? Even if we bracket for a moment the forms of "endo-" and "exo-" colonization that would make primitive accumulation a point of transition which continually repeats itself, these questions are difficult to answer owing to the intimate relationship that the violence of primitive accumulation has with the new order it engenders. Marx demonstrates that primitive accumulation involves a relation of force, power, and, more important the powers of the state, which give birth, as it were, to a new society. Poised at the point of transformation the moment of violence almost disappears in its execution. Gilles Deleuze and Félix Guattari have related Marx's critique of political economy to a particular type of violence that is difficult to critique because it is always presented as pre-accomplished and carrying with it its justification.

Hence the very particular character of state violence: it is very difficult to pinpoint this violence because it always presents itself as pre-accomplished. It is not even adequate to say that the violence rests with the mode of production. Marx made the observation in the case of capitalism: there is a violence that necessarily operates through the state, precedes the capitalist mode of production, constitutes the "primitive accumulation" and makes possible the capitalist mode of production itself. From a standpoint within the capitalist mode of production, it is very difficult to say who is the thief and who is the victim, or even where the violence resides. That is because the worker is born entirely naked and the capitalist objectively "clothed" an independent owner. That which gave the worker and the capitalist this form eludes us because it operated in other modes of production.[20]

Thus, the violence of primitive accumulation is immediately justified within and by the new order that it constitutes. For example, the destruction of the common lands by the enclosure acts only appears violent from the perspective of the old order and practices that it destroys. As Michel Foucault argues, the period of primitive accumulation entails a fundamental transformation of the definition of illegality and property: the longstanding relations of traditional use surrounding land (free pasture, wood collecting, and so forth) were replaced by a new regime of property: "[L]anded property became absolute property; all the tolerated 'rights' that the peasantry had acquired or preserved were now rejected by the new owners who regarded it simply as theft."[21] Primitive accumulation is the point of transition between violence and right. As Antonio Negri writes, "Violence thus constitutes the vehicle between accumulation and right."[22]

If the violence of primitive accumulation is difficult to locate as an event because it loses itself in the law and the new society that it produces, it is also difficult to locate because it is always situated with respect to a transformation of violence and the emergence of a new type of violence. In the long passage from feudalism to capitalism this transformation is in the first instance the passage from the dispersed violence of feudal lords to violence monopolized and standardized by law and the bourgeois state. As Marx states, in the beginning, "[T]he rising bourgeoisie needs the power of the state, and uses it to 'regulate' wages, i.e., to force them into the limits suitable for making a profit, to lengthen the working day, and to keep the worker himself at his normal level of dependence. This is an essential part of so-called primitive accumulation" (CI 899/764). In the first instance the sporadic and excessive feudal forms of violence passes into the universality of law, but this is not the entirety of the transformation. Marx also seems to indicate a second moment of this transformation of violence in which violence disappears not into the neutrality of law but into the quotidian relations that the law makes possible. In Marx's words, "The silent compulsion of economic relations sets the seal on the domination of the capitalist over the worker. Direct extra-economic force is still of course used, but only in exceptional cases" (CI 899/764).

Marx is somewhat ambiguous with respect to the closure of primitive accumulation and its relation to the mode of production it engenders. At times, Marx appears to argue that primitive accumulation and the overt violence it involves ends in the day-to-day relations of exploitation; while at other times it appears that the violent lawmaking power of primitive accumulation is merely privatized and brought indoors into the factory.[23] Marx emphatically illustrates the order of discipline imposed by the factory codes: "The overseer's book of penalties replaces the slave-driver's lash. All punishments naturally resolve themselves into fines and deductions from wages, and the law-giving talent of the factory Lycurgus so arranges matters that a violation of this laws is, if possible, more profitable to him than the keeping of them" (CI 550/447).

Marx suggests that there is a qualitative difference between primitive accumulation and the capitalist economy it engenders, in terms of the former's bloody discontinuity and the latter's continuity and silent functioning. At the same time, however, Marx would suggest that this qualitative change is best understood perhaps as a change in the form of violence itself, capitalist accumulation is nothing other than primitive accumulation continued onto the shop floor, and thus nothing other than a continuation of the modification of violence begun with "bloody legislation" and the enclosure acts. The violence of law and the police gives way to the coercive force of the shop supervisor and the rhythm of machines.[24]

The problem of the relation between primitive accumulation and the capitalist mode of production opens onto yet another problem: the definition of the capitalist mode of production, or stated otherwise, the difference between capitalism thought as a mode of production and capitalism thought as an "economy." What is at stake in such a distinction is the understanding of the continuity of capital, the reproduction of the forces and relations of production over time. To understand capital as a mode of production is, in some readings, to insist on the necessarily complex conditions of this continuity—an entire series of complex factors including the state, law, and ideology are necessary to the functioning of capital. To understand capital, or any other mode of production, as an economy is to lapse into what has been called "economism." Economism, briefly, is the guarantee of the adequacy of the economy to its own reproduction without the necessary implication of other factors, or elements, such as the state, ideology, law, or subjectivity. Economism takes the lawlike nature of the economy as a given and understands its effects on other elements to be that of a simple linear cause. To return to ambiguity indicated above with respect to the closure of primitive accumulation, we can see the possibility of interpreting the "silent compulsion of economic relations" as either the dominance of the economy over other instances of the social or, following Marx's statements regarding the disciplinary power of the capitalist, as the internalization of the violence within the system itself.

At the level of individual quotes and citations the problem of the contours and complexity of the mode of production is, strictly speaking, irresolvable; it will always be possible to oppose an "economist" Marx to a "noneconomist" Marx—the entire history of Marxism bears witness to this possibility. To get beyond the seemingly endless back and forth of this or that statement, or concept, of Marx's writing, it is necessary to pose another seemingly unrelated question, the question of the place of primitive accumulation in the exposition, or logic, of Marx's *Capital*. Louis Althusser has argued that Marx's later writings, especially the first volume of *Capital* (since it was completed by Marx) engage philosophical problems articulated through their very exposition, in the order of chapters, and the logic of categories. Marx himself writes in the afterward to the second edition of *Capital*: "Of course the method of presentation [*Darstellung*] must differ in form from that of inquiry [*Forshung*]. The latter has to appropriate the material in detail, to analyze its different forms of development and to track down their inner connection. Only after this work has been done can the real movement be appropriately presented" (CI 102/27).

Capital, according to Althusser, is not an incomplete manuscript, a manifesto, or a series of notes "written for self clarification"; it is a completed text, or at least part of one, and as such it engages and enacts a particular question, the question of its exposition or logic. That is, the relation between abstract concepts, examples and historical events, a relation that poses the problem of the presentation, or even the representation of something called the capitalist mode of production itself.

We have already glimpsed something of this problem in the critique of so-called primitive accumulation. In part, and if it is possible to put aside the clear differences of ideology and politics, *the difference between the bourgeois theory of primitive accumulation and Marx's theory can be expressed as a difference of representation.* The violence and historicity of primitive accumulation cannot appear within classical political economy. It does not fit within the manner in which classical political economy constructs its object: the market as an invisible hand functioning without state intervention.[25] For Marx the presentation of primitive accumulation and the formation of capital involved not only fundamentally different elements, such as the entire history of the dissolution of the feudal mode of production, the violent formation of the capitalist mode of production, and the history of colonialism, but also the question of the relations between these elements.[26] If there is a specifically materialist dialectic, as a thought of contradiction, antagonism, and relation, or if Marx is something other than G. W. F. Hegel turned upside down (Hegel applied to the material world), then this dialectic (if that word is still appropriate) would have to be found in the logic of the presentation of *Capital.*

This problem of presentation is not limited to *Capital*; it is given a stronger and more forceful theoretical formulation elsewhere. In the "1857 Introduction" (Notebook M of the *Grundrisse*) Marx wrestles with a question that we have already touched upon: How is it possible to give a historical presentation of the capitalist mode of production? The obvious answer would be a linear historicism in which the concepts and relations follow each other as they have chronologically from primitive forms of ground rent to finance capital and so on. What such a presentation misses, however, are the relations of priority and determination within the capitalist mode of production itself; that is, the particular relations of dominance and subordination established between the "old" and "new" economic forms within the capitalist mode of production. As Marx writes:

> For example, nothing seems more natural than to begin with ground rent, with landed property, since this is bound up with the earth, the source of all production and of all being, and with the first form of production of all more or less settled societies—agriculture. But nothing would be more erroneous. In all forms of society

there is one specific kind of production which predominates over the rest, whose relations thus assign rank and influence to the others. It is a general illumination
which bathes all the other colors and modifies their particularity. (G 106/40)

And, later:

It would therefore be unfeasible and wrong to let the economic categories follow one
another in the same sequence as that in which they were historically decisive. Their
sequence is determined, rather, by their relation to one another in modern bourgeois
society, which is precisely the opposite of that which seems to be their natural order
which corresponds to historical development. The point is not the historic position
of the economic relations in the succession of different forms of society. Even less is
it their sequence "in the idea'" (Proudhon) (a muddy notion of historic movement).
Rather, their order [*Gleiderung*] within modern bourgeois society. (G 108/41)

The sequence of categories and concepts in Marx's texts are neither chronological nor determined by a purely logical or conceptual relationship (their sequence "in
the idea") but a presentation, or articulation, of the particular relations in capitalist
society. This "presentation" is a necessary abstraction in order to go beyond any
fetishization of the concrete, any theorization that remains at the level of a particular phenomenon or element and tries to grasp capital from this concrete element (as
classical political economy understood the formation of capital from the particular
memory of saving or accumulation). It is through the presentation (or articulation)
that the particular relations constituting the capitalist mode of production can be
grasped in their stability and instability.[27]

Reading Marx's works such as *Capital* and the *Grundrisse* for such an articulation
has particular theoretical and philosophical effects: Most important, it allows one
to read for an "object" and a "problem" which is never named or announced as such
by Marx. I have already preemptively titled this object/problem "the representation"
of the capitalist mode of production. This is perhaps something of a misnomer, or
it could be correct provided that what is being "represented" here, the capitalist
mode of production, actively transforms the contours and terrain of representation
itself.[28] What is being represented is not an object for thought, but a relation or series of relations and their particular dynamism and tensions (G 102/36). That is,
Marx's text deals with the problem of the relations between structures, the division
of labor, relations of production, and so on, which are different elements of a larger
structure: the capitalist mode of production.[29]

The relation between these structures cannot be contained or presented within
existing models of causality (they are not simply the causes or effects of each other
in a mechanical or expressive sense) or presentation (most notably the often presupposed division between essence and appearance); rather, this relation is one of
immanent causality: The cause, or structure, is immanent in its effects; there is
nothing outside of its effects. Thus there is no simple division or priority between
cause and effect: Every effect is equally and at the same time a cause.[30] This cause

is both immanent and absent, because to be immanent and present in its effects is also to be unlocalizable. This cause cannot be present or empirically given at any one point, hence the other name that Althusser gives it: "metonymical causality." To risk something of an example (risk because it is not quite clear if the traditional philosophical presuppositions regarding the relation between universal and particular, concept and example, are at work here): Elements of the capitalist mode of production that would appear to be its effects, such as the desire for accumulation on the part of the capitalist, or "rationalized" hoarding, must equally be thought of as causes and elements of its functioning. Louis Althusser compares this presentation/articulation/structure to a new theater, a new machinery.

> Now we can recall that highly symptomatic term *"Darstellung"* compare it with this "machinery" and take it literally, as the very existence of this machinery in its effects: the mode of existence of the stage direction [mise en scène] of the theatre which is simultaneously its own stage, its own script, its own actors, the theatre whose spectators can, on occasion, be spectators only because they are first of all forced to be its actors, caught by the constraints of a script and parts whose authors they cannot be, since it is in essence an authorless theatre.[31]

Without necessarily following all of the ramifications of Althusser's reading of *Capital*, although we will return to many of these points, it is important to indicate that his insistence on the intimate relation between presentation, or philosophical exposition, and structure and the relations of the mode of production, displaces the earlier question regarding the place of transition or transformation in the mode of production from the infinite and inexhaustible series of quotes and counter-quotes of what "Marx thought" to another and different problem: that of the exposition or logics (holding open for a second that there at least may be more than one) at work in Marx's text.

Marx's rewriting of the fantasy of primitive accumulation poses particular problems when placed within this question of textual presentation. Although primitive accumulation deals with the intersecting questions of the real relations that have formed the capitalist mode of production, the dissolution of feudalism, and the imaginary apprehension of those relations (the morality tale), it is placed at the end of *Capital*, in the final chapters. Thus there is a considerable difference between the presentation of primitive accumulation within the articulation of *Capital* and its place in the historical formation. The text begins with the famous analysis of the commodity form which constitutes the phenomenological appearance and common sense of the capitalist mode of production, where " [t]he wealth of societies in which the capitalist mode of production prevails appears as an 'immense collection of commodities [*ungeheure Warensammlung*]'" (CI 126/49). The commodity is presented as both the unexamined material of day-to-day experience under capitalism and the key to all of its riddles.[32] Marx does not begin *Capital* with the question of origins but with an element of capital that is at once quotidian and all encompassing in its scope. From the starting point of the commodity form, Marx develops the contradictory relationship between exchange and use values and abstract and concrete labor. Without attempting to offer anything like an overview or synopsis of the exposition of *Capital*, I will attempt to indicate something of the difference between primitive accumulation as the historical emergence of capital and the commodity form as the starting point for the presentation of capital. The difference between these two points is not only the difference between the synchronic articulation of the relations of capital and its historical emergence, it is also the difference between two different tendencies within the presentation [*Darstellung*] of the capitalist mode of production.

Althusser argues in a later text entitled "Marx dans se limites," in a point that could be understood as both a radicalization and a destabilization of his earlier insistence on the relation between presentation [*Darstellung*] and structural causality, that Marx's writings, in even mature texts such as *Capital*, cannot be reduced to the articulation of a single presentation but rather must be understood as themselves determined and constructed by multiple presentations and multiple logics.[33] To follow the two different presentations I have indicated, the commodity form and the first chapter of *Capital* proceed by a series of internal contradictions: from use value and exchange value, to abstract and concrete labor, and finally to surplus value itself. This movement is also the movement from the indeterminate abstraction of the commodity or value to what is finally the specific articulation of the capitalist mode of production including the day-to-day relations and struggles on the factory floor. The first chapters of *Capital* would seem to participate in a logic that is at once a sort of crude Hegelianism (passage from the indeterminate abstract to the concrete through contradiction) and an economism (understanding capitalism entirely from the commodity form).[34]

In Althusser's earlier writings he attempted to show how the supposedly opposed camps within Marxism, Hegelian or historicist Marxism (Antonio Gramsci, Jean-Paul Sartre, and others) and economistic Marxism (Second International), were actually two sides of the same "problematic."[35] Although such an argument may appear to be completely dated, and thus barely warranting a footnote, it is worth returning to Althusser's argument for the simple fact that today the conjunction of economism and Hegel is often invoked as grounds for a complete rejection of Marx. According to Althusser, economistic Marxism, or Stalinist Marxism, is focused on one central contradiction: between forces and relations of production. All other contradictions and conflicts then are merely effects, or conditions, of this dominant contradiction that proceeds unhindered until its eventual collapse. Such an interpretation bases itself on an emphasis on the first part of Marx's famous paragraph from the preface to *A Contribution to the Critique of Political Economy* (and perhaps never really goes beyond it):

> In the social production of their existence, men inevitably enter into definite relations, which are independent of their will, namely relations of production appropriate to a given stage in the development of the material forces of production. The totality of these relations of production constitutes the economic structure of a society, the real

foundation [Basis], on which arises a legal and political superstructure [Überbau] and to which correspond definite forms of social consciousness. . . . The changes in the economic foundation lead sooner or later to the transformation of the whole immense superstructure . . . in short ideological forms in which men become conscious of this conflict and fight it out.[36]

Most historicists, or Hegelian Marxists, oppose themselves to this by emphasizing the conflicts in the superstructure, arguing that it is the conflict of the ideological forms that determine the actual fate of the class struggle and the direction of history. In each case "there is never more than one *structure* of identification at work—the structure of the problematic which, by reducing one to the other, *theoretically* identifies the levels present."[37] What is retained across the theoretical divide that separates Hegelian Marxism from economism is expressive causality, the idea of a society structured by one single contradiction. Thus, in "Marx dans se limites" Althusser recognizes both of these tendencies: to understand society as structured by a single contradiction in the logic of the commodity form.

The "logic" that opens *Capital Volume I,* a logic that is one part a crude Hegelianism and one part economism, does not account for the entirety of the text. Althusser contends that it is continually interrupted by chapters and analyses that incorporate relations and levels irreducible to the enfolding of the internal contradictions of the commodity form, and are outside the order of presentation [*hors ordre d'exposition*], constituting a break with a Hegelian, or economistic logic.[38] Even though this rupture includes the chapters on primitive accumulation, and thus the problem of the foundation of the capitalist mode of production, it is not limited to it. This other logic in tension with economism includes the chapters on cooperation, the working day, and machinery and large-scale industry (all of these chapters and the logic they suggest will be returned to later). What is at stake in this other logic that remains outside of the dominant order of exposition? How might an alternative be thought of in other than negative terms, as other than an interruption or an outside to the dominant logic? Put otherwise, What is it that economism and Hegelianism, or the shared space between the two that has comprised much of what has been designated Marxist thinking, necessarily exclude to constitute themselves as a discourse of the social?[39]

The beginning of a response to these questions can be found in the disparity between the two starting points: the commodity form and primitive accumulation. The first assumes what the second puts into question by historicizing the commodification of labor itself. Whereas primitive accumulation reveals the violent operations necessary to constitute a laboring subject, to constitute those who have only their labor power to sell, the analysis of the commodity form takes this condition as an already accomplished fact. One might even claim that this is the difference of historical perspective. It is the difference between the capitalist mode of production viewed as completed, on the one hand, and the problem of the formation of the capitalist mode of production, on the other hand. At the same time, and as the first logic progresses from use value/exchange value to abstract and concrete labor and to the definition of surplus value as the chapter progresses, the assumption of the commodification of labor becomes inseparable from a purely quantifiable understanding of surplus value itself.

> When you read Section 1 Book 1 of *Capital*, you find a theoretical presentation of surplus value: it is an arithmetical presentation, in which surplus value is calculable, defined by a difference (in value) between the value produced by labor power on the one hand and the value of the commodities necessary for the reproduction of this labor power (wages) on the other. And in this arithmetical presentation of surplus value, labor figures purely and simply as a commodity.[40]

As Althusser argues, what this presentation excludes are the conditions necessary to the constitution of labor as commodity, both in terms of its organization, for example, on the factory floor according to the division of labor, cooperation, and discipline and its reproduction beyond the factory floor; that is, the "organized social forces" (state, law, ideology) necessary to the formation of the economy as such. The difference is profound at the basis of the chapter on the commodity for there is the idea of labor as a commodity, and thus the possibility of a purely economic analysis, while the section on primitive accumulation points to a "politics of production," the relations necessary to convert labor power into a commodity.[41] The profound statement of such a difference makes it possible to understand what was politically at stake in the idea of immanent causality. Immanent or structural causality as the recognition of the overdetermined conditions of any economy, of any mode of production, is related directly to the political and philosophical problem of thinking the materiality of social relations.

In underscoring the destruction and violence necessary to the constitution of the free worker, and thus of capital, the chapters on primitive accumulation begin to outline the materiality of social relations. As Antonio Negri indicates, the destruction and violence that defines primitive accumulation can be understood only if one posits forms of cooperation and social relations that preexist capital, and must be destroyed or seriously modified to produce the "free worker" necessary to capitalist accumulation. Negri writes that "in the period of primitive accumulation, when capital enveloped and constricted pre-existent labor forms to its own valorization, it was capital which posed the form of cooperation—and this consisted in the emptying of the pre-constituted connections of the traditional laboring subjects."[42] The intimate relation between the formation of the capitalist mode of production and violence found in primitive accumulation has as its correlate the materiality of social relations that preexist capital.[43] This "other side" of primitive accumulation persists in the spontaneous and resistant social relations, from primitive cooperative exchanges to criminal expropriations, that mirror the violent history of primitive accumulation, from the enclosure acts to bloody legislation. Just as primitive accumulation as institutionalized violence never properly ends but instead migrates into the enclosed spaces of the factory, these forms of cooperation and sociality are not destroyed but rather fundamentally transformed by the formation of capital. As

Negri argues, the entire history of the capitalist mode of production can be interpreted as the changing antagonism between forms of accumulation, with their corresponding regimes of power and violence, and forms of cooperation, with their
corresponding forms of counter-power.[44] This conflict continually destroys and creates new forms of accumulation and cooperation.

The destruction and creation of new forms of cooperation entails the destruction and creation of the old forms of sociality and subjectivity. Thus it is possible
to find in Marx a third moment of primitive accumulation, after the expropriation
or destruction of the previous mode and its violent legislation, a moment of normalization that bears on subjectivity and sociality itself. As Marx writes: "The advance of capitalist production develops a working class which by education
[*Erziehung*], tradition, and habit [*Gewohneit*] looks upon the requirements of that
mode of production as self evident natural laws" (CI 899/765). The violence and
dissolution of the old mode of production is followed by the normalization of the
new mode of production, which obliterates the memory of the past mode of production as well as any traces of the violent foundation of the new mode of production. This normalization constitutive of the regularity and functioning of the
capitalist mode of production is actualized not only at the levels of laws or institutions but also at the level of subjectivity.[45] *There is a production of subjectivity necessary to the constitution of the capitalist mode of production.* For a new mode of
production such as capital to be instituted it is not sufficient for it to simply form
a new economy, or write new laws, it must institute itself in the quotidian dimensions of existence—it must become habit.

What is at stake in these different logics thus is sociality and subjectivity itself,
as both produced by and in excess of the economy. "Produced" and "in excess" are
perhaps crude ways to indicate that what is in question here is a relation, one of sociality and subjectivity to or in the mode of production. Such vagueness is, at this
point, necessary in that we are only beginning to glimpse the contours of this relation, which is to assert that we are glimpsing the contours of the mode of production itself. Although we can know very little at this stage about what this
relation is, it is not the simple production of an obedient and docile form of sociality by the economy, as is suggested by various economisms and even Althusser's
earlier works. Nor is it a relation of exteriority and transcendence, as it is in various forms of voluntarism and various metaphysics of alienation. The basic idea underlying such conceptions of subjectivity is theoretically complicit with classical
political economy and its theory of so-called primitive accumulation: in both cases
subjectivity is capable of acting on history insofar as it is placed outside of history
as a timeless possibility. Change and transformation can only be imagined by re-
sorting to the image of a transcendental subject who is not touched by the violence
of history. To begin to articulate an affirmative, rather than simply negative, understanding of this relation between subjectivity and the mode of production, we
must examine this "other logic," while at the same time remaining aware of its
constitutive co-implication with, and contamination by, the "major" logic of
Marx's texts.

THE PREHISTORY OF CAPITALISM

The problem of economism and the critique of economism is a problem and conflict interior to the space opened by Marx's work; it is not named as such by Marx and is thus in some sense a problem of Marxism and not of Marx.[46] Within Marx's works there are somewhat different problems, ones that prefigure the problem of economism, such as the nature of the difference between the capitalist mode of production, as a mode of production constituted by the dominance of the economic relations (the production of commodities, realization of surplus value, and so on), and other precapitalist modes of production that perhaps have other relations of determination and domination. Although this problem is not the same as the problem of economism, that is, it is not a matter of differentiating between those societies (precapitalist) for which economism is false and those for which it is true, it is similar in that it deals with the relation between the conditions for the constitution of something called the economy in its differential effectivity within different modes of production. This is one of the questions at stake in Marx's notebook on "Pre-Capitalist Economic Formations" [*Formen, die der kapitalistischen Produktion vorhergehen*] in the *Grundrisse*.

The primary question for Marx in "Pre-Capitalist Economic Formations" is the nature of the distinction between precapitalist modes of production (Asiatic, ancient, feudal, and so forth) and the capitalist mode of production in terms of the grounds and consequences of such a distinction. Claude Lefort contends that Marx is primarily concerned with the major division between precapitalist modes of production and the capitalist mode of production rather than what he considers to be the minor differences between the various precapitalist modes of production.[47] This distinction, however, does not exhaust the entirety of the questions traversed in the notebooks. Since the precapitalist modes of production constitute the prehistory of the capitalist mode of production, providing the elements which in their dissolution become constitutive of the capitalist mode of production, there are relations of descent and transformation that exceed a simple comparison. Thus there are multiple points of intersection between these notebooks and Marx's analysis of primitive accumulation. For these different modes, or forms, to occupy the same terrain, of either comparison or historical descent, there must be some commonality, something that makes them a mode of production, and thus the text also broaches the general problem of the definition of a mode of production. It is in relation to this third problem that this text most explicitly intersects with the minor logic outlined previously. The notebook on precapitalist economic conditions, like most of the *Grundrisse*, is developed on a conceptual terrain that acknowledges the constitutive force of subjectivity and sociality in determining and transforming a mode of production.[48]

Finally, it is important to add after the enumeration of these different problematics at work in this text, all of which will have to be both justified and elaborated, that there is a fourth aspect that is not necessarily a problematic in itself, although it does pose a problem for reading; that is, the specific articulation of the relation between these different problems. The articulation of "Pre-Capitalist Economic Formations" follows the open, overlapping, and discontinuous nature of the notebooks in the *Grundrisse*, which often repeat with slight modifications and transformations earlier statements and analyses and at times drop analyses only to redevelop them later. The *Grundrisse* also follows an articulation that does not neatly divide between general theory and specific articulation, or concept and example, in which the particular is generally only an illustration or an instance of an already pre-given concept or generality.[49] This destabilization of the priority of the general and the particular, like the earlier features I have indicated, could be chalked up to the incomplete status of the notebooks, but it could also be understood as an opening to another question, What is at stake in these notebooks, other than a contribution to the fields of speculative anthropology and history? What is at stake in these notebooks is not only a complex thought of the relation between subjectivity and the mode of production but a different and original thought of historical transformation.

Marx's "Pre-Capitalist Economic Formations" begins by introducing the basic historical preconditions and presuppositions of the capitalist mode of production. As with Marx's account of primitive accumulation, the presuppositions and preconditions of the capitalist mode of production, the conditions that constitute its formation and yet cannot be derived from it, are the separation of the "worker" from the means of production and the freeing up of a flow of money that is capable of becoming capital; or the naked worker and free wealth. From this starting point Marx both investigates the historical formation of these specific presuppositions [*Voraussetzung*] and historical preconditions [*Bedingungen*] in the dissolution of the precapitalist economic formations and develops a major distinction between precapital and economic formations according to not only their different presuppositions and preconditions but a different treatment of, or relation to, their presuppositions. All of the precapitalist economic formations (Asiatic, ancient, feudal, and so on) have as their presupposition not the separation of the worker from the means of production or the separation of money from wealth but their integration within a particular community or sociality. As Marx writes:

> This naturally arisen clan community, or, if one will, pastoral society, is the first presupposition—the communality [*Gemeinshaftlichkeit*] of blood, language, customs—for the appropriation of the objective conditions of their life, and of their life's reproducing and objectifying activity (activity as herdsmen, hunters, tillers, etc.) The earth is the great workshop, the arsenal which furnishes both means and material of labor, as well as the seat, the base of the community. They relate naively to it as the *property of the community* [*Eigentum des Gemeinwesens*], of the community producing and reproducing itself in living labor [*lebendigen Arbeit*]. (G 472/385)

There are at least two theoretical effects of this particular approach to the relation between precapitalist and capitalist modes of production. First, it includes and intertwines the problem of genesis of the latter with the problem of their distinction: In both cases it is a matter of presuppositions. Second, it imposes a some-what different theoretical problem of thinking the mode of production from its presuppositions; that is, thinking it from that paradoxical instance of formation that is exterior to a particular mode of production, since it is constituted by other forces and relations and the dissolution of another mode of production, and, at the same time, interior to a particular mode of production, since it is the reproduction of these presuppositions that sets the terms and relations for the continuity and survival of the mode of production. For example, the capitalist mode of produc-tion not only presupposes the "naked laborer" and "free wealth" as preconditions, it also must continually reproduce these presuppositions to survive.

Thinking the mode of production from its presuppositions entails thinking the mode of production from the moment at which these presuppositions come to-gether in time and space, it entails thinking the mode of production from the "en-counter." The constitutive elements of the formation of any mode of production, the elements that enter into relations such as free laborers and money freed from any productive use as in the formation of the capitalist mode of production, have different and divergent histories.[50] Once these elements encounter each other, once an excess of money encounters a population with only its labor-power to sell, there is the emergence of a particular mode of production with its attendant forms of necessity and stability. (To continue our example, one could think here of the multiple necessities of the capitalist mode of production, the necessity of getting a job, to produce commodities, to extract surplus value, and to realize a profit, to name a few, all of which impose themselves to different degrees and for different groups within the mode of production.) The encounter itself is contingent. As Deleuze and Guattari argue, "The encounter might not have taken place, with the free workers and the money-capital existing 'virtually' side by side."[51] Necessity, or the regular reproduction of a mode of production, is itself generated by contin-gency, and as such it is perhaps never free of it. This imposes a particular demand on how one thinks of the mode of production. As Althusser writes, "Instead of thinking of contingency as a modality of or an exception to the necessary, one must think necessity as the becoming-necessary of contingent encounters."[52] A "becoming necessary," a process and not a simple transition from contingency to necessity, because the different elements of a mode of production, the social, tech-nological, and political conditions have independent histories and relations, and this independence threatens any mode of production with its dissolution or trans-formation. As Marx has repeatedly indicated, capital is constantly threatened by the unhinging of its two constitutive elements: The flow of workers could dry up or leave, and capital could be "wasted" rather than invested.[53] In "Pre-Capitalist Economic Formations" the "becoming necessary of the contingent" is translated, or expressed, in two specific problems: the relation that any mode of production has with its preconditions and the relation between production and reproduction within any mode of production.

The presuppositions of any mode of production are the conditions that consti-tute a mode of production but are not produced from it. Their original appearances are unimaginable or unexplainable according to the particular protocols and practices of that mode of production. Thus, as we saw with so-called primitive accumulation, the very question of these presuppositions is concerned with the question of what could be called "ideology," or the manner in which a particular mode of production justifies itself by rewriting, or over-coding, its own emergence. In the case of so-called primitive accumulation this over-coding proceeded through a moralization of the difference between capitalist and workers as those who saved and those who squandered. Marx recognizes a similar type of problem with respect to the precapitalist economic formations, all of which entail a particular appearance or coding of their presuppositions.[54] As Marx writes:

> The *real appropriation* through the labor process happens under these *presuppositions,* which are not themselves the *product* of labor, but appear as its natural or *divine* presuppositions [*natürlichen oder göttlichen Voraussetzungen erschein*]. This form, with the same land-relation as its foundation, can realize itself in very different ways [*kann sich selbst sehr vershieden realisieren*]. (G 472/385)

These natural or divine preconditions include the relation with the earth, cited previously, as well as the particular communal and social relations that appear to preexist any productive activity. Marx gives these presuppositions, or this "form" that entails a particular relation with these presuppositions, a broad scope. This form that defines the precapitalist economic formations is broad enough to include not only the social relations of primitive tribes, a sort of primitive communism, but also the Asiatic despot. In the Asiatic mode of production, it is the despot himself or herself and not the earth who appears as the precondition and presupposition for any productive activity. As Marx argues:

> E.g. it is not in the least a contradiction to it [the form] that, as in most of the *Asiatic* landforms, the *comprehensive unity* standing above all these little communities appears as the higher *proprietor* or as the *sole proprietor*. Because the *unity* is the real proprietor and the real presupposition of communal property, it follows that this unity can appear as a *particular* entity above the many real particular communities, where the individual is then in fact propertyless, or, property—i.e. the relation of the individual to the *natural* conditions of labor and of reproduction as belonging to him, as the objective, nature-given inorganic body of this subjectivity [*als unorganische Natur vorgefundener Leib seiner Subjektivität*]—appears mediated for him through a cession by the total unity—a unity realized in the form of the despot, the father of many communities [*für ihn vermittelt erscheint durch das Ablassen der Gesamteinheit, die im Despoten realisiert ist als dem Vater der vielen Gemeinwesen*]—to the individual, through the mediation of the particular commune. (G 473/385)

The fact that Marx includes within the same form, without contradiction as it were, the earth and the despot as conditions of production would seem to indicate the relation, if not the indissociability, of the question of the appearance or coding of the mode of production with the question of the presuppositions of any mode of production. Thus what would seem to be a relatively banal point, that every mode of production, or all productive activity, is inseparable from certain preconditions or presuppositions, or that one always begins somewhere in history, is paired with a more difficult question: that of the generation and constitution of certain forms of stability, or becoming necessary through the appearance, or coding, of these presuppositions. This second problem would begin to suggest that the "reproduction of the relations and forces of production," which every mode of production must manage, involves the generation and normalization of beliefs, appearances, and desires, and thus the creation and generalization of particular quotidian practices, habits, or subjective comportments, as much as it involves the creation of new institutions, laws, and practices.[55]

The normalization and reproduction of a particular mode of production entails the construction of the appearance of the mode of production. As Marx stated with respect to the emergence of the capitalist mode of production, "[T]he requirements of that mode of production must appear as 'self-evident' natural laws" (1899/765). Following Marx's assertion, one may suggest this appearance is both a reification and a naturalization, but also an "inversion" of sorts, in that it proceeds through an effacement of the practices, the habits, and violence that constitute and make possible the mode of production. In each of the precapitalist economic formations what is an effect of the mode of production and its particular extraction of surplus labor, the particular type of sociality such as in despotism, is mis-recognized as a cause (and thus in some sense functions as a cause) working to guarantee and normalize the relations proper to that mode of production. This is the problem of what Althusser called the "society effect" (*l'effet de société*) or what Deleuze and Guattari call the "socius." For Althusser, any attempt to historicize the formative elements of a mode of production is incomplete unless it poses a second, different problem, the problem of the society effect: the manner in which these elements cohere together to form a particular type of social existence.[56] Beyond the history of the complex conditions that have constituted a mode of production, expropriation of peasants, usury, colonialism, merchant capital, and so on in the case of the capitalist mode of production, there is the manner in which these elements are articulated together constituting a particular mode of production with its own regularity, stability, and rules.[57] The society effect is this stability, or rather it is one of the causes that produces stability, the element of normalization and cohesion that is both an effect and a precondition of the regular function of the mode of production. As Althusser argues:

> The mechanism of the production of this "society effect" is only complete when all the effects of the mechanism have been expounded, down to the point where they are produced in the form of the very effects that constitute the concrete, conscious or unconscious relation of the individuals to the society as a society, i.e., down to the effects of the fetishism of ideology (or "forms of social consciousness"—*Preface* to *A Contribution.* . . .), in which men consciously or unconsciously live their lives, their projects, their actions, their attitudes and their functions as *social*.[58]

As a mechanism the society effect must be grasped as a series of effects or over-lapping levels—from institutions and structures to habits and attitudes, from economic relations to social relations—without necessarily establishing an auto-matic priority between these levels.[59] As was indicated by Marx's remarks con-cerning the presuppositions or appearance of the various precapitalist modes of production, this society effect entails a particular appearance of, or attitude to-ward, the mode of production. This appearance is often described as an inversion of cause and effect, in which the effects of a particular activity or practice appear as its cause. This appearance or attitude, however, cannot be dismissed as a sim-ple effect or epiphenomenon—it has its own effectivity as it is incorporated into the acts, ideas, and behaviors of the ensemble of human relations within a par-ticular mode of production. It is thus what Deleuze and Guattari call a quasi-cause. As Deleuze and Guattari write in relation to the text from Marx in the previous quote:

> [T]he forms of social production, like those of desiring production, involve an un-engendered nonproductive attitude, an element of anti-production coupled with the process, a full body that functions as a *socius*. This socius may be the body of the earth, that of the tyrant, or capital. This is the body that Marx is referring to when he says that it is not the product of labor, but rather appears as its natural or divine presuppositions. In fact, it does not restrict itself merely to opposing productive forces in and of themselves. It falls back on [*il se rabat sur*] all production, constitut-ing a surface over which the forces and agents of production are distributed, thereby appropriating for itself all surplus production and arrogating to itself both the whole and the parts of the process, which now seem to emanate from it as a quasi-cause.[60]

For Deleuze and Guattari a quasi-cause is a paradoxical entity because it involves the retroactive causality and effectivity of what is itself an effect. This effect, the appearance or attitude toward that which appears as the presupposition of a mode of production, or more generally that which appears to be outside the historicity and history of practice and production, is itself a cause in that it shapes and affects the attitudes of those who live within that particular mode of production.

One could extend this society effect, as Althusser and Deleuze and Guattari have, into the general problem of the mode of production, and thus into Marx's analysis of capital. There are within Marx's writings at least several points that would serve as footholds for this extension. First, as I have already indicated, for Marx the very problem of the "presuppositions" and "historical preconditions" of a mode of production is inseparable from the ideological appearance or coding of those presuppositions. Second, there is a general thematic, which of course runs throughout most of Marx's texts from *The German Ideology* to all of *Capital*, con-cerning the simultaneous "separation" and inversion of appearances. Without at-tempting to follow this second theme, which traverses such diverse concepts and problematics as ideology and fetishism, I can at least follow those points where the appearance of capital takes on a similar form or structure of appearance as the precapitalist or Asiatic mode of production. Capitalism, like the world of the Asiatic despot, would seem to constitute its own particular "mode of appearance." It constitutes a bewitched world in which capital seems prior to and independent of labor. As Marx writes:

> This natural power of labor appears [*erscheint*] as a power incorporated into capital for the latter's own self preservation, just as the productive forces of social labor appear as inherent characteristics of capital, and just as the constant appropriation of surplus labor by the capitalists appears as the constant self-valorization of capital. All the powers [*Kräfte*] of labor project themselves as powers of capital, just as all the value-forms of the commodity do as forms of money. (CI 756/633)

Capital, like the Asiatic despot, becomes a "mystical being" appearing to generate its own conditions of possibility, in this case the work that produces surplus labor.[61] As Marx indicates, the earth or the despot as the presupposition of productive activity is always a half-real and half-imagined (or godlike) being (G 493/401). This mystified appropriation is an appropriation of the social forces of cooperation, the supplementary productivity of a large group of individuals working together, and thus it would appear to belong to whatever force or power appears to organize the group of workers (CI 451/352). Marx goes on to argue in a more polemical tone that it is this real power of the Asiatic despot, the power of cooperation and the multitude, as well as the particular mystified form of appearance that accompanies it, that is revived and reborn with the capitalist mode of production. As Marx writes, "The power of Asiatic and Egyptian kings, of Etrusan theocrats, etc. has in modern society been transferred to the capitalist, whether he appears as an isolated individual or, as in the case of joint stock companies, in combination with others" (CI 452/353).

Unless these arguments regarding the similarity of the Asiatic mode of production and capitalism are to be left as elements of a polemic, a matter of Marx revealing that supposedly "enlightened" bourgeois society is constituted by the same myths as its other, oriental despotism, then there must be some sort of link, conceptually or historically, between the two modes of production and their mode of appearance. This structural or formal similarity between two modes of production separated by an immense gulf of space and time has been bridged, at least conceptually, by Balibar. He argues that this structural or formal similarity of the specifically Asiatic and capitalist modes of production, their tendency to produce not only an inversion between cause and effect but a specific image of the social that appears to generate social relations as if from within itself, can be explained given the specific relations of determination at work in each mode of production. According to Balibar, other modes of production, such as the feudal mode of production, are founded on a distinction and difference between the dominant instance, or the instance determined as dominant, and the determinate instance, which is the economy.[62] He writes, "In different structures, *the economy is determinant in that it determines which of the instances of the social structure occupies the determinant place.* Not a simple relation, but rather a relation between relations; not a transitive causality, but rather a structural causality."[63]

The distinction and difference between the determinant and dominant is articulated and institutionalized through the particular conditions under which surplus is extracted within the different modes of production. Balibar argues that in the feudal mode of production labor and surplus labor are distinct in both time and space, and this distinction is both reflected and constituted in a series of legal, juridical, and religious relations and practices.[64] Relations of domination such as servitude and peasantry, are thus determined as dominant by this division in the extraction of labor. Capital and the Asiatic mode of production are similar, at least at the level of form or structure, in that there is no lived division between labor and surplus labor; in capital this division is imperceptibly woven into the core of every workday, while under the Asiatic despot, all property is property of the despot, and thus labor, or necessary labor, is derived from labor performed for the despot (G 473/385). In each of these modes of production it is the same instance, institution, or practice that occupies the site of determination and domination: economy in the capitalist mode of production and political power in the Asiatic mode of production. This overlapping of the site of determination and domination produces its own appearances, or optical effects. For Balibar this mis-recognition can be called "fetishism" because of its thematic linkages with Marx's famous short chapter on commodity fetishism: In both cases the determinate site, or scene, is itself mis-recognized.[65] Determination is not displaced to another scene, such as religion or politics, but what is fetishized is the determinant instance itself in that it appears to be entirely self-sufficient and autonomous, not to mention transcendent and perhaps even metaphysical: In the Asiatic mode the despot seems to be prior to and independent of the social relations, and, in capital, it would appear that the economy functions through its own laws, independent of and prior to human action.

Any such attempt to construct a general theory of the society effect or the appearance of the mode of production, must, as Althusser has indicated, be developed to the point of expounding the lived, unconscious and conscious, effects and relations of this effect at the most minute and quotidian level.[66] Without such an exposition a thought of the society effect remains at the level of either a purely formal theory of the necessary mis-recognition of consciousness or a purely polemical association that links the power of capital with the ancient and mystical powers of Asiatic despotism.[67] A purely formal, or "optical," theory is both imprecise in terms of the functioning and relations of the different elements and ultimately static in its conception of the particular mode of production. What such a theory misses are the differences that throw into question the possibility of locating a discrete and determinant instance of the "economic" or the "political" within a particular social formation; that is, the manner in which the society effect functions differently in different modes of production as a determinant element. More important, such a theory overlooks the manner in which the relations of tension and transformations that underlie any existing mode of production are themselves interior to the society effect. Thus, with respect to "Pre-Capitalist Economic Formations," any similarities between the Asiatic and capitalist mode of production at the level of an optical effect must be thought against not only the specificity of each mode of production—for example, the different sense or function of "surplus" in each mode of production—but, more important, the specific historical tensions and relations of transformation at work within each mode of production.

According to Marx, the Asiatic mode of production, like all precapitalist modes of production, is more properly a mode of reproduction in which productive activity and developments have as their telos and aim the reproduction of communal and social relations that are its presuppositions. Precapitalist modes of production are forms of stasis and repetition, aiming to repeat rather than invent.[68] It is against the backdrop of a fundamental repetition that their particular transformations and eventual demise must be thought. As Marx writes:

> In all these forms—in which landed property and agriculture form the basis of the economic order, and where the economic aim is hence the production of use values, i.e. the *reproduction of the individual* within the specific relation to the commune in which he is its basis—there is to be found: 1) Appropriation not through labor, but presupposed to labor; appropriation of the natural conditions of labor, of the earth as the original instrument of labor as well as its workshop and repository of raw materials. The individual relates simply to the objective conditions as being his; [relates] to them as the inorganic nature of his subjectivity . . . 2) but this relation to land and soil, to the earth, as the property of the laboring individual—who thus appears from the outset not merely as a laboring individual, in this abstraction, but who has an *objective mode of existence* in his ownership of the land, an existence *presupposed* to his activity, and not merely as a result of it, a presupposition of his activity just like his skin, his sense organs, which of course he also reproduces and develops in the life process, but which are nevertheless presuppositions of this process of his production—is instantly mediated by the naturally arisen, spontaneous, more or less historically developed and modified present of the individual *as a member of a commune*. (G 485/393)

Marx's remarks on the precapitalist, and specifically the Asiatic, modes of production, which place them outside of history, would seem to repeat the basic Hegelian theme that makes the West the locus of history and progress.[69] Although it would be absurd to pretend that Marx's theory of the Asiatic mode of production is free of such fantasies and themes, it is also important to pose the question of what is at stake for Marx on a purely textually immanent level, that is, posing the question of the manner in which this problem functions within the text, and what it makes possible, rather than dealing with the adequacy of this theory to a supposed referent.[70] Thus the question becomes, What, according to Marx, are the conditions, limits, and effects of repetition in history? Marx goes on to argue that what is repeated most of all is a particular type of subjectivity, "the reproduction of the individual," within the specific communal and social relations that constitute his or her subjectivity, its "inorganic nature." "Individual" here does not designate the isolated individual separated from these bonds; as Marx writes, "The positing of the individual as worker, in this nakedness, is itself a product of history" (G 472/385). Marx argues that the reproduction of particular forms of the intersection of individuality and social bonds in the precapitalist modes of production provides the mode of production with a particular type of stability that may underlie and survive other forms of historical transformation.[71] Marx asserts that the condition of this repetition is a certain type of production: the production of use values. The link between the production of use values (the production for consumption and use rather than exchange) and the reproduction of presuppositions and sociality is not immediately clear. There is the possibility that the link between the production of use values and the reproduction of sociality will be forged by a purely anthropological understanding of "reproduction" in which production corresponding to need automatically reproduces, rather than changes, the sociality or subjectivity. According to this view capital, or the capitalist mode of production, would be the deviation from the realm of natural needs, a perversion of this natural harmony between economy and need. As Marx writes:

> Thus the old view, in which the human being appears as the aim of production, regardless of his limited national, religious, political character, seems to me to be lofty when contrasted to the modern world, where production appears as the aim of mankind and wealth as the aim of production. In fact, however, when the limited bourgeois form is stripped away, what is wealth other than the universality of human needs, capacities, pleasures, productive forces etc., created through universal exchange? The full development of human mastery over the forces of nature, those of so-called nature as well as humanities own nature? The absolute working out of his creative potentialities, with no presupposition other than the previous historical development. . . . Where he does not reproduce himself in one specificity, but produces his totality? Strives not to remain something he has become, but is in the absolute movement of becoming? In bourgeois economics—and in the epoch of production to which it corresponds—this complete working-out of the human content appears as a complete emptying out, this universal objectification as total alienation, and the tearing down of all limited, one-sided aims as sacrifice of the human end-in-itself to an entirely external end. (G 488/396)

However, as much as Marx's writing (not to mention that of Marxists) has tended in this direction, the division between reproduction and production cannot be the division between "nature" and the realm of need and capital and the realm of overproduction/alienation. This theme begins to unravel even in citing the passages from the *Grundrisse* that would seem to support it. First, as I have already noted, the "form" of which the precapitalist economies of reproduction are realization includes the Asiatic despot as well as the primitive community. What is placed in the space of reproduction is not the natural individual "man" but a series of different possibilities and constraints of subjectivity (the subject of despotism, the slave, or serf). Reproduction does not simply conform to some natural or pre-given community or subjectivity. Rather, it includes within its general schema different possible relations of power. Precapitalist modes of production reproduce use values, but the "uses" that these values are put to include the maintenance of relations of power. Reproduction is not a simple natural regeneration of the species but the regeneration of the social demands of the mode of production.

In *The German Ideology* the reproduction of the basic material conditions of life is presented as always already implicated with a particular social relationship. Even this early text in which Marx and Engels famously invert the Hegelian schema of history—placing the production and reproduction of life as the basis of human history—reproduction is presented as inseparable from production, which is in turn presented as inseparable from the relations of domination and subordination. As Marx and Engels write, "The production of life, both of one's own in labor and of fresh life in procreation, now appears as a double relationship; on the one hand as a natural on the other hand as a social relationship."[72] Marx and Engels's assertion of the double nature of production, as natural and social, or, to return to the terms discussed previously, the claim that every reproduction is also and at the same time production, does not in itself resolve the issue. In *The German Ideology*, as well as later texts, biological production and reproduction—the reproduction of human individuals—is understood as the initial intersection of the relationship between the social and natural dimensions of production. The site of this intersection is the family. As such the family does not provide a theoretical clarification of the "double relation"—natural and social—but is alternatively described as "a natural division of labor" and as the original social relationship of exploitation. As Engels writes,

> The first class antagonism which appears in history coincides with the development of the antagonism between man and woman in [monogamous] marriage, and the first class oppression with that of the female sex by the male. Monogamy was a great historical advance, but at the same time it inaugurated, along with slavery and private wealth, that epoch, lasting until today, in which every advance is likewise a relative regression, in which the well-being and development of the one group are attained by the misery and repression of the other. It is the cellular form of civilized society, in which we can already study the nature of the antagonisms and contradictions which develop fully in the latter.[73]

Any attempt to maintain "natural" and "social" as normative concepts underlying the distinction between reproduction and production comes up against Marx's (and Engels's) ambiguous position with respect to the family, or the sexual division of labor. Marx and Engels locate a natural sexual division of labor at the basis of all later divisions, stating famously in *The German Ideology* that division of labor was "originally nothing but the division of labor in the sexual act."[74] However, Marx and Engels do not "naturalize" the family as the basic pre-political ground of any and all society, in fact it is one of the primary aims of Engels's *The Origin of Family, Private Property, and the State* (a work heavily indebted to Marx's anthropological research in the *Grundrisse*) is to historicize the family. The family (in its modern patriarchal and monogamous sense) arises not out of biological necessity, or of a deep-hidden drive, it is a social and political relationship that develops out of the transformation of property and the mode of production.[75] As the previous quote indicates, it is the primal scene of exploitation and domination, thus containing in a condensed form the relations of later complex societies. It is possible to locate in Marx and Engels's thought a natural division of labor, grounded in part on sexual difference, and the political and social transformation of that basic relation into specific sociocultural institutions such as the "modern family."[76] As this natural division constitutes something of the raw material of later articulations of the reproduction of individuals, a material that is reworked into such entrenched social institutions as the division between housework and productive labor, it is uncertain to what extent it continues to exist as anything like a natural basis, as a reproduced element of nature.[77] Whatever natural basis this division might have in sexuality, or reproduction, would seem to be significantly transformed by vicissitudes of history: the sexual division of labor is continually transformed by and transforming the social division of labor.[78] In brief, it is possible to say that if capitalism does not create the family it at least thoroughly modifies it, in part by its isolation, which is produced by primitive accumulation's destruction of other relations of cooperation in which the family is embedded.[79]

If reproduction cannot be understood as natural, in anything resembling a normative sense, then at the same time production cannot be understood as a deviation from nature. In the passage from the *Grundrisse* cited previously Marx poses the following questions, "In fact, however, when the limited bourgeois form is stripped away, what is wealth other than the universality of human needs, capacities, pleasures, productive forces etc., created through universal exchange? The full development of human mastery over the forces of nature, those of so-called nature as well as humanities own nature?" (G 488/396). Thus, Marx recognizes a positive nature to production freed from the fetters of reproduction, alluding to an idea of wealth as the universality of need and the creation of new needs.[80] Even taken in isolation, such a statement begins to suggest exigencies for the critique of capital other than the liberation of a naturally preexisting subjectivity and sociality. Thus, reproduction and production cannot be simply related by analogy to nature and culture, as Marx's statement regarding use value would seem to suggest, but must have their own specific theoretical development, which would entail different grounds than and assumed division between supposedly natural needs and their cultural deviation.

PRODUCTION

To follow the development of the theoretical articulation of the division between production and reproduction, it is instructive to turn to "Notebook M" of the *Grundrisse,* or what is otherwise known as the "1857 Introduction." Originally intended as an introduction for *A Contribution to the Critique of Political Economy,* Marx delayed publishing it, leaving it as part of the notebooks which make up the *Grundrisse.*[81] Even though the relationship of this notebook to the rest of the notebooks of the *Grundrisse* has been debated, it seems that the structure that Marx sets up in that text among production, distribution, and consumption relates to the problem broached above concerning the ground of Marx's division between precapitalist and capitalist modes of production on the basis of reproduction and production. More specifically, it relates to the theoretical ground such a distinction rests on. In the introduction Marx explicitly addresses and thematizes the difference between an historical—contingent and finite—and an ahistorical—necessary and natural—account of bourgeois society. As Marx argues, bourgeois or classical political economy proceeds through a particular articulation of the relation between production, distribution, exchange, and consumption; a particular logic that is informed by and constitutes a particular idea of the "economy" and its relation to an idea of human nature. Marx writes:

> Thus [in political economy] production, distribution, exchange and consumption form a regular syllogism; production is the generality, distribution and exchange the particularity [*Besonderheit*], and consumption the singularity [*Einzelnheit*] in which the whole is joined together. This is admittedly a coherence, but a shallow one. Production is determined by general natural laws, distribution by social accident, and the latter may therefore promote production to a greater or lesser extent; exchange stands between the two as a formal social movement; and the concluding act, consumption, which is conceived not only as a terminal point [*Endziel*] but also as an end-in-itself [*Endzweck*], actually belongs outside of economics except in so far as it reacts in turn upon the point of departure and initiates the whole process anew. (G 89/25)

Within this conception of political economy—production and consumption, the starting point and end point of political economy—are outside political economy, or, at least, outside the history of political economy. Consumption and production are governed by natural laws, by the anthropological constant of need.[82] Thus they function as the "given," as the assumed ground from which political economy proceeds. Only distribution and circulation are recognized as properly historical: There are only different types of property, different forms of law, mediating and interrupting an otherwise natural relation between product and need. History is never internal to economy but rather exterior to it, hence the intimate relation between this concept of the economy and history figured as the history of wars and conquest. (These events are the only possible interruptions and transformations of a homogenous and continuous history of human nature producing for itself.) Classical political economy is determined, in the first and last instance, by an anthropology that is wise enough to remain out of sight, directing the action from offstage.[83] Althusser suggests that what this anthropology determines is an entire conception of the social as a homogenous space; that is, it makes possible an entire discourse within which the assumption of needs, and the correlative production for those needs, as given, is raised and preserved into a conception of society as a subject with its own needs and rationality. From this understanding of the relation between need, the economy, and society, it becomes possible and obligatory to speak in terms of society's needs: The space that anthropology opens is closed off by an anthropomorphic conception of society, society has needs and acts to meet those needs. What is foreclosed by such a conception is not only history (as a history of production, consumption, and distribution) but also the differences that this history inscribes at the center of social existence, differences of hierarchy, conflict, and separation—differences of class. (G 94/29)

It is against this conception of the social, of the anthropological foundation of the social, that Marx presents a fundamentally different relation between production, distribution, exchange, and consumption that is thoroughly historical. Or, put differently, rather than maintaining the simple and linear causality of natural needs and historical mediations, Marx develops a thought of the complex relations of production, distribution, exchange, and consumption in which all act on and determine each other and, to a certain extent, produce each other. To translate this into another philosophical language, the interrelations of production, consumption, and distribution could be considered as the exposition of a thought of immanence in that it is opposed to both the theoretical assertion of a transcendental scene of determination that remains exterior to that which it determines (as in most forms of economism) or the assumption of a concealed transcendental foundation (as in the anthropological ground of classical economics). A thought of immanence requires that all of the relations (production, distribution, and consumption) must be thought both as effect and cause of each other.

The simultaneity of a relation of cause and effect can be demonstrated with respect to production and consumption. As Marx indicates, production and consumption seem to have an immediate identity, as well as an opposition, in the simple fact that all production involves consumption of raw materials, and all consumption would seem to immediately produce something, if only the energy for production. Beyond this immediate identity Marx asserts that there is a more intimate relation of co-implication that encompasses and enfolds the supposed exterior and ahistorical ground of need and subjectivity. As Marx writes:

> Production not only supplies a material for the need, but it also supplies a need for the material. As soon as consumption emerges from its initial state of natural crudity and immediacy—and, if it remained at that stage, this would be because production itself had been arrested there—it becomes itself mediated as a drive by the object. The need which consumption feels for the object is created by the perception of it. The object of art—like every other product—creates a public which is sensitive to art and enjoys beauty. Production thus not only creates an object for the subject, but also a subject for the object. . . . Consumption likewise produces the producers *inclination* by beckoning to him as an aim determining need. (G 92/27)

Production produces consumption, producing not only its object but its particular mode and subject, and in turn consumption acts on production, in effect producing it. Similarly, Marx explains that "consumption ideally posits the object of production as an internal image, as a need, as a drive and a purpose. It creates the objects of production in a still subjective form" (G 92/27). As much as this formulation of the relation between production and consumption ascribes an active sense to consumption, the relation of causality between the two still appears hierarchically organized in that consumption supplies a need or a desire, while production completes this need producing its material and means; consumption produces only an indeterminate provocation, while production completes and determines this provocation giving it its form.[84] "Production thus produces not only the object but also the manner of consumption, not only objectively but also subjectively. Production thus creates the consumer" (G 92/21). Or, as Marx describes suggesting something of a residual element of the nature/culture distinction, "Hunger is hunger, but the hunger gratified by cooked meat eaten with a knife and fork is a different hunger from that which bolts down raw meat with the aid of hand, nail, and tooth" (G 92/21). The relations of immanence are interrupted by this latent transcendence, this residue of hierarchy, which is not the transcendence of the economy to the social, but the primacy of production over the other elements of the social. This primacy appears even stronger with respect to distribution, which Marx states has often served as the determinant historical instance in classical political economy. Marx argues that there is only an apparent primacy of distribution

> If it is said that, since production must begin with a certain distribution of the instruments of production it follows that distribution at least in this sense precedes and forms the presupposition of production, then the reply must be that production does indeed have its determinants and preconditions, which form its moments. At the very beginning these may appear as spontaneous, natural. But by the process of production itself they are transformed from natural into historic determinants, and if they appear to one epoch as natural presuppositions of production, they were its historic product for another. (G 97/32)

Thus, Marx would appear to bend the stick in the other direction, so to speak, where classical (bourgeois) political economy saw distribution, property relations, as the historical variant, Marx argues that it is production that changes over time, transforming the other relations.

The difference between Marx and classical political economy is not a simple inversion; that is, it is not a matter of a shift of emphasis from distribution to production within the same logic. The primacy that Marx ascribes to production is not placed on production in a limited sense, as the production of things, but on the mutual relations of causality and effectivity underlying production, consumption, and distribution. Production is inscribed twice in the series, as one of the terms alongside the others, and as the relation of effectivity structuring the entire series.[85] According to Marx: "Production predominates not only over itself, in the antithetical definition of production, but over the other moments as well. . . . A definite [bestimmte] production thus determines a definite consumption, distribution and exchange as well as *definite relations between these different moments*. Admittedly, however, in its *one sided form*, production is itself determined by the other moments" (G 99/34). This definite production, or the relation between a determinant production, consumption, and distribution, is one definition given by Marx of a mode of production.

The question remains regarding how to interpret the larger sense of production constituting a mode of production. This question is integral to how one understands the relation between production and reproduction that founds the major distinction between precapitalism and capitalism. There are at least two possibilities that roughly correspond to the division between "forces" and "relations" of production in Marx's (or Marxist) thought.[86] The first asserts that production is primary in that it is the history of technology, or the history of the means of production, which transforms and determines production, distribution, and consumption.[87] This view can be found in Marx's statement: "The hand-mill will give society with a suzerain; the steam mill, society with industrial capitalism."[88] The second would argue that the relations of production determine production itself. Thus the social relations are prior to, and determinate of, the technological relations. Polemics and arguments over the primacy and definition of these two terms have riddled the history of Marxist thought, working from ambivalences and instabilities in Marx's thought. Marx asserts, in "Pre-Capitalist Economic Formations," in a particularly ambivalent definition of the mode of production that:

> [t]he original unity between a particular form (clan) and the corresponding property in nature, or relation to the objective conditions of production as a natural being, as an objective being of the individual mediated by the commune—this unity, which appears in one respect as the particular form of property—has its living reality in a specific *mode of production* itself, a mode which appears both as a relation between the individuals, and as their specific active relation to inorganic nature, a specific mode of working (which is always family labor, often communal labor). The community itself appears as the first great force of production; particular kinds of production conditions (e.g. stock-breeding, agriculture), develop particular modes of production and particular forces of production, subjective, appearing as qualities of individuals, as well as objective [ones]. (G 495/403)

Within this passage both the communal or social relations and technological or productive developments are given the determinate role: It is equally unclear to what extent social relations and technological relations can even be separated ("the community itself appears as the first great force of production"). Thus, it would appear from this passage that the polemics regarding the primacy of forces or relations of production misses a more difficult question: How to think forces and technology as relations, and how to think relations as forces? Marx's famous remarks regarding the manner in which transformation of means of production function as indices of relations of production also suggests that for Marx "forces" cannot be separated from social relations.

Relics of bygone instruments of labor possess the same importance for the investigation of extinct economic formations of society as do fossil bones for the determination of extinct species of animals. It is not what is made but how, and by what
instruments of labor, that distinguishes different economic epochs. Instruments of
labor not only supply a standard of the degree of development which human labor
has attained, but they also indicate the social relations within which men work.
(CI 286/194)

The effects of this suggestion extend beyond the possibilities it offers for a social
history or archaeology: They extend into the problem of immanence as I have indicated. I would argue that production understood as the interrelation of social
and technical relations restores the immanence I have suggested; that is, while production would still preside over the other moments (consumption, distribution,
and production), this production constitutes a social relation, a type of cooperation and way of life that must necessarily be affected by transformations of consumption, distribution, and quotidian practices.

There is, however, a theoretical and political risk that immanence will be reduced to a formulation of society producing itself, or man making man. In other
words there is a risk of a return of a model of expressive causality, of the idea of
society as the expression of one dominant ideal of production. The detour through
the forces of production is thus something other than the recuperation of technological history by social history; it is the necessary interruption of any such humanist recuperation of a mode of production. As Althusser asserts: " For Marx, the
social relations of production do not bring *men alone* onto the stage, but the agents
of the productive process and the material conditions of the productive process in
specific 'combinations.' "[89] What is determinate is not the forces or relations but
the "relation between relations," relations that can only be thought through immanence, by discarding any dimension of existence—the economy or human nature—that would stand outside of history. Immanence is not the "mirror of
production," the immanence of man to man through production, but it includes
the relation with nature and technology—it is a nonhuman immanence. As
Deleuze and Guattari write, in an oblique citation of the "1857 Introduction":

It is probable that at a certain level nature and industry are two separate and distinct
things: from one point of view, industry is the opposite of nature; from another, industry extracts its raw materials from nature; from yet another it returns its refuse to
nature; and so on. Even within society, this characteristic man–nature, industry–
nature, society–nature relationship is responsible for the distinction of relatively autonomous spheres that are called production, distribution, consumption. . . . [T]he
real truth of the matter . . . is that there is no such thing as relatively independent
spheres or circuits: production is immediately consumption and a recording process
[*enregistrement*], without any sort of mediation, and the recording process and consumption directly determine production, though they do so within the production
process itself. Hence everything is production: *production of productions,* of actions
and of passions; *production of recording processes,* of distributions and of co-ordinates

that serve as points of reference; *productions of consumptions,* of sensual pleasures, of anxieties, and of pain.[90]

For Deleuze and Guattari, immanence, the immanence of production, breaks down not only any division between forces and relations of production but also any division between the production of material things and the production of modes of existence and subjectivity: Consumption, production, and distribution are not only related to things or objects but to the desires, inclinations, and needs related to those things.

The term that Deleuze and Guattari reserve for this immanent relation of production, subjectivity, and technology is *machine,* or *social machine.* In part, their use of this term follows Althusser's use of the word *combination,* or *ensemble,* in that it stresses the irreducibility of the mode of production to an intersubjective relation, to a particular "manner of producing." However, Deleuze and Guattari's use of the term *machine* includes not only the combination of social relations and technical forces but also their necessary overlap with particular apparatuses, or material conditions, for the production of subjectivity. They argue that

> [t]he social machine, in contrast, has men for its parts even if we view them with their machines, and integrate them, internalize them in an institutional model at every stage of action, transmission, and motricity. Hence the social machine fashions a memory without which there would be no synergy of man and his (technical) machines. The latter do not in fact contain the conditions for the reproduction of the process; they point to the social machines that condition and organize them, but also limit and inhibit their development. . . . The social machine is literally a machine, irrespective of any metaphor, inasmuch as it exhibits an immobile motor and undertakes a variety of interventions: flows are set apart, elements are detached from a chain, and portions of the tasks to be performed are distributed. Coding the flows implies all of these operations. This is the social machine's supreme task, inasmuch as the apportioning of production corresponds to extractions from the chain, resulting in a residual share for each member, in a global system of desire and destiny that organizes the productions of production, the productions of recording, and the productions of consumption.[91]

The social machine includes not just the relations between humans and machines but also the appearances and coding of these relations.[92] Codes are nonhuman, nonintersubjective, elements of subjectivity in that they pass through subjectivity, through desires, knowledge, and language, without necessarily originating from them; they are elements of what Marx designated "inorganic subjectivity." For Deleuze and Guattari, rituals, apparatuses, and ideologies, are quite literally machines for the production of subjectivity.[93] (Marx's analysis of hoarding, or the production of hoarding by the very qualities of the money form, provides something of an indication of the relation between objects and practices and the production of a particular kind of desire.) To understand how this works, in relation to "Pre-Capitalist Economic Formations," we could take, for example, the Asiatic mode of production: Following Deleuze and Guattari, this would designate not only particular forms of cooperation and labor—small-scale communal cooperation organized and coordinated by a centralized bureaucracy—and a particular technological development—centralized irrigation projects and waterworks—but also the Asiatic despot as a ritualized object of awe and fear. This third element would constitute a particular form of subjectivity or belief, a society effect, which is no less integral to the longevity and survival of the mode of production than are particular social relations and technological relations.[94] The social machine is the particular interaction, or coding, of the relation between these elements: No machine can outlive its political, technical, or subjective conditions of possibility. As a reading of the *Grundrisse,* Deleuze and Guattari's terminology of machines and codes underscores one important fact: It is impossible to consider a mode of production apart from the production of subjectivity that it both produces and presupposes. Deleuze and Guattari's reading for an ontology of production follows Althusser's concept of structural causality: In each case there is the development of a concept of the mode of production that goes beyond both economism and humanism.

A mode of production is inseparable from the production of a particular social relation, and a particular subjectivity, which it needs to reproduce itself. Engels writes that "the production and reproduction of immediate life . . . is of a two fold character": It is the production of the means of subsistence but also a production of "the species."[95] It may be incorrect to identify this second dimension with "the species," as if it were ever a matter of the reproduction of human life. Or rather, it might be more correct to argue that all production and reproduction has a three-part character: means of production, biological existence, and particular form of subjectivity. (Remembering that Marx also adds in *The German Ideology* that every mode of production is also the production of a particular relationship of production, of a particular division of labor.) It is the articulation of the relation between these three dimensions that constitutes the mode of production, what Deleuze and Guattari call "coding," at least insofar as a definition of the mode of production is given in "Pre-Capitalist Economic Formations." Such a definition then comes up against the limitations of these notebooks outlined earlier; that is, the subordination of the general task of theorizing the mode of production to a representation of the epochal division between precapitalism and capitalism, and the incomplete and fragmentary nature of the notebooks themselves. The particular contours of these limitations come to light whenever one attempts to rigorously develop the relationship, the levels of effectivity, and determination between these different "aspects" of production.

What is lacking from the "Notebooks" is a rigorous sense of the articulation of the different dimensions of the reproduction and production of existence. Marx's focus in the treatment of the precapitalist modes of production is to show how the presuppositions constitutive of capitalism—the flow of money and the flow of labor power—are nonexistent prior to the dissolution of these specific modes of production. Or, more exactly, they are nonexistent as separate flows. In the various precapitalist modes wealth does not yet exist as abstract wealth, it is thoroughly implicated with a structure of belief and domination, and labor does not exist as abstract labor, it is embedded within particular structures of subordination. This focus on the overall historical difference between capitalism and precapitalist modes of production, in which the various aspects of these modes of production are presented as elements of the "genealogy" of capital, is written at the expense of any specific investigation of the concrete relations constitutive of the different pre-capitalist modes of production.[96] Marx's notebooks articulate the immanence of the production of subjectivity to the mode of production, destroying any rigid and ahistorical hierarchy of base and superstructure or forces and relations of production, but they do so as a problem—leaving the specific relations, the specific causality or relations of determination, to be thought from the ground up.

ANTAGONISTIC LOGIC (PART ONE)

It may seem that we have drifted far from the matter at hand: the distinction that Marx draws between precapitalist modes of production, as modes of reproduction, and capitalist modes of production, as the mode of production proper. However, it is important to grasp not only this distinction but also the logic of this distinction, the particular foundation such a distinction rests upon. I have argued that this distinction cannot take as its foundation either an assumed natural ground of need and its deviation or a particular idea of the history of technological transformation, but, rather, it must be sought in an expansive sense of the mode of production, as the immanent relations of production, consumption, and distribution, relations which include subjectivity as both a complex effect and a cause. I have argued that this relation undoes any a priori figure of causality or effectivity between the different elements; it is not given in advance what effects a particular transformation of productive technologies, relations of property, beliefs, and desires will have. This does not mean that all things are absolutely equal, however, or that politics, power, and history are reduced to absolute contingency where anything is possible at any moment. Rather, what this means is that the particular possibilities and limits must be thought from the ground up, from the particular conjuncture and mode of production. The particular causality that makes possible reproduction and production in the precapitalist and capitalist mode of production must be thought from the specific elements and relations of each mode of production.

"Pre-Capitalist Economic Formations" constitutes something of an interruption of the dominant versions of a philosophy of history at work in Marx's texts. Unlike other texts, most famously *The Communist Manifesto*, the history or genealogy that Marx gives in "Pre-Capitalist Economic Formations" does not rest on universal principles or causes, such as class struggle or the relation between forces and relations of production. In fact, Marx does not present the different modes of production along a linear history (from Asiatic, to ancient, to feudal, to capital, and so on) at all; rather, as I have already indicated, Marx presents the various precapitalist modes of production as different realizations of a particular

form. This formal presentation, however, does not entirely prevent Marx from inserting elements of each mode of production's particular conditions of stability
and dissolution.

As I have already noted, all of the precapitalist modes of production are explained from the perspective of their dissolution—it is a retrospective account,
what Balibar calls a "genealogy." Marx's development of the particular form the
dissolution of a particular mode of production at times verges on the contingent
and even the anecdotal. For example, Marx indicates that the wars of conquest
necessarily threaten the very mode of production they are fought to preserve because they transform both the objective forms of property and the subjective forms
of rank and title. In Marx's words:

> In particular, the influence of warfare and conquest, which e.g. in Rome belonged
> to the essential conditions of the commune itself, suspends the real bond on which
> it rests. In all these forms, the *reproduction of presupposed* relations—more or less
> naturally arisen or historic as well, but become traditional—of the individual to his
> commune, together with a *specific, objective* existence, *predetermined* for the indi-
> vidual, of his relations both to the conditions of labor and to his co-workers, fel-
> low tribesmen etc.—are the foundation of development, which is therefore from
> the outset *restricted,* but which signifies decay, decline and fall once this barrier is
> suspended. (G 487/396).

Warfare, slavery, the concentration of land, and usury are specific occurrences and
marginal developments within each of the precapitalist modes of production. Each
of these developments has its condition of possibility and perhaps even its rationale
within the particular mode of production from which it develops; at the same time,
each of these developments has effects on the relations of production, distribution,
and consumption, and on subjectivity that are unintended and eventually corrupt
their own foundations. Each precapitalist mode of production is threatened by unintended consequences. Technological, social, and political transformation all open
up the space of uncontrollable effects.[97] As Claude Lefort argues with respect to the
precapitalist modes of production, "History, one could say, comes to it from the outside."[98] Such a statement, however, has as its necessary corollary that if history comes
to the precapitalist modes of production from outside, it does so only to the extent
that the conditions for such an entry are within the particular mode of production
itself. It is because the precapitalist modes of production are conservative, because
they necessarily repeat and conserve their presuppositions that are at once social,
technological, and political, that they are necessarily threatened by unintended effects. As Negri contends: "Each determined social formation is then this complex of
conditions and limits whose interrelationship is constitutive of both the existence
and crisis of the given formation."[99]

With this intersection of conditions and limits we arrive at something like a
general concept, a general figure, or even a dialectic of historical causality and
transformation, although it is one that is without telos or end and continually

short-circuits the division between necessity and contingency. This logic is framed by the necessarily dialectic interrelation of reproduction and production, which cannot simply be opposed: Every reproduction, and thus every mode of reproduction, must produce, and every production must reproduce its conditions to survive. This is not simply a matter of the identity of opposites because it is impossible, almost physically impossible, for production and reproduction to ever coincide or to reach the same ends. Production always pushes ahead of and beyond the demands of a particular reproduction. Marx claims, "This reproduction, however, is at the same time necessarily new production and destruction of the old form" (G 493/401). This "dialectic," although it is perhaps too loose to entail such a term, passes through subjectivity, and it is this detour through the production of subjectivity that gives it its specificity and dynamism. As Marx states:

> Not only do the objective conditions change in the act of reproduction, e.g. the village becomes a town, the wilderness a cleared field etc., but the producers change, too, in that they bring out new qualities in themselves, develop themselves in production, transform themselves, develop new powers and ideas, new modes of intercourse [*Verkehrsweisen*], new needs and new language. (G 494/402)

It is not only that production exceeds reproduction, that there is a surplus, but that this surplus becomes truly disruptive to the mode of production only to the extent that it is embodied in particular desires, needs, and beliefs. The aleatory and sporadic excess of production to reproduction within any precapitalist mode of production becomes necessary once it is inscribed within comportments, beliefs, and practices. Hence, the importance that Marx ascribes to money in the dissolution of the precapitalist modes of production. The importance ascribed to money, of the hoards of money accumulated by usury and mercantile capitalism, is not a slippage back into so-called primitive accumulation, but instead it is the positing of a dense nodal point at which material practices, objects, desires, and forms of subjectivity coincide. Money has a corrosive aspect; it destroys the relations of prestige, knowledge, and desire that constituted the old communities and forms of labor, effectively decoding the old codes.[100] Money constitutes the material possibility of a new form of greed: Desire is no longer the desire for a specific object but for that object which stands in for all others. A similar argument could be made for the emergence of the new subjects of labor, the bird-free [*vogelfrei*] laborer: This worker is "naked" stripped of the codes that would subject him or her to a narrow form of belief, and desires, as a necessary condition for labor (as in feudalism). The encounter between the flows of money and the flow of those who have nothing but their labor power to sell is constitutive of and constituted by new desires, new habits, and new subjectivities.

The high point of "Pre-Capitalist Economic Formations," the theoretical development of a thought of a mode of production which is immanent to and interspersed with sociality and subjectivity, is also the limit, the edge, of the analysis. As Negri indicates, the abstract and general tendency of production exceeding and transforming reproduction, the expanding sphere of what is considered necessary for existence, begins to take on a specific, determinant, and subjective character at the point when it develops into the specific antagonism of the capitalist mode of production. I have already noted that the analysis of "Pre-Capitalist Economic Formations" dovetails with the analysis of primitive accumulation; in each text there is a consideration of the complex conditions of dissolution that constitute the material conditions from which the capitalist mode of production arises. Negri argues that it is at the precise point that the analysis of precapitalist economic formations merges with the analysis of the formation of capital that the abstract dialectic of production and reproduction ceases to be indeterminate. This logic is determined by constituting subjects and antagonisms.[101] As Marx argues:

> The production of capitalists and wage laborers is thus a chief product of capital's realization process. Ordinary economics, which looks only at the things produced, forgets this completely. When objectified labor is, in this process, at the same time posited as the worker's non-objectivity, as the objectivity of a subjectivity antithetical to the worker, as a property of a will alien to him, then capital is necessarily at the same time the capitalist. . . . It is posited within the concept of capital that the objective conditions of labor—and these are its own product—takes on a *personality* towards it, or what is the same, that they posited as the property of a personality alien to the worker. The concept of capital contains the capitalist. (G 512/420)

It is with the formation of classes, and with class antagonism, that subjectivity ceases to be an indeterminate element attached to a thought of community, or certain presuppositions of a particular mode of production. With the antagonism and conflict of classes, production and reproduction cease to be generic tendencies of any social formation, as sort of social or natural laws, and become elements of particular wills and conflicting strategies. Up until this point, until the analysis of capital, subjectivity was thought of as unified as an element of species-being [*Gattungswesen*] or herd mentality, and although there were different conditions for the formation of subjectivity within the different modes of production (from the subject of Asiatic despotism immersed in mystical fear and awe, to the frustrations of the mercantilist hoarder), there was not an analysis of the difference and antagonism internal to a singular mode of production. Even the Asiatic despot was more of an appearance, an optical effect of the Asiatic mode of production, than a subjective element of forces engaged in a conflict. (Or, if one wanted to draw out the similarities between Marx's theory of the Asiatic mode of production and Hegel's *Philosophy of History*, one could say that in the Asiatic mode of production only the despot has subjectivity.) It is possible that Marx's point is quite simply that prior to any division of class, the subjective conditions and effects of any mode of production are relatively uniform. If this is the case, then the emergence of the division into classes, with its accompanying social and technical division of labor, adds new levels of complexity. The various practices and comportments of the social would have to be posited twice, according to the division between classes that they constitute and reflect.[102]

Posing the problem of the mode of production and its relation to subjectivity from the perspective of Marx's analysis of precapitalist modes of production does not simply historicize the former; rather, it articulates a specific theoretical concept, immanence, or immanent causality. Immanent causality destroys any reference to a static or ahistorical locus of determination, a human nature or an idea of an economy, as a transcendent structure. At the same time, the concept of immanent causality, and the ontology of production it rests on (or makes possible), poses a specific problem: of the relations of effectivity, and causality, between the different dimensions of the mode of production—consumption, distribution, and production. If the notebooks on precapitalist modes of production left this question somewhat obscure, it did so to underscore the major difference between precapitalism and capitalism: a difference that in part concerns a fundamental transformation of the production of subjectivity. Precapitalist modes of production are for the most part modes of *reproduction,* reproducing their objective and subjective conditions, while capitalism must at the same time reproduce and revolutionize its conditions.

Marx's writings on the prehistory of capitalism have an ambiguous relationship to the problem of subjectivity in the capitalist mode of production. On the one hand, there is the general theoretical assertion of the immanence of the production of subjectivity to the mode of production, while on the other hand, there is assertion that "everything changes" when it comes to capital. As much as the writings on the prehistory of capitalism underscore the centrality of the production of subjectivity, they do so primarily as a point of contrast with the problem of subjectivity in capitalism. Thus as much as the reading of primitive accumulation points to the persistence of the problem of the production of subjectivity in Marx's thought on the capitalist mode of production, several questions remain to be explored in relation to Marx's writing on capitalism. First, What is the status of the production of subjectivity in the capitalist mode of production; what are its conditions and effects? And at the same time, What happens to Marx's thought on the production of subjectivity when he turns to critique capitalism, a mode of production he more than often refers to as constituted in its indifference to and abstraction from subjectivity?

TWO

WHAT IS LIVING AND WHAT IS DEAD IN THE PHILOSOPHY OF KARL MARX

THE POLITICS AND ONTOLOGY OF LIVING LABOR

———————————

In effect when Marx concerns himself with the essence of capitalism, he begins by invoking the establishment of a single global and nonqualified subjectivity, which capitalizes all the processes of subjectification. And this unique subject ("the unique subjective essence of wealth") expresses itself in "whatever" object. According to Marx capitalism liberates the subjectivity of all of the traditional codes which limit it, only to fall back on [rabattre sur] it in the production of value.

—Maurizio Lazzarato and Antonio Negri, "Annex 2"

ABSTRACT LABOR

For Karl Marx the two constitutive components of the capitalist mode of production are labor, or the capacity for labor freed from the means of its employment, and wealth, freed from the objective means of its investment. The capitalist mode of production is formed in the encounter between a free flow of labor and a flow of undifferentiated wealth. The encounter of these two flows, in the form of wage labor, are sufficient to constitute what Marx calls "formal subsumption," the initial stage of capitalism.

In the previous chapter we examined the particular historical argument entailed in ascertaining the capitalist mode of production from the point of view of the "encounter"; an argument that entailed a recognition of the role of the encounter in history—history as the history of the encounter of various ensembles (subjective, technical, and political) and their effects on each other. Marx's assertion of the foundational role of labor and wealth in the formation of the capitalist mode of production must also be placed in relation to the discourse of political economy not only in terms of the moral, anthropological, or ideological elements underlying its philosophy of history, as in so-called primitive accumulation, but also in terms of the dominant question of its problematic. This dominant question is the connection between labor and wealth (or as it is called later, "value") as it is elaborated and developed by the physiocrats Adam Smith and David Ricardo. Many have argued that Marx's formulations involving labor power, living and dead labor, and capitalist valorization are merely a continuation of "the labor theory of value" begun with Smith and Ricardo. I will argue, however, that Marx's thought of the conjunction of labor and wealth at the formation of the capitalist mode of production cannot be understood simply as a response to a question already posed but is itself the formulation of another question that develops into a problem unique to Marx. This other problem, or rather, series of problems, can be indicated by the specific antagonistic nature of the conjunction of labor and wealth: Labor and wealth come together in time and space in a particular relation, between laborer and capitalist, and thus the problem for Marx is articulating the particular antagonistic logic produced in and through this relation with its overlapping structures and strategies of exploitation, domination, and transformation. Marx begins with the problem inherited from bourgeois political economy—the relation between labor and wealth—and translates this into another problematic that is strictly unthinkable from the perspective of political economy: the conflictual and historical logic of the relationship between capitalist demands and the working class resistance.[1]

At the heart of this problematic is the production and constitution of subjectivity. In the previous chapter we saw that in the precapitalist modes of production the intersection between subjectivity and the mode of production was framed by reproduction, by what Marx saw as the intrinsically conservative nature of the precapitalist forms. The precapitalist forms repeat and conserve their conditions and presuppositions, which are technical, political, and subjective. This repetition exposes the precapitalist forms to a particular type of vulnerabilty: They are threatened by changes in the production of subjectivity and in the production of material life. In contrast to this, the capitalist mode of production has at its formation and foundation a collective subject that is "free" from the constraints and guarantees of a particular form of life. Thus the problem of subjectivity enters into the capitalist mode of production in a fundamentally different way: It is not a matter of the reproduction of a fixed subject but instead the extraction of wealth from a multitude of subjects that are constituted as basically interchangeable. This fundamental difference, which will be explored in this chapter, does not change a basic fact that is true for all modes of production: The conditions and limits of a mode of production, everything that causes the dissolution of one and the formation of another, necessarily pass through the production of subjectivity.

The disparity between the two problems of political economy—the determination of value and Marx's problem, the "antagonistic" structure of the capitalist mode of production—gives us a sense of the gulf that separates Marx from political economy proper; however, it does not provide us with a map of this distance. The outlines of such a map are provided in the various statements in which Marx summarizes the distance between his thought and that of classical political economy. This difference would seem to lie, at least in part, in the naming or conceptualization of those two "flows": wealth and labor. As Marx tells Frederick Engels in a letter, the first distinction between his conception of capital, and those of his immediate predecessors (Smith and Ricardo) is that rather than thinking wealth from the determinate forms in which it is given (rent, profit, interest, and so on) he considers it first abstractly as undifferentiated surplus value.[2]

The second crucial difference is that rather than attempting to directly relate labor and value, Marx insists that labor, like the commodity, must have a double character. With respect to the double character of labor Marx argues that it is "the secret to the whole critical conception."[3] The conceptualization, or name, of the differences between Marx and political economy are as follows: abstract surplus value, rather than the concrete figures of profit, interest, and rent, and labor as the conjunction of "abstract" and "concrete" labor. At first glance these appear to be simply terminological differences. However, the terminological difference only begins to indicate a fundamental difference of problematic. The contours of this distinction become manifest in the form of a paradox. Despite the fact that Marx identified himself as a materialist, and thus offered a materialist critique of political economy, the critical difference here would seem to be the insistence on the abstract itself; that is, Marx separates himself from political economy by thinking in terms of abstract surplus value, rather than more concrete forms of profit, rent, or wealth, and by positing abstract labor as a necessary complement to concrete and particular labor. Marx's materialism is not grounded on a simple dismissal of abstraction, or of form, in the name of concrete materiality of particular things, instead, it is on the recognition that abstraction itself has very real material conditions and effects. Case in point: What matters most about the commodity form, in terms of its effects on subjectivity, culture, and politics is that it is absolutely indifferent to its material content. Its materiality and effectivity is in its abstraction.[4]

The paradox of "abstract materiality" deepens if one takes into consideration Marx's early criticisms of G. W. F. Hegel and the young Hegelians in which one of his central points of criticism is the replacement of concrete and determinate relations of politics and the economy with the indeterminant relations of the concept. Marx's *Critique of Hegel's "Philosophy of Right"* provides a prime example of such a criticism. Marx summarizes the relation between concept and existence at work in Hegel's philosophy of right: "The philosophical task is not the embodiment of thought in determinate political realities, but the evaporation of these realities in abstract thought. The philosophical moment is not the logic of fact but the fact of logic."[5] Hegel, and the young Hegelians, think only of the concept, and relations between concepts, even when they claim to grasp the concrete reality of existence. It is from the context of this criticism of the young Hegelians that Marx develops his early theory of ideology in *The German Ideology*. In that text abstraction, the removal of ideas from their particular context and condition, is the primary condition of the ideological conception of history.[6] Once ideas are removed from their sociohistorical conditions of emergence it is then possible to understand history as not only the progression of different ideas, but as the self-development of the idea, or spirit. It is against this conception of history, history as the progress of spirit or the idea, that Marx proposes a concrete history, one that does not begin with abstraction but the concrete facts of the necessary material interaction between man and nature.[7]

Even at the early stage of *The German Ideology* Marx is not satisfied with a static opposition between abstract and concrete history. First, the latter must include the former; Marx sets himself to the task of giving the sociohistorical conditions that make it possible for history to appear as a history of ideas. Thus, Marx's remarks concerning the relation of German idealism to the backward political conditions of Germany (Germany as a nation in which there has only been a revolution in and of ideas) are not just polemical remarks; they are integral to the concept of ideology. Second, ideology is not only explained materially in terms of its conditions, but it is material in terms of its effects, most notably effects of domination and subjugation. The dominating and subjugating power of ideas, or of ideality in general, stems from the division between mental and manual labor, which is itself the condition and effect of class division. From this division it is possible to divide the social between those who possess the means to distribute and circulate ideas and those who are left to passively receive these ideas. "The class which has the means of material production at its disposal, has control at the same time over the means of mental production, so that thereby, generally speaking, the ideas of those who lack the means of mental production are subject to it."[8] Subjection here is at one and the same time subjection to particular ideas and ways of viewing the world and a particular class rule. Thus, these two elements necessarily imply each other. Marx does not rigorously develop this recognition of the material force of ideas, in fact he interrupts it, returning to the opposition between idea and reality in the figure of the proletariat in the final pages of *The German Ideology*, which is understood to be free of ideology because of its position with respect to material production.[9]

Marx's "1857 Introduction" returns to the first two of the problems introduced in *The German Ideology*: the critique of the ahistorical and idealizing tendency of the abstract and the historical conditions that produce abstract concepts. (Which is not to suggest that the third problem, the relation between abstraction and domination, is entirely absent.) Marx's return to the problem of the abstract is framed through a reconsideration of the distinction between political economy and the critique of political economy, from the place of abstraction in each. Marx introduces this distinction by stating that political economy that begins from the concrete datum of the "population" presupposed as the foundation and subject of the entire social act of production seems to begin from the concrete—after all what is more concrete than the factual verifiable number of individuals residing in the same place (G 100/35). However, Marx states that the population, considered apart from and prior to its constitutive antagonisms and divisions, is itself an "imagined concrete" [*vorgestellten*

Konkreten]. Marx argues for something of an inversion: Rather than start from the presumption of a concrete starting point such as the population, which is nothing but a confused thought of the totality, one must start from the abstract. This inversion is not just an inversion of priority between the abstract and concrete, but is founded on the recognition of the difference between the production of abstraction in existence and their production by and through thought (G 101/36).

The world that we inhabit practically and concretely is produced according to its own "rules," which are not the rules of the concept. This division does not preclude there being any relation between thought and the concrete, but makes possible their reconciliation in the "real abstraction."[10] Marx contends that Smith's immense discovery, discarding any limiting specification of labor tying it to a particular type of employment such as agriculture or industry, is itself a product of a particular history that is not reducible to the history of political economy. The simple category "labor in general" appears only with the emergence of capitalist wage labor.

> As a rule, the most general abstractions arise only in the midst of the richest possible concrete development where one thing appears common to many, to all. Then it ceases to be thinkable in a particular form alone. On the other side, this abstraction of labor as such is not merely the mental product [*geistige Resultat*] of a concrete totality of labors. Indifference towards specific labors corresponds to a form of society in which individuals can with ease transfer from one labor to another, and where the specific kind is a matter of chance for them, hence indifference. Not only the category, but labor in reality [*Wirklichkeit*] has become the means of creating wealth in general, and has ceased to be organically linked with particular individuals in any specific form. (G 104/38)

Marx's statement regarding the appearance of labor as abstraction could be understood in part as a repetition of Hegel's regarding the modern condition: whereas the philosophical task of antiquity was to wrest the concept, or the abstract, from sensuous immediacy—"in modern times the individual finds the abstract form ready-made."[11] Thus, Marx could be understood as extending Hegel's problem: The task of modern philosophy is to wrest thought from the static and reified abstractions found ready to hand, whether in philosophy, political economy, or everyday existence. The problem then is one of recognizing the effectivity of the "abstract" not only in thought but in existence, and liberating oneself from its rusted chains. For Hegel this liberation entailed reflexivity, self-consciousness, and the dialectic, in short recognizing oneself in the supposedly autonomous and stubborn concepts and setting them in motion.[12] For Marx, given that abstraction is not just a matter of thought, but concerns all of activity, liberation necessarily passes through different channels.

Marx's understanding of the abstract is only in part indebted to Hegel. Mario Tronti has argued that Marx's development of the concept of abstract labor, or of the relation between abstract labor and concrete labor, can be understood as the convergence of problematics inherited in part from political economy, specifically

Ricardo, on one side, and Hegel on the other.[13] It is from the combination of these two problems that Marx develops his thought of the materiality of the abstract. From Ricardo, Marx inherited a specific problem; that is, the relation between labor-as-such, as abstract subjective activity, and value.[14] Ricardo does not locate the source of wealth in a specific object, such as gold in the case of the mercantilists, or in a specific type of labor, as the physiocrats did with agricultural labor, but in the capacity for subjective productive activity in general.[15] Value, for Ricardo, is determined not by any specific object, or type of labor, but by the cost of labor or abstract productive activity. As Gilles Deleuze and Félix Guattari write, "Marx said that Luther's merit was to have determined the essence of religion, no longer on the side of the object, but as an interior religiosity; that the merit of Adam Smith and Ricardo was to have determined the essence or nature of wealth no longer as an objective nature but as an abstract and deterritorialized subjective essence, the activity of production in general."[16] Abstract subjective activity—activity indifferent to its means and object—capable of being employed anywhere, is at the basis of the production of wealth in capitalism.[17] However, as much as Ricardo separated labor from any privileged type of labor, such as agricultural labor, he did not arrive at abstract labor, and continued to see labor as a cost of production bound up in its particularity. Even though this failure may have produced problems at the level of political economy, in terms of its specific questions and discourse, in itself it is indicative of problems at the heart of the capitalist mode of production. As Deleuze and Guattari make clear, the recognition of subjective activity as the source of wealth in political economy is combined with its alienation.

> Here we have the great movement of decoding or deterritorialization: the nature of wealth is no longer to be sought on the side of the object, under exterior conditions, in the territorial or despotic machine. But Marx is quick to add that this essentially "cynical" discovery finds itself rectified by a new territorialization, in the form of a new fetishism or a new "hypocrisy." Production as the abstract subjective essence is discovered only in the forms of property that objectifies it all over again, that alienates it by reterritorializing it.[18]

Deleuze and Guattari locate in the distinction between classical political economy and Marx not just a break between two different discourses but a central contradiction of the capitalist mode of production: "Capitalism can proceed only by developing the subjective essence of abstract wealth or production for the sake of production . . . but . . . at the same time it can do so only in the framework of its own limited purpose, as a determinate mode of production . . . the self expansion of existing capital."[19] While Deleuze and Guattari locate in abstract labor something of the dynamic of the entire capitalist mode of production, a point that we will return to, Tronti recognizes something of this double-sided nature of abstract labor already at work in the particular way in which Marx develops this concept from two sources. Which is to suggest that the problem for Tronti is not simply one of Marx's two or three sources, but rather it is a problem of the antagonistic dynamic of capitalism itself.

If, according to Tronti, Ricardo was in some sense the thinker who recognized the relation between labor in general and value, in effect separating value from this or that objective measure and referring it to the productivity of subjectivity, it was Hegel who posed the problem of "abstract labor." The concept of abstract labor is a thread running from Hegel's early Jena philosophy through the *Philosophy of Right*. In part this thread concerns the rise of "abstraction" as a defining element of lived experience. At the same time, what is at stake politically for Hegel in abstract labor is not the determination of value, but rather the *Aufhebung* of the particularity of concrete labors.[20] Labor is the space of mediation where the blind and animalistic concrete labor, often described as the labor of peasants, embedded in the brute immediacy of need, is subjugated and subjected to universality, making possible its incorporation into the state.[21] Labor is the education [*Bildung*] of particularity. The education into universality is found in the technical conditions (machinery), social conditions (cooperation/division of labor), and political conditions (trade unions) of work.[22] As Hegel describes this process:

> Practical education through work consists in the self perpetuating need and habit of being occupied in one way or another, in the limitations of one's activity to suit both the nature of the material in question and, in particular, the arbitrary will of others, and in a habit, acquired through this discipline, of objective activity and universally applicable skills.[23]

Civil society is the society of the organization, education, and control, of abstract labor.[24] Thus, to extend Tronti's suggestion, two "discoveries" converge in Marx: the productivity of an indifferent subjective force (Ricardo) and the need to continually subject this force to discipline (Hegel). The coexistence of these two problems imposes on Marx's thought a demand that is alien to Ricardo and Hegel: the demand to consider the coexistence of an abstract subjective force (labor power) that is extremely powerful, productive of the realm of value, and the necessary discipline and control of that force (capital). As a sort of provocation, which will be justified later, it is possible to suggest that this combination of Ricardo and Hegel in Marx can be understood to entail the same political problem that Michel Foucault argues underlies disciplinary power: "Discipline increases the forces of the body (in economic terms of utility) and diminishes these same forces (in political terms of obedience)."[25] In each case the political problem is not simply one of exploitation or domination, but of the necessary provocation of a "counter-power"—capitalism is dependent on the productivity of the laboring subject, which it must also control.[26]

It is perhaps because of the novelty of this problem that Marx is forced to rethink what Hegel understood by abstract labor and thus the abstract itself. Abstract labor, the labor constitutive of value, becomes itself the site of conflict and control, and thus it cannot be a simple "generalization." To return to the passage from the "1857 Introduction" cited previously:

Such a state of affairs is at its most developed in the most modern form of existence of bourgeois society—in the United States. Here, then, for the first time, the point of departure of modern economics, namely the abstraction of the category "labor," "labor as such," labor pure and simple becomes true in practice [*praktisch wahr*]. The simplest abstraction, then, which modern economics places at the head of its discussions and which expresses an immeasurably ancient relation valid in all forms of society, nevertheless achieves practical truth as an abstraction only as a category of the most modern society. (G 104/38)[27]

Marx seems to suggest in this passage that "labor," abstract and indifferent from this or that specific task or activity, is not merely a concept that is applicable to capital but is itself actual and effective with the emergence of capital. Labor has become "true in practice," prior to or at the same time that it is discovered by political economy. Marx is not simply concerned with the history or the historical emergence of abstract thought, as in the case of Hegel, but with the way in which abstraction, in terms of ideal identity and indifference to qualitative content, is itself practically produced in history, and not simply in thought.[28] But what sort of practice produces this abstraction? How? And what is the relation of this practice/production to the simultaneous discovery of subjective activity as the source of value along with the need to subject this activity to the demands of discipline?

In the opening chapter of the first volume of *Capital*, Marx demonstrates that just as the commodity must be understood as the coexistence of use value and exchange value, labor also must be understood as both concrete and abstract labor. Tronti argues that, unlike the double character of the commodity, which has found its way into the heart of Marxist economics and philosophy, the double character of labor, as concrete and abstract labor, has often been overlooked.[29] Furthermore, it is possible to add, following Tronti, that the latter division has been overlooked, or even missed, insofar as it exceeds a purely conceptual determination; that is, insofar as it is something other than the coexistence of the particular (this or that labor) and the universal (labor in general). Often abstract labor has been understood as "labor in general" and as such would be a simple "mental generalization," necessary to understanding capital, and the production of value in capital. In other words, abstract labor would only be a mental approximation.[30] What this understanding of abstract labor misses is how such a mental generalization produces value; or more than that, how abstract labor and the social average of labor has real effects insofar as value and surplus value are necessarily dependent on it. Seeing abstract labor as simply a mental generalization of different particular labors makes it impossible to recognize the particular force of abstract labor. Marx rhetorically indicates this failure by ridiculing the naivete of trying to draw a direct link between particular concrete labor and value.

It might seem that if the value of a commodity is determined by the quantity of labor expended to produce it, it would be the more valuable the more unskillful and lazy the worker who produced it, because he would need more time to complete the article. However, the labor that forms the substance of value is equal human labor, the expenditure of identical human labor power. (CI 129/53)

Such a direct connection fails because it does not recognize the effectivity of abstract labor. The effectivity of the social average of all labors is that which imposes itself on this or that particular labor as a norm: failure to produce according to the speed and productivity of this norm is a failure to produce value or a profit. This norm makes necessary the equalization of the diverse and heterogeneous labors of diverse and distinct individuals into an average capable of being measured. At this point, however, Marx presents this average as sheer fact without indicating its ground, in other words, without indicating what makes such an equalization of the diverse possible. At the same time that Marx accepts this as fact, as a given, he seems to indicate both by his criticisms of classical political economy, which failed to recognize the necessary abstract nature of value-producing labor, and by his own statements regarding abstract labor as a "process which goes on behind men's backs," that this equalization is, if not unconscious, at least not recognized as such. Neither the worker struggling to keep up to speed nor the economist searching for the secret of wealth recognizes abstract labor. Abstract labor has the paradoxical status of a fact that is lived in its effectivity, in terms of the demands it imposes to produce according to the speed and rate of this average, but never recognized as such. The abstraction of abstract labor is neither arrived at nor recognized by thought alone, but is lived in its concrete effects.

The intersection of the facticity of abstract labor and the seeming inability to recognize this fact is obliquely developed through the definition of commodity fetishism placed at the end of the first chapter of *Capital*. This assertion seems somewhat paradoxical since, on a first reading, commodity fetishism and labor would seem to be opposed as falsity to truth. If commodity fetishism is on some basic level the false attribution of a social quality, value, to things, to the point where it would seem that objects and not social relations, specifically labor, produce value, then labor would seem to be the truth to the illusion. For Marx, however, an opposition between truth and falsity misses the central question—the question of the particular appearance, or form, itself. It is by answering this question that we can approach an understanding of the simultaneous "factual" and unconscious nature of abstract labor. In the section on commodity fetishism Marx refuses any psychological or intentional understanding of this illusion. It is not, like Immanuel Kant's famous antinomies, an illusion hard wired into human consciousness, nor has anyone been deceived by a ruling class—operating the smoke and mirrors from offstage. "It constitutes, rather, the way in which reality (a certain form or social structure) cannot but appear."[31] For Marx the source of this appearance is to be found in activity itself, in the ensemble of relations. It is not so much that value is believed to be in commodities but, rather, that one acts in the process of exchange as if commodities, despite their distinct and different natures, were all reducible to some abstract equivalent that constitutes the possibility of exchange. This abstraction is necessary to the act of exchange, although it is quite possible that it is not recognized as such. In fact, in the act of exchange what is recognized is the concrete particularity of this or that specific commodity. Alfred Sohn-Rethel writes, "In commodity exchange the action and the consciousness of people go separate ways. Only the action is abstract; the consciousness of the actors is not."[32] It is this production of abstraction in exchange that is in part constitutive of abstract human labor. In the case of both the commodity form and abstract labor the issue is how things, or practices, in their diverse and heterogeneous particularity can be subject to some standard or measure, and Marx would seem to argue that this happens through exchange.

> Men do not therefore bring the products of their labor into relation with each as values because they see these objects merely as the material integuments [*als bloß sachliche Hüllen*] of homogeneous human labor. The reverse is true: by equating their different products to each other in exchange as values, they equate their different kinds of labor as human labor. They do this without being aware of it. (CI 167/88)

This unrecognized abstract equivalent that makes the exchange of diverse and disparate objects possible is itself produced by the practice of exchange of commodities; it is materialized through these practices. The abstract equivalent is material in at least two senses: It is produced in the quotidian practices of exchange that continually bring into relation the different products, and different labors, as units of abstract homogenized labor; and this equivalent is materialized in money. Or it would be more accurate to say, placing paradox upon paradox, it is simultaneously materialized and idealized; that is, money is a material object but it is also a material object that stands in for pure abstraction as a unit of pure quantity.[33] The relations of exchange, the commodity form, and money are relations of consumption, and thus they constitute an exemplary instance of consumption acting on and determining production.[34] Because consumption is also a practice it would not be incorrect to say, referring to Marx's expansive definition of production, that consumption produces the particular appearance of abstract labor. The practices of commodity consumption produce abstract labor as a necessary unconscious presupposition.

It is not exactly correct to say that abstract labor is unconscious. In fact, returning to the earlier epochal distinction between precapitalist and capitalist modes of production, it might be more useful to employ the distinction between "codes" and "axioms" to clarify how abstract labor and exchange value are produced through quotidian practices without being recognized or interiorized as belief. One of the central elements of codes, or coding, is that they are meaningful, attached to belief. When the precapitalist modes of production code their presuppositions, placing one set of difference over another, presenting the despot as founder and origin of community, for example, it establishes a relation of belief that is necessary to the functioning of the mode of production.[35] Axioms are distinct from codes in that they do not require belief in order to function. It might be more accurate to say that axioms are concerned more with what should be done rather than what must be believed. Axioms relate to no other scene or sphere, such as religion, politics, or law, that would provide their ground or justification. They are merely differential relations between abstract and quantitative flows.[36] In capitalism two such flows are the flow of labor power available on the market and the flow of capital. These two flows conjoin at a particular time and place, and this conjunction establishes a differential relation between the two flows.[37] Once such a relation is established, setting up a particular relation between a particular quantity of labor and a particular quantity of capital, or wage, the axiomatic is effective. It cannot be avoided; one can only add new axiomatics to the system. There is no possible contestation at the level of code or belief, in fact the differential relations and their concrete effects remain in place; they are functional whether or not they are believed.[38] The "setting up" of axioms between abstract quantities is an aspect of what Deleuze and Guattari call "reterritorialization," the regulation of the abstract quantities as abstract quantities.[39] To return to the example of commodity fetishism, the equivalence between a quantity of abstract labor and money displaces the abstract potentiality of labor onto money itself, setting up an artificial territory—it now appears as if it is money itself that is productive. The epochal distinction between precapitalist and the capitalist mode of production is not only a distinction between subjective and objective domination but also a shift in how this domination is lived. Whereas prior to capitalism it is lived through the coded structures of belief and personal subjugation, in capitalism it is lived through abstract operative rules, which are not necessarily believed or even grasped. As Marx writes, "These *objective* dependency relations also appear, in antithesis to those of *personal* dependence . . . in such a way that individuals are now ruled by *abstractions*, whereas earlier they were dependent on one another" (G 164/98).

In the case of commodity fetishism, value is not something one necessarily believes to be an attribute of commodities or money; at the end of the day one is willing to admit that things are "just things" and money is only paper, but one acts, and must act, "as if" value is an attribute of commodities or expressed in money.[40] Commodity fetishism is an element of the society effect: It is produced through actions but it is not recognized as something produced or historical.[41] It is at this point, where the appearance of value in the commodity form immediately relates to a series of practical comportments and behaviors, that Marx's theory proceeds from a theory of social objectivity (the "socially uniform objectivity as values," or "phantom objectivity," which commodities are seen to possess) to a theory of social subjectivity.[42] The value that things possess, and the fluctuating relations and transformations of value, is not something that one simply observes or perceives as an optical illusion, but is something that determines or affects behavior. The worker approaches these commodities, and the values between them, as one who also has a commodity to sell—labor power—and this commodity is fetishized as much as the other commodities in the world. Labor power—human activity— becomes a thing, a value, whose relation to other things must be evaluated and calculated.[43] Thus, abstract labor, which is produced by a particular practical activity, is posited as a necessary presupposition of exchange value and in turn falls back on the practical activity governing it.[44] Marx shows that labor would seem to preexist the labors of the specific individual: "Labor, thus measured by time, does not seem, indeed, to be the labor of different persons, but on the contrary the different working individuals seem to be mere organs of this labor."[45] Just as one necessarily sees all the diverse commodities as different expressions of the substance exchange value one necessarily treats ones own labor power, or subjective potential, as a share of a labor to be sold.

The interrelation between the social practical production of a particular form of objectivity (objects as commodities/values) and a particular form of subjectivity (individuals as instances of abstract labor) is by no means an incidental or secondary point for Marx. It is from the equivalence of the diverse labors in the particularity that it becomes possible to speak of humanity in general.

> For a society of commodity producers, whose general social relation of production consists in the fact that they treat their products as commodities, hence as values, and in this material [*sachlich*] form bring their individual, private labors into relation with each other as homogenous human labor, Christianity with its religious cult of man in the abstract, more particularly in its bourgeois development, i.e. in Protestantism, Deism, etc. is the most fitting form of religion. (CI 172/93)

Abstract labor, as the possible comparison and equalization of diverse activities, and humanity, as the essence underlying any particular identity, appear at the same time historically. As Marx argues, it is because this historical conjunction of abstract labor and abstract humanity had not yet taken place that Aristotle could not discover the secret of value (CI 152/72).[46] Rather than founding an anthropology in which labor is the essence of man—the link between abstract labor, labor in general, and humanity—refers back to a radical historicization in which both terms must be seen as themselves historically and socially produced. It is the social relation that is prior to either abstract labor or abstract humanity. In Marx's words: "However, let us remember that commodities possess an objective character as values only in so far as they are all expressions of an identical social substance, human labor, that the objective character as values is therefore purely social" (CI 139/62). Abstract labor and humanity are both grounded on a social relation, on the production of commodities.[47] From this perspective it is possible to reread the opening passages of *Capital* as proceeding from radical rethinking of human needs and human activity from the abstract indifference of the commodity form.[48] The indifference of commodity production to the needs the commodity satisfies is the precondition of the indifference of abstract labor. "The commodity is, first of all, an external object, a thing which through its qualities satisfies human needs of *whatever* kind [*irgendeiner Art*]. The nature of these needs, whether they arise, for example, from the stomach, or the imagination, makes no difference" (CI 126/49). *Capital* opens with the materialization of the abstract.

At this point, it might be necessary to pause over Marx's assertion that abstract humanity arrives with the commodity form. Clearly at the time of Marx's writing, and today, this abstract humanity produced by the demands of abstract labor has yet to arrive: Differences of race and gender continue to structure the world of labor. For Marx machinery constituted the possibility of abstracting labor from the strength, skill, and ultimately gender of the one performing it, producing an abstract indifference. "The labor of women and children was therefore the first result of the capitalist application of machinery" (CI 517/416). In *The Communist Manifesto* the patriarchal structure of the family is presented as a feudal residue soon to be drowned in the "icy waters" of capitalist calculation, which exposes everyone to an equal exploitation. That such a transformation has not come to pass, despite the entry of many women into the workforce, has been the critical focal point of much work in Marxist feminism. Without attempting a thorough consideration of this debate, it is at least imperative to indicate its importance for the discussion of abstract labor.

As Heidi Hartmann argues, Marx's understanding of the tendency toward the abstract interchangeability of labor regardless of gender is incapable of explaining the subordination of the family as anything other than a residue of previous feudal modes of production. There is nothing within the Marxist critical conceptual apparatus to directly account for the fact that gender continues to be operative in allocating positions in the economy in the absence of any "natural" justification, or the subordination of women to men generally.[49] Not only is it operative but the patriarchal family—a family in which the surplus of household labor (cleaning, child rearing, and so on) is performed by the woman—is functionally beneficial to capital, reproducing labor power inexpensively.[50] It is the question of how do we account for the simultaneous independence and interdependence of capitalism and patriarchy that is addressed in much of the Marxist feminist writing.[51]

The very question would seem to invalidate Marx's assertion of the materiality of abstract labor in the capitalist mode of production, or at least limit its scope, in that it points to a concrete difference—the difference of gender—that has not been leveled by the abstract flexibility of work. However, as Leopoldina Fortunati indicates, the coexistence of capitalism and patriarchy is at the same time the coexistence of different realms of work: abstract labor, or wage labor, which is public and productive and reproductive work, which is nonwaged and does not even appear as work. Reproductive work, the work done to care for and reproduce men and children physically and emotionally, is not subject to the wage, and thus it appears a "natural" attribute of social relations.[52] Whereas labor done for the wage is abstract and interchangeable, reproductive labor is situated within a network of personal connections that obscure its status as labor, its productivity. Thus the intersection between abstract labor and value does not simply work in one direction; it is not just that abstract labor produces value but also that value, through the distribution of the wage and capital, determines what activities constitute labor proper, or abstract labor.[53]

Despite the fact that Marx argues for a historical and social understanding of abstract labor, he also presents abstract labor—the equivalence between different types of labor—as a biological fact or residue. As he states in the first section of *Capital*:

> If we leave aside the determinate quality of productive activity, and therefore the use-
> ful character of the labor, what remains is its quality of being an expenditure of
> human labor-power. Tailoring and weaving, although they are qualitatively differ-
> ent productive activities, are both a productive expenditure of human brains, mus-
> cles, nerves, hands, etc. and in this sense both human labor. They are merely two
> different forms of the expenditure of human labor. (CI 134/58)

If the coexistence of these two seemingly opposed statements in the same presentation is understood to be anything other than confusion and self-contradiction,
then it must indicate a specific problem; that is, the necessity of thinking abstract
labor at one and the same time as historical and natural—as being produced from
a certain ensemble of relations and also involving and implicating subjectivity to
the point at which it appears be coexistent with the biological basis of subjectivity
("brains, muscles, and nerves, etc.").[54]

The seemingly contradictory combination of the natural and the historical is in
some sense provocative: It reveals that Marx is not simply concerned with the co-
implication of certain subjective states such as greed—and the formation of the
capitalist mode of production—but with the production of subjectivity down to
its apparently natural and biological ground. Marx's interest in producing a historical account of the apparently biological or natural dimensions of subjectivity is
already somewhat ambitiously indicated in *The Economic and Philosophic Manuscripts of 1844* in which Marx writes, "The forming of the five senses is a labor of
the entire history of the world down to the present."[55] The contradictory and
paradoxical description of abstract labor as biological and historical, however, begins to indicate the limitation of the perspective followed in the first part of *Capital.* The first part of *Capital* limits itself to a consideration of circulation and the
market, whether it be the market of commodities or the labor market. In each
case, following the expansive sense of production—the production of production—outlined in the *Grundrisse* and in the previous chapter, it is clear that these
relations of distribution and consumption are in themselves productive in that
they produce abstract labor as their unrecognized yet effective presupposition. It is
unclear, however, whether these relations are entirely adequate to the "production"
of abstract labor; that is, it is questionable if abstract labor can be seen to derive entirely from the commodity form. Or put otherwise, Can the entirety of social relations in capital be derived from the commodity form? There have been many
attempts to present the commodity form, or commodity fetishism, as expressing
the essential and central element of the capitalist mode of production.[56] Without
attempting anything like a thorough criticism of these arguments, which make up
a long-standing tendency of Marxist thought, it is important to at least point out
their limitations if only to stress the importance of extending the analysis of abstract labor into the "hidden abode of production."

As Louis Althusser characterizes it, "expressive causality" is the attempt to present the social totality as the expression of one central contradiction. Any attempt
to deduce the dynamics of capitalism from the overlapping contradictions of the

commodity (the contradictions of use and exchange value, abstract and living labor) necessarily participates in this logic.[57] This logic runs into problems in terms of the representation of social relations. In the first section of *Capital* Marx presents commodity production as production carried out by isolated producers whose only social relation is the act of exchange itself. "Since the producers do not come into social contact until they exchange the products of their labor, the specific social character of their private labors appears [*erscheinen*] only within this exchange" (CI 165/87). The first problem with this presentation is that it is not a necessary element of capitalist production: commodity production preexists capitalist production, and the scenario of isolated commodity producers coming into contact only through exchange is more likely to take place at the margins of precapitalist society.[58] More important, such formulations, which posit isolated commodity producers coming into contact through exchange, would seem to make exchange the central nexus of capitalist socialization, leaving labor outside, or prior to, sociality.

As I argued in the previous chapter, the section on the commodity forms in the opening of *Capital* assumes that labor is a natural human attribute; it does not engage with the problem of the production of the subjectivity of labor. In this point of view, labor is the natural ground of a history, which is only the history of different modes of distribution. Following this presentation many writers have elevated this difference between exchange and production to the point at which it is a matter of two different or opposed worldviews: exchange is the locus of the production of abstract labor, if not abstraction itself, and production—labor—is entirely other from this process. In this view, exchange both requires and makes necessary a world seen as a world of exchange values, of identical quantitative units. Labor is an engagement with the concrete in its dynamic particularity.

Even though there is no doubt a necessary connection between commodity production and abstract labor, presentations that focus on Marx's early presentation of production as isolated and asocial have a tendency to occlude the social and conflictual nature of production that Marx develops in the later chapters of *Capital*.[59] Such criticisms, which stop at the commodity form, are implicitly criticisms of the mode of distribution in capital—commodity production and market relations—rather than the mode of production of capital.[60] These criticisms focus on the commodity form and market relations as the object of their critique, leaving labor and production relatively untouched. Thus they fail to grasp the extent to which abstract labor acts not only in the market of commodities and labor but also in the production process itself as a norm that is forcefully imposed on the diverse bodies of different labors.[61] In Marx's terms they are attentive to "how capital *produces*, but not how capital is itself *produced*." What is overlooked is the manner in which the capitalist mode of production must be made and remade, not just at the level of economic relations but also at the intimate level of power relations affecting the body, habits, and subjectivity of the worker. Furthermore, by deriving abstract labor solely from the commodity form, they present it as a deed already accomplished with the emergence of commodity production, thus overlooking the antagonistic relations internal to the social production of abstract labor. What is missed is not only that the demand to make labor quantifiable and calculable comes up against certain limits, but also, as we shall see, the most powerful limitation that capital comes up against is its own tendency to produce an active and cooperative working class.

LIVING LABOR

Before proceeding to consider the ensemble of relations that constitute abstract labor and the antagonistic and conflictual terrain that these relations produce, it is necessary to examine the other side of the problematic Marx inherited from Ricardo and Hegel. If the Hegel side of this problematic is an examination of the practices and processes that discipline labor, subjecting it to the equalization and normalization of abstract labor (practices necessary to the production of value), then the Ricardo side of this problem is the former's condition of possibility in that it presents labor in general as productivity, or subjective potential. Although, as we shall see, "condition of possibility" is meant here only in a logical sense, rather than a chronological sense—it is not a matter of a pure undifferentiated potential existing first only to be contained and trained by practices and forces subjecting it to quantification and standardization. The names "Hegel" and "Ricardo" indicate two different complementary examinations: one into the power relations imposed on bodies and individuals to standardize and regularize their productivity to given ends; the other into the productivity of bodies and individuals—their superadequacy to their own self-maintenance.[62] These two different sides correspond to different sides of abstract: The first (Hegel) side corresponds to the interchangeability, the reduction, of diverse bodies to units of abstract labor power; while the second (Ricardo) side refers to the potentiality and flexibility of labor power: its ability to exceed the given.

Although Marx's concept of abstract labor is explicitly framed as part of his critical break with bourgeois political economy—the secret to the whole "critical conception," the development of which takes up most of the opening pages of *Capital*—"living labor" is only explicitly named in a few scant passages in the *Grundrisse*. However, just because the concept is only referred to a few times does not mean that it is not operative throughout Marx's writing. Thus, defining and explicating Marx's idea of living labor demands subjecting Marx's various critiques of labor to "symptomatic reading." Moishe Postone broadly distinguishes between two different critical strategies in Marxism: the first one that makes labor the object of its criticism and a second in which labor is the subject of its criticism.[63] To make labor an object of criticism is to criticize the reduction of all human activities to labor; in short it is to criticize the instrumentality and teleology implicit in the idea of labor. Such a criticism is situated against the idea that human beings are primarily "*homo laborans*" and seeks to undercover the historical, political, and cultural transformations that have reduced human beings to "organs" of labor; while a critique articulated from the standpoint of labor takes labor for granted as a fundamental element of existence and from this criticizes the relations of distribution that exploit labor, alienating it from its own activity. Labor is assumed to be productive, and creative of value, and the critical question is how this power is turned against it. These two critiques are assumed to be fundamentally opposed. The opposition between these two critical strategies generally assumes that labor itself is one-sided, thus forgetting the duality of labor. An examination of the relationship between abstract and living labor makes possible a criticism in which labor is both the object, in the sense that it is a criticism of the apparatuses and structures that constitute abstract labor, and the subject, in the sense that it places the potentiality of labor at the center of this critique. As Tronti argues, the working class must struggle against itself, against its constitution as abstract labor power as much as it must struggle against capitalism, against the exploitation of labor power.[64]

The critique that takes labor as its subject would seem to apply most directly to Marx's earliest writings, *The Economic and Philosophic Manuscripts of 1844* (also known as the "Paris Manuscripts"). On first glance the development of the idea of estranged labor, or alienation, would seem to follow the lines of a critique written from the standpoint of labor as subject. Labor is assumed to be the "concrete essence" of humanity, and it is because it is the essence of humanity that its alienation, in the products and labor processes which are not under its control, becomes nothing less than the alienation of human essence itself. However, in this text there is already a tension between two different definitions of production: on the one hand, an immanent definition of production—production as the mutual causality of production, consumption, and distribution—and, on the other hand, a reduction of not only this conception of production but also all of political economy to an anthropological meaning of the expression and loss of the essence of man.[65] The space between these problematics is not clearly demarcated, and their differences can only be identified retrospectively from the perspective of later developments. It is from this perspective that it is possible to isolate a thoroughly immanent articulation of the relation between man, nature, and history, prefiguring the immanent sense of production developed in the *Grundrisse*:

> Nature is man's *inorganic body*—nature, that is, insofar as it is not itself the human body. Man *lives* on nature—means that nature is his *body*, with which he must remain in continuous interchange if he is not going to die. That man's physical and spiritual life is linked to nature means nothing else than nature is linked [*zusammenhängt*] to itself, for man is a part of nature.[66]

At the same time this immanent terrain of nature reaches its completion in man, who has the ability to exceed its limitations. As Marx writes in a latter section of the same passage, "[An animal] produces one sidedly, whilst man produces universally. It produces only under the dominion of immediate physical need, whilst man produces even when he is free from physical need and only truly produces in freedom therefrom. And animal produces only itself, whilst man reproduces the whole of nature."[67] Without ascribing too much importance to this one passage, or attempting a reading of the entire manuscript, we can argue that this problematic remains in itself thoroughly ambiguous, in that it seems to affirm at one and the same time an immanence of man, nature, and history as well as a residual transcendence that ascribes to "man" the active part of the relation.[68] (It would even be possible to suggest that this ambiguity persists in Marx's texts up through the definition of the labor process in chapter 7 of *Capital*.) It is through this ambivalent insistence of man, nature, and history, that Marx redefines Ludwig Feuerbach's term *species-being* [*Gattungswesen*]: Man is a species-being because he takes his species, or the universal as his object, or rather, man is a species-being insofar as he interacts with nature as such.[69] This definition of species-being seems to turn the previous insistence of immanence definitely toward a humanism, and it is in this capacity that it grounds the definition of alienation [*Emfremdete*].

Alienation can be described in part as an objectification; that is, as labor losing itself in becoming object, or property, which stands opposed to it. "With the *increasing value* of the world of things proceeds in direct proportion the *devaluation* of the world of men."[70] Alongside this first sense of alienation—alienation as objectification—there is a second sense of alienation that necessarily follows from the first: alienation in the activity itself. "But the estrangement is manifested not only in the result but in the act of production, within the producing activity itself."[71] This second sense of alienation is founded on a contradiction and an inversion between the undetermined possibility of life activity—one possible understanding of species-being—and this or that specific labor. The worker is alienated insofar as the former is subsumed under the latter. This transformation is an inversion: Species-being, the undetermined possibility of this, that, or whatever activity, is subordinated to one specific activity—labor—necessary to the maintenance of bare life, of living altogether.[72] Species-being as potential indifference to whatever activity, or the open possibility of any activity, thus seems to prefigure, one important part of Marx's definition of abstract labor, although the sense is entirely inverted: Abstract indifference to activity appears as a quality that is alienated in capitalist labor and not presupposed by it. Marx's theory of alienated labor could also be understood as a theory of labor as alienation: Labor, the forced constraint to one particular limited activity, is an alienation of the openness of activity that constitutes species-being and will in turn prove to be integral to the concept of living labor.

The first of the "Theses on Feuerbach" would seem to develop this thought of species-being in that it suggests that subjectivity must be thought as activity.

> The chief defect of all hitherto existing materialism (that of Feuerbach included) is that the thing, reality, sensuousness, is conceived only in the form of the *object or of contemplation*, but not as *sensuous human activity, practice,* not subjectively. Hence in contradistinction to materialism, the *active* side was developed abstractly by idealism—which of course does not know real sensuous activity as such.[73]

Marx's criticism reveals that materialism conceals idealist tendencies in that it posits the material object as an object that can be represented, and that idealism, specifically German idealism with which Marx was familiar, has a materialist tendency in the priority it gives to activity, or practical activity.[74] From this two-pronged criticism one can extract the positive content of Marx's thesis: an attempt to go beyond all hitherto concepts of both materiality and subjectivity. Thus it is possible to read the first thesis as both a redefinition of materialism, positing matter or materiality as practice and activity rather than mute objectivity, and a redefinition of subjectivity, subjectivity as activity rather than contemplation. It is this reworking of materiality and subjectivity, subjectivity as material activity, that runs through Marx's latter concepts of labor power and living labor.[75]

In Marx's later writings, the opposition, or relation, between undetermined activity and labor ceases to be a static opposition, one that situates species-being as a potentiality that is already alienated with the onset of capitalism.[76] The relation between the abstract potential of labor and its actual existence becomes a dynamic condition of conflict. In *The German Ideology* indifference to whatever activity appears as a positive figure, one of the few Marx provides, of communism. Marx writes that:

> in communist society, where nobody has one exclusive sphere of activity but each can become accomplished in any branch he wishes, society regulates the general production and thus makes it possible for me to do one thing today and another tomorrow, to hunt in the morning, fish in the afternoon, rear cattle in the evening, criticize after dinner, without ever becoming hunter, fisherman, shepherd or critic."[77]

However, the ground of this utopian possibility is ultimately unclear. We might ask whether it refers to the prior conception of species-being as the central concept of a philosophical anthropology, in which man's own proper activity is the impropriety of any activity. Or is it grounded historically in the existent social relations as an immanent contradiction between the historically emergent flexibility demanded of the new proletariat and the social division of labor that chains each individual to a specific field of activity? This ambiguity seems to be resolved in the *Grundrisse* when Marx posits living labor as the historically constituted, and contradictory facet of abstract labor.

> This living labor, existing as an *abstraction* from these moments of its actual reality [raw material, instrument of labor, and so on] (also, not value); this complete denudation, purely subjective existence of labor, stripped of all objectivity. Labor as *absolute poverty*, poverty not as shortage, but as total exclusion of objective wealth . . . Labor not as an object, but as activity; not as itself value, but as the *living source of value*. . . . Thus, it is not at all contradictory, or, rather, the in-every-way mutually contradictory statements that labor is *absolute poverty as object,* on one side, and is, on the other side, the *general possibility* [*allgemeine Möglichkeit*] of wealth as subject and as activity, are reciprocally determined and follow from the essence of labor, such

as it is *presupposed* by capital as its contradiction and as its contradictory being [*gegensätzliches Dasein*], and such as it, in turn, presupposes capital. (G 296/217)

In this passage the same terms of the *1844 Manuscripts* are employed—subject, object, activity in general, poverty—only their previous sense has been rewritten. It is no longer the simple contradiction between poverty (labor) and wealth (capital) but a dynamic contradiction in which labor must be recognized as absolute poverty and the source of all wealth. Furthermore, it is because it is poverty, stripped of any means of production and any specific character, that labor is the source of all wealth. Marx develops a somewhat different sense of abstract labor and its confrontation with abstract wealth than those previously explored, "[S]ince capital as such is indifferent to every particularity of its substance, and exists not only as the totality of the same but also as the abstraction from all of its particularities, the labor which confronts it likewise subjectively has the same totality and abstraction in itself" (G 296/218). Abstract labor, the capacity for any-labor-whatsoever as opposed to the determinate fixed activity, appears here in a manner akin to species-being with the exception that rather than appearing prior to capital, as a lost presupposition, it appears internal to it as both effect and necessary cause. Moreover, this passage from the *Grundrisse* develops a definition of abstract labor that has an antagonistic character not found in *Capital*.[78] Abstract labor is defined here, not as a presupposition of commodity exchange nor as a process of equalization and simplification that goes on behind the backs of producers but as a specific power in its indifference to its activity.[79] Abstract labor is infused with living labor.[80]

The term *living labor* [*lebendig Arbeit*] plays both a rhetorical and a conceptual role in Marx's thought. Rhetorically, it informs and underlies an entire metaphorics that presents the opposition between living labor, in the form of the working class, and "dead labor," as capitalist wealth and machinery, as the opposition between "life" and "death"; or, more dramatically, life and the "living-dead monstrosity of capital" (CI 302/210). Alongside, and implicated within, this rhetorical use, there is a somewhat different sense of living labor: not so much opposed to the dead labor of capital—fixed capital—but understood as the aspect of labor implicated with the needs and demands of the working class.[81] This aspect of living labor is ultimately unruly in that it is labor as activity, as creative power, as the pure power to produce the new.[82] As Marx writes, "Labor is the living, form-giving fire; it is the transitoriness of things, their temporality, as their formation by living time" (G 361/281). This labor not only produces things—objects—it is also productive of needs and sociality; living labor produces for itself, for its need, as much as it produces for capital.[83] What unifies the first (rhetorical) sense and the latter (antagonistic) sense is that in each case activity, power, and transformation are placed on the side of labor, and it is this power that capital must utilize.

Living labor is labor power defined in opposition, or better, in antagonistic relation to, capital. If the capitalist mode of production is founded on valorization, the increase of surplus value, then living labor is self-valorization. As capital seeks to reduce necessary labor and increase surplus value, living labor seeks to increase necessary labor and thus increase the effectivity of needs and desire.[84] Self-valorization, as Antonio Negri develops it through a reading of the *Grundrisse*, is situated on the intersection between production and reproduction. Stated somewhat briefly, and cryptically, self-valorization is the nonidentity of production and reproduction. The space of their relation and conjunction is defined by the conflict over needs and desires, over necessary and surplus labor. In the first place, the expansion of need is made necessary by the process of capitalist accumulation itself: To realize surplus value there must be new needs, new products. Marx describes it as "the discovery, creation and satisfaction of new needs arising from society itself; the cultivation of all the qualities of the social human being, the production of the same in a form as rich as possible in needs, because rich in qualities and relations . . . is likewise a condition of production founded on capital" (G 409/323). The expansion of the sphere of needs is not entirely produced, or imposed by capital; however, it is, after all, necessary for capital to simultaneously reduce "necessary labor," to reproduce labor power at the absolute minimum of cost, and at the lowest level of existence, and to expand the terrain of needs, produce new needs, and new desires.[85] Thus, the tendency for needs to increase cannot be entirely explained by capital's drive to create artificial needs because capital is caught in a conflict of drives working in the opposite direction.

For the tendency to increase the sphere of need to be realized, or actualized, struggle and conflict from the side of living labor is necessary. This struggle is made possible by the fact that in capital the worker does not simply work for the specific and determinate conditions of reproduction, as in slavery or feudalism, but for the wage—the abstract conditions of reproduction.

> The free worker receives [the means of subsistence] in the shape of *money, exchange-value,* the abstract social form of wealth. Even though his wage is in fact nothing more than the *silver* or *gold* or *copper* or *paper* form of the necessary means of subsistence into which it must constantly be dissolved—even though money functions here only as a *means of circulation . . . abstract wealth,* remains in his mind as something more than a particular use value hedged round with traditional and local restrictions. It is the worker himself who converts the money into whatever use values he desires; it is he who buys commodities as he wishes and as the *owner of money . . .* he stands in precisely the same relationship to the sellers of goods as any other buyer. Of course, the conditions his existence—and the limited amount of money he can earn—compel him to make his purchases from a fairly restricted section of goods. But some variation is possible as we can see from the fact that newspapers, for example, form part of the essential purchases of the urban English worker.[86]

Of course the worker's share of this abstract wealth is limited. More important, it is from the ground of this abstract potential that the worker asserts his or her particular desires, a particular form of life. As Marx writes,

> [T]he number and extent of [the worker's] so-called necessary requirements, as also the manner in which they are satisfied, are themselves products of history, and depend

therefore to a great extent on the level of civilization attained by a country; in particular they depend on the conditions in which, and consequently on the habits
[*Gewohnheiten*] and expectations with which, the class of free workers has been
formed. In contrast, therefore, with the case of other commodities, the determination
of the value of labor power contains a historical and moral element. (CI 275/185)

This historical and moral dimension constitutes the difference between wages
within different national cultures and traditions (the English need their newspa-
pers and so on). Deleuze and Guattari refer to these moral and historical components, these values and desires, as "neoterritorialities" or reterritorializations. These
are not the codes or territories of the precapitalist modes of production that tie
production to particular social relations but, rather, the insistence of particular values that are instituted in and through the abstract universality of the wage.[87] Thus,
if these traditions and values are going to have an effect in determining the wage,
they do so only through self-valorization, through the struggles of the working
class, which demands them as necessary conditions of its reproduction.[88] It is this
struggle that renders the increase of needs practically irreversible.[89] It is not impossible to reduce needs, but it is difficult in that needs inscribe themselves in the
habits and patterns of the working class. Self-valorization exposes the pressures
that "reproduction," the reproduction of the working class, places on production.

As much as living labor and abstract labor constitute two sides of an antagonistic struggle, the stake and scope of which will be clarified in the following sections, they do not directly coincide or match up. As the connection between living
labor and reproduction suggests, living labor exceeds the labor that is directly com-
pensated for the wage. The reproductive work of the family constitutes a realm of
need and desire that is incredibly productive of subjectivity and social networks. It
reproduces the labor power necessary to abstract labor. Moreover, such labor is all
the more productive for capital in that it does not assume the form of abstract
labor.[90] The immense productivity, flexibility, and potentiality of the living labor
of reproductive work is obscured by its appearance as nonwaged work, as a series
of social relationships that are outside of the economy.[91] The wage is necessary to
appear to be productive. Wage labor's appearance as productive is derivative of
capital's appearance as self-generating wealth; it is an afterimage of the society effect of capital. Living labor confronts abstract labor as its internal condition and
its constitutive outside.

The capitalist mode of production emerges when a flow of "free" labor meets a
flow of "free" wealth. It is clear now that this freedom on the side of labor is the
simultaneity of poverty and indeterminacy. It would not be improper to think of
this indeterminacy, this abstraction, as a kind of power, the power to bring the new
into the world; after all it produces not only things—commodities—but also the
capitalist mode of production itself. It would also be correct to identify this abstract subjective potential as something new, and thus as something that emerges
with, and is the condition for, capitalist accumulation. It would be incorrect, however, to identify this with freedom in the conventional sense because this abstract

subjective potential cannot but sell itself as labor power. It must subject itself to whatever-capitalist enterprise, to the job and task available.[92] Abstract labor, or abstract labor as living labor, is free to develop and consume "whatever" forces and possibilities—forces and possibilities unimaginable and impossible within the narrow spheres of precapitalist reproduction. At the same time, it is also freely exposed to the demands and transformations of the labor market. The old guarantees that limited production, tying it to a determinate sphere of reproduction, political and social, have disappeared. In the absence of old guarantees and the former limitations, there is a new struggle, a new antagonism: It is a struggle that seeks to reduce living labor, the flexibility and productivity of a new subject, to abstract labor, to a homogenization and standardization that is the precondition for surplus value.

DISCIPLINARY POWER

At the end of part one of *Capital*, with the completion of the famous section on commodity fetishism, abstract labor is presented as a concept whose particular domain of applicability is exchange. Abstract labor is produced by and productive of commodity exchange: It is the presupposition of any such exchange and in turn it acts on and regulates the actions of individuals on the labor market. Thus, when Marx turns from an analysis of exchange to the analysis of production at the end of part two of *Capital*, a transition that is presented as stepping into the hidden abode of production past the sign that reads "No admittance except on business," it would follow that abstract labor would pass out of the picture along with its attendant concept commodity fetishism. Despite what one would be lead to believe in reading part one of *Capital*, which presents abstract labor as constituted and completed by commodity exchange, *Marx presents abstract labor, the equalization and reduction of diverse labors and practices to the same standard, as a problem that is continually reposed.* In fact over the course of the presentation of *Capital*, Marx enumerates several conditions—technical, social, and legal—for the production of abstract labor which are intertwined with the larger problem of the text: the struggle between capitalist valorization and self-valorization. Abstract labor is not only a precondition of exchange in that it provides a standard by which to measure the diverse commodities and products of labor, it is also a precondition of production, or more specifically of the valorization process. For there to be surplus value—the difference between the cost of labor power and its productivity—there must first be a standard, a norm, of production.

Marx uses the same term, *abstract labor*, to refer to two different, but not necessarily contradictory, problems and practices. In the first, abstract labor is the unrecognized equivalent produced by and underlying the diverse exchanges of the market. An equivalent that is not only the precondition of the exchange of goods but also the exchange of labor on the market. Thus insofar as abstract labor, in this first sense, is inseparable from a posited equivalent between goods on the market and an hour of labor, it serves as a "spontaneous" ideology.[93] The second problem encompasses a different practice, and a different production: the production of abstract labor within diverse sites of production—abstract labor not as appearance, or ideology, but as an effect of the power relations and technological transformations that cancel out individual differences of strength, skill, and resistance. The unification of these different problems and senses under the same name could be seen as an unfortunate "poverty of language," the confused mingling of two different concepts under the same term, or it could be an indication of the intersection and inseparability of consumption and production, ideology and power, as constitutive elements of the mode of production.[94]

In the labor process the capitalist employs diverse individuals, or bodies, and must extract from these individuals not just labor power, but the social average of labor power. As Marx writes,

> A further condition is that the labor-power itself must be of normal effectiveness [*normale Charakater*]. In the trade in which it is being employed, it must possess the average skill, dexterity and speed prevalent in that trade, and our capitalist took good care to buy labor-power of such normal quality. It must be expended with the average amount of exertion and the usual degree of intensity; and the capitalist is as careful to see that this is done, as he is to ensure that his workmen are not idle for a single moment. He has bought the use of the labor-power for a definite period, and he insists on his rights. He has no intention of being robbed. Lastly—and for this purpose our friend has a penal code of his own—all wasteful consumption of raw material or instruments of labor is strictly forbidden. (CI 303/211)

Even though the production of abstract labor involves the transition from quality—the diverse bodies that are put to work—to quantity—the calculable hour of labor time—it is not reducible to such a dialectical transition. Labor is not an inert manifold of qualities that is homogenized and quantified here; instead, it is a multitude of bodies that resists through its irreducible plurality and heterogeneity. Thus the transition from quality to quantity opens onto another problem: the political problem of the control of living labor.

In the previous chapter we saw that primitive accumulation was not just a violent transformation—the violent birth throes of the rise of the capitalist mode of production—but was itself a transformation of the form of violence—from the sporadic and bloody violence of the feudal mode of production to the more or less quotidian acts of exploitation and domination. Marx indicates the transformation through a series of figures, or allegories, in which aspects of sovereign power, or even ancient power, are displaced from the political sphere and placed within the capitalist mode of production. For example, Marx writes in the same paragraph of "the law giving talent of the factory Lycurgus" and that "[i]n the factory code, the capitalist formulates his autocratic power over his workers like a private legislator, and purely as an emanation of his own will, unaccompanied by either that division of responsibility otherwise so much approved by the bourgeoisie, or the still more approved representative system" (CI 550/447). Marx employs all the characters and figures of world history from ancient

Greece to Asiatic despotism to present the power of capital. Beyond and within these rhetorical figures of power, Marx entertains a sustained comparison between the supervision of workers within the capitalist mode of production and military discipline.

> The technical subordination of the worker to the uniform motion of the instruments of labor, and the peculiar composition of the working group consisting as it does of individuals of both sexes, and all ages, gives rise to a barrack-like discipline [*kasernenmäßige Disziplin*], which is elaborated into a complete system in the factory, and brings the previously mentioned labor of superintendence to its fullest development, thereby dividing the workers into manual laborers and overseers, into the private soldiers and the N.C.O.s of an industrial army. (CI 550/447)

These figures and formulations could be understood in the manner of an Althusserian symptomatic reading, as figures standing in the place of a concept that is absent: the concept of the form of power produced by and productive of the capitalist mode of production.[95]

This absent concept has perhaps been produced by Foucault. Even though Foucault did not intend to complete, or stitch together, Marx's remarks on the formation of power in the capitalist mode of production, by providing an investigation of power in capitalism, his analysis of disciplinary power converges with Marx on several points: First, as I have already noted, there is the transition from power organized according to the "law" and its "transgression" to power organized according to a norm. Power organized according to the law, what Foucault calls "sovereign power," can only respond or punish with respect to a transgression. It is thus by nature binary: There are only two terms: legal and illegal.[96] A "norm," however, allows for an infinite gradation of distinctions—one can always fall short of a norm—thus there is the possibility for an infinite intervention, continual surveillance, and improvement.[97] This is perhaps the distinction that Marx presented in the figure of the penal code operative on the factory floor: It is not simply a matter of the movement of political power to a different space but a transformation of that power in such a way that its manner of functioning, objectives, and techniques have fundamentally changed.

The history of the formation of capital is also a history of different techniques and technologies of power. As Foucault summarizes, "[O]ne can find between the lines of *Capital* an analysis, or at least the sketch of an analysis, which would be the history of the technology of power, such as it was exercised in the workshops and factories."[98] At the center of this "sketch" is a specific problem: the modification of the structure and terrain of violence that is part of the formation of the capitalist mode of production. In the passages on primitive accumulation Marx illustrates this passage by setting the sporadic, excessive, and bloody feudal violence—a violence that passes through the state—against the quotidian, standardized, coercion of the capitalist factory. On this point as well, Foucault's analysis of disciplinary power can be read as an elaboration of a nascent theory of the transformation of power and violence in Marx. Foucault argues that disciplinary power is both an effect of and condition of the emergence of capitalism.[99]

Prior to the formation of capitalism, in feudalism wealth rested in land and in the accumulated hoards of lords and sovereigns, relatively and secure. With the development of capitalism, wealth or the production of value became dependent on the intersection between the bodies of workers and an increasingly expensive productive apparatus (machinery, tools, transportation networks). This transformation exposes the wealth and power of the newly emergent bourgeois class to new types of illegality: An entire level of quotidian "illegalities"—thefts, sabotage, and occupation—that the old system could tolerate now become intolerable. "The way in which wealth tended to be invested, on a much larger scale than ever before, in commodities and machines presupposed a systematic, armed intolerance of illegality."[100] At the same time as the new grid of power inserts itself into the networks of property, defending it and guarding, it also acts on subjects—making them not only obedient but productive. "The problem is then to attach workers firmly to the production apparatus, to settle them or move them where it needs to subject them to its rhythm, to impose the constancy or regularity on them that it requires—in short, to constitute them as a labor force.[101] Thus with capitalism there emerges an "ensemble of techniques through which the bodies and time of men become labor-time and labor-power."[102] Disciplinary power produces a population, or a laboring subject, which is both productive, according to the norms and demands of abstract labor, and docile.

Although Foucault's analysis of disciplinary power offers something of an elaboration and clarification of the form of power that coincides with the development of the capitalist mode of production, there remains a profound difference between Foucault and Marx on the historical progression and formation of this type of power. Foucault's analysis of "disciplinary power" has its place in a genealogy of the contemporary structures of modern power, while Marx's comments or figures of the formation of power in capitalism are situated against the backdrop of a larger examination, or series of examinations, most notably the history of the formation and transformation of the capitalist mode of production and the increasing intensive and extensive extraction of surplus value. This difference is not just a distinction of the respective backdrop of a concept, it is ultimately a distinction in what I referred to earlier as a logic of presentation. Which is to suggest that what is at stake between these two different presentations is not simply a matter of competing philosophies of history—a history of the different power formations and their investment of the body as opposed to a history of the capitalist mode of production—but rather an understanding of the materiality of power. By materiality here I mean the multiple and complex effects that power has, not only on other powers, or strategies, but also the inscription of the effects of power in different practices and institutions.

Framed in these terms we can see the most striking similarities and differences between Marx and Foucault's conceptions of power. In terms of similarities we can locate in each a "transversal" conception of power: Power is not located in one level or instance of the social field, as in the state, but traverses different institutions and practices.[103] Power is heterogeneous; one can only speak of powers and their diverse interactions.[104] A consequence of this conception of power is that despite Foucault's and Marx's attentiveness to the concrete history of institutions (prisons, hospitals, and factories, etc.) these institutions are not themselves explanatory of social relations and conflict, but must be explained by the relations of power.[105] Thus Marx and Foucault are perhaps linked in the simple fact that they both must produce a concept of a higher order of "abstraction" to account for the power relations that traverse the social field. For Marx this concept is the mode of production, which is not simply the economy but the complex and mutually determinate relations between economic, political, and social relations. In Marx's words:

> It is in each case the direct relationship of the owners of the conditions of production to the immediate producers—a relationship whose particular form naturally corresponds always to a certain level of development of the type and manner of labor, and hence to its social productive power—in which we find the innermost secret, the hidden basis of the entire social edifice, and hence also the political form of the relationship of sovereignty and dependence, in short, the specific form of state in each case.[106]

The concept of the mode of production short-circuits any a priori division between the political sphere and the economic sphere, a division constitutive of not only bourgeois political economy but also political theory in general.[107] It replaces this division with a history of the complex relation between a particular relation of labor—the technological conditions—and the state. A similar violation of the divisions between the economic and the political runs through Foucault's understanding of disciplinary power. Disciplinary power intersects with new technologies and demands of production as much as it intersects with new developments in the penal code. As Balibar argues:

> "Discipline" and "micro-power" therefore represent *at the same time* the other side of economic exploitation and the other side of juridico-political class domination, which they make it possible to see as a unity; that is to say, they come into play exactly at the point of the "short-circuit" which Marx sets up between economics and politics, society, and state.[108]

Moreover, Foucault's thought of an apparatus (*Dispositif*) is written against any presupposed division or causal structure of divergent practices. An apparatus is constituted by a heterogeneous set of practices—for example, in the case of the "disciplinary apparatus" this would include a particular legal relation, an economic relation, architectural forms (the prison and the factory), as well as an entire set of discourses and forms of knowledge. Thus Foucault's apparatus comes close to certain dimensions of Marx's concept of the mode of production: In each case it is the articulation of the relations between disparate elements. For Foucault, the connection between these diverse elements is only generated by a specific relation of power, or strategic situation.

[T]he apparatus as such is constituted and enabled to continue in existence insofar as it is the site of a double process. On the one hand, there is a process of *functional overdetermination*, because each effect—positive or negative, intentional or unintentional—enters into resonance or contradiction with the others and thereby calls for a readjustment or a re-working of the heterogeneous elements that surface at various points. On the other hand, there is a perpetual process of *strategic elaboration*. Take the example of imprisonment, that apparatus which had the effect of making measures of detention appear to be the most efficient and rational method that could be applied to the phenomenon of criminality. What did this apparatus produce? An entirely unforeseen effect which had nothing to do with any kind of strategic ruse on the part of some meta- or trans-historic subject conceiving it or willing it.[109]

In each case the apparently static and stable forms and institutions of the political and social field must be connected to the power relations and conflicts of power that provoke and determine them.

Negri suggests that Marx's use of the term *mode of production* encompasses both a world historical sense—the passage from the Asiatic to the capitalist mode of production, developed most strongly in the notebook on precapitalist economic formations—and, on a smaller scale, the transformation of the technological and social conditions of labor from handicrafts to large-scale industry, analyzed in *Capital*.[110] Bracketing for a moment Negri's decision to identify the second as the "appropriate" definition of the mode of production, it is possible to find another important parallel with Foucault. As Deleuze writes with respect to Foucault:

> This thesis concerning *dispositifs* of power seemed to me to move in two directions, in no way contradictory, but distinct. In both cases, these *dispositifs* were irreducible to a State apparatus. But according to one direction, they consisted of a diffuse and heterogeneous multiplicity, "micro-dispositifs." According to another direction, they referred to a diagram, a kind of abstract machine immanent to the entire social field (hence panopticism, defined by the general function of seeing without being seen and applicable to any multiplicity). These were, so to speak, the two directions of microanalysis, both equally important, since the second showed that Michel was not satisfied with a "dissemination."[111]

For both Foucault and Marx the "structure," apparatus or mode of production, is stretched to include, on the one hand, the entire social field, while it is also reduced, on the other hand, to include the multiplicity of specific spatial instantiations of this structure. As Marx writes in the *Grundrisse*: "Production is always a *particular* branch of production—e.g. agriculture, cattle raising, manufactures etc.—or it is a *totality*" (G 86/21). It is with respect to this first direction, the specific apparatus or particular branch of production, that the structure is more thoroughly identified and implicated within a concrete and even technological instance, such as the factory or the prison. If these directions are, as Deleuze argues with respect to Foucault, noncontradictory, they are also nonidentical. The relation between the two directions is one of tension: between the immanent cause and its specific instances. Capitalism, the capitalist mode of production, cannot be identified with the factory, just as "disciplinary" power cannot be identified with the prison. The immanent social field is constituted by a multiplicity of apparatuses or relations, in the case of capitalism, the mode of production is also constituted by relations of distribution and consumption, which, although constitutive of the social field, have differing and divergent logics from those found in production proper.[112] The nonidentity of the two directions of analysis—the immanent relations of the social field and the concrete structures—is also the nonidentity of the antagonistic strategies across these vectors. Resistances on the smaller scale, in the factory or prison, have different effects on the larger scale.

It is also on the issue of the logic and relations of antagonism that Marx and Foucault diverge. For Marx the multiplicity of instances of struggle are always reducible, at least virtually, to the conflict over exploitation, with the reduction of labor time and the materiality of need, on one side, and the demand for exploitation—the reduction of necessary labor and the increase of surplus value—on the other side. Whereas in Marx there is a primacy of antagonism, with its implicit bifurcation of the social, in Foucault one finds agonism, the multiplicity of conflictual relations.[113] Marx gave different versions of this reduction: At times, as in *The German Ideology*, it is based on the historic tendency of "proletarianization," the reduction of all social functions to labor and the reduction of all labor to its simplest and most precarious forms; while at other times, most notably in the *Grundrisse*, the simplification of antagonisms is based on the development of the forces of production to the point at which labor exhausts itself as the basis of value.[114] On the other hand, Foucault maintains a fundamental plurality or multiplicity of relations of power. Any division or duality of power into two camps must itself be produced by an interlinking of the various and singular sites of power.[115]

Marx and Foucault can also be distinguished, or even opposed, with respect to the manner in which they situate the problem of subjectivity.[116] For the most part, Marx subordinates the analysis of the production of subjectivity to an analysis of material production: Transformations of subjectivity are addressed only insofar as they intersect with the transformations and conflicts of material production. However, this marginalization of the problem of the production subjectivity is profoundly complicated by Marx's recognition of the co-implication of capitalism and an abstract subjective power of living labor. *In Marx there is the recognition of an abstract subjective activity that is constitutive of the capitalist mode of production combined with incomplete fragments toward an analysis of how this potential is formed into concrete and determinate subjects.* It is possible to find not so much an opposing emphasis in Foucault's work but at least an emphasis that can be productively opposed to Marx. Foucault focuses almost exclusively on the manner in which different regimes of power constitute different subjects, and at times this focus seems to virtually exclude anything like a thought of abstract subjective activity that exceeds this process of subjection.[117] However, in Foucault's later works, the immanence of the production of subjectivity to power and knowledge relations is paired with an increasing insistence on the irreducibility of subjectivity to the conditions of its production. *It is an effect of power, but it is never merely an effect of power.* As Deleuze writes, "Foucault's fundamental idea is that of a dimension of subjectivity derived from power and knowledge without being dependent on them."[118] Subjectivity is not exterior to the relations of power, but it constitutes an added dimension, which is the possibility for resistance, for an invention irreducible to its conditions. Thus, what appears at first as a difference of emphasis, or even a different understanding of the term *subjectivity*—Marx focuses on an abstract subjective potential prior to subjection, while Foucault focuses on the particular modes of subjection—can also be understood as a different way of framing the immanence of subjectivity to the "structure."[119] In Marx the immanence of subjectivity to the capitalist mode of production is posited through the immanence of living labor to capital—for Foucault it is the immanence of subjectivity to the relations of power and knowledge that produce it. The relation between the two ideas borders on an inversion: With Marx, subjectivity—living labor power—is immanent to the structure—capital—which it produces; while for Foucault, subjectivity—the specific historically constituted subjectivity—is immanent to the structures—the relations of knowledge and power—that produce it.

The point here is not to develop an exhaustive account of the relation between Foucault and Marx but to develop specific problems in the logic of the relation between living and abstract labor. Thus what is framed above as a series of sharp divergences between Marx and Foucault will be rephrased as a series of questions or problems for the examination of this relation.[120] First, What is the relation between the plurality of conflictual instances and the duality of antagonism? In other words, What is the relation between the complexity of the mode of production—the intersection of political, economic, social, and technical practices—and the dualistic antagonism between labor turned toward the needs, desires, and creative power of the laboring subjects and labor as the activity subordinated to the demand for surplus value? Second, how is it possible to think of living labor, and the subjectivity it entails, as fully immanent to capital (as both productive of and produced by) without reducing it to a mute effect of capital? Inversely, How is it possible to think invention or resistance without recourse to a dimension of transcendence? If one has a taste for generality, or intellectual history, these two problems could be rephrased as a question of the relation between subjectivity and structure.

ANTAGONISTIC LOGIC (PART TWO)

Although the investigation of abstract labor as normalization and domination is developed throughout *Capital*, there is no systematic use of the term *living labor*. However, in *Capital* there is an insistence of not only the irreduciblity of labor power to its commodification but the tendency for resistance and practice to change, to intersect transversally with the different elements of the mode of production, and expand. This tendency appears sporadically alongside and within the dominant exposition of *Capital:* The analysis of the development of the capitalist mode of production—a development that is also the progression from absolute to relative surplus value.

Absolute surplus value is surplus value that is extracted by the simple extension of the working day beyond the time necessary for the reproduction of labor power; it is not only the condition and effect of the emergence of the capitalist mode of production, since it entails nothing other than imposition of the capitalist relation over already existing social and technical conditions, it is also a figure of sheer exploitation, a pure quantifiable difference between necessary and surplus labor. Relative surplus value is produced through the intensification of the labor process; it entails a transformation of the technological and social conditions of labor (CI 645/533). The transition from the former to the latter is presented according the "dominant" or major logic of *Capital*: not only a purely conceptual transition, from quantity to quality, but a transformation in which the demands of the capitalist mode of production are imposed upon an inert and passive ground. The commodification of labor, its reduction to abstract labor without remainder or residue, thus is assumed. This dominant presentation is continually undercut by a series of examples and instances, drawn mostly from Marx's study of the historical conditions of the emergence of the capitalist mode of production in England, which introduces conflict and antagonism to this logic.

If these examples are to be something more than impurities or exceptions that confront the development of capital, only to be digested and neutralized, if they are to be more than historical footnotes and constitute an affirmative investigation of the social and political effects and conditions of the development of the capitalist mode of production, the logic of their articulation must be given. The excavation of this articulation follows not so much the term *living labor* but the logic of living labor; that is, the production by and for capital of an abstract subjective potential that continually exceeds and evades the conditions of its production. As with Foucault's reading of disciplinary power behind the figures of abstract labor, living labor demands a symptomatic reading.

The chapter on cooperation is central to the overt concerns of Marx's text: the presentation of the production of abstract labor and the creation of absolute and relative surplus value as the central dynamic of the capitalist mode of production. At the same time it is also one of the points at which living labor shows itself without being explicitly named. In "Co-operation" Marx argues that the assembling together of a group of workers in one productive operation is at first a normalizing force: It is the material basis for the average. As Marx asserts:

> In every industry, each individual worker differs from the average worker. These individual differences, or "errors" as they are called in mathematics compensate each other and vanish whenever a certain minimum number of workers are employed together. . . . The law of valorization therefore comes fully into its own for the individual producer only when he produces as a capitalist and employs a number of workers simultaneously, i.e. when from the outset he sets in motion labor of a socially average character. (CI 441/342)

Cooperation does not only produce the socially average labor necessary for capitalist valorization, it also produces a particular type of surplus: the surplus of sociality. Marx shows that the causes for this surplus are manifold:

> Whether the combined working day, in a given case, acquires this increased productivity because it heightens the mechanical force of labor, or extends its sphere of action over a greater space, or contracts the field of production relatively to the scale of production, or at the critical moment sets large masses of labor to work, or excited rivalry between individuals and raises their animal spirits, or impresses on the similar operations carried on by a number of men the stamp of continuity and many-sidedness, or performs different operations simultaneously, or economizes the means of production by use in common . . . whichever of these is the cause of the increase, the special productive power of the combined working day, is under all circumstances, the social productive power of labor, or the productive power of social labor. This power arises from cooperation itself. When the worker co-operates in a planned way with others, he strips off the fetters of his individuality, and develops the capabilities of this species [*Gattungsvermögen*]. (CI 447/349)

First, this paragraph, in its sheer indifference to the causes of this sociality, or social labor, as a spatial contraction caused by some sort of psychological compulsion to imitate, produced by low-grade antagonisms and rivalries, can be understood as a further step separating Marx's thought of sociality from either a theory of intersubjectivity or collectivity.[121] Neither preexisting individuals nor a preexisting collectivity are assumed as elements of the capitalist mode of production, rather the capitalist mode of production produces a type of sociality—that is, also a type of subjectivity—which it requires in order to produce surplus value. In this passage species-being, or the capacity of the species, returns, not as an abstraction inherent in each single individual but as an ensemble of social relations, to use Marx's terminology. The capitalist mode of production not only produces a "collective labor power," but there is a tendency for the mode of production to extend this "collectivity" both extensively and intensively.[122] The extensive movement occurs as more and more productive processes are brought into the factory or other productive spaces organized on a massive scale. Collectivity is extended "intensively" when the division of labor and tasks in the productive process continually extends the social dimension of production: when cooperation, coordination, and integration of tasks becomes an integral element of production.

With the development of capitalism, all labor tends to become collective labor, the isolated worker producing commodities for the market is a rarity. Collective labor power is subjected to complex and interrelated forms of organization. This production is not reducible to the demands of capitalist socialization; there is always a surplus of collectivity. This passage indicates a tendency of the capitalist mode of production, which is perhaps in tension with what Marx identifies as the dominant tendency of the labor process in *Capital*, the tendency of proletarianization. Proletarianization is the dual process of the breakdown of the stability, security, and sociality of precapitalist forms of labor, on the one hand, and the reduction of all labor to simple labor, on the other hand. Alongside and opposed to this tendency, there is a second tendency or direction, what Tronti calls "socialization."[123] Socialization is also a dual process, encompassing the increasing creation and incorporation of social relations into the site of production as well as the extension of capitalist relations throughout social space.[124]

The extension of this "collective productive power" imposes a particular demand on the disciplinary power of capital. In the first instance, disciplinary power was necessary to oversee labor, to guarantee its "average productivity" against the minute differences of aptitude and skill, as well as the passive resistances of work slowdowns or simply "slacking." This disciplinary power now confronts a collective power that is capable of resisting it. "As the number of co-operating workers increases, so to does their resistance to the domination of capital, and, necessarily, the pressure put on by capital to overcome this resistance" (CI 449/350). Capital finds itself face to face with a collectivity and subjectivity that it created but which is nonetheless irreducible to its needs.[125] Supervision and control become more and more necessary to the production process. Marx states, drawing his metaphor from what he considers to be the very model of disciplinary power, the army, "[t]hat a capitalist should command in the field of production is now as indispensable as that a general should command on the field of battle." This necessity is imposed by the collective powers of labor, the socialization of labor power.[126] The capitalist must necessarily deal with a collective power and render this power productive and profitable.

Marx's descriptive statements regarding the form of power necessary to regulate the increasingly collective and socialized force of living labor follow the same series of figures and allegories indicated previously: The control capital exercises over this social power is described as both the command of "an industrial army of workers" and as power akin to, and descended from, the power that the despots of ancient Egypt and China wielded over their subjects to produce the monuments of the ancient world. Beyond these figures Marx begins to introduce an element integral to the analysis of manufacture and large-scale industry in the later chapters. The power relation between the capitalist, or its agents dispersed throughout the productive process, and the collective worker is displaced onto the division between mental and manual labor. Control is exercised not only by the direct activities of supervision and discipline but indirectly through the separation of conception and execution. The "plan," execution separated from activity, is the correlate of the authority and power of capital over labor. Marx writes, "Hence the interconnection between their various labors confronts them, in the realm of ideas, as a plan drawn up by the capitalist, and, in practice, as his authority, as the powerful will of a being outside them, who subjects their activity to his purpose" (CI 450/351). The plan is not only parallel, in the "realm of ideas," to the power of the capitalist in the realm of power but is a displacement and concealment of this power—it is no longer the gaze of the supervisor that confronts the laborer but the order of production itself.

Marx's statement regarding the plan, and its role in the control of the collective laborer, could be understood as the return of a prior theme from *The German*

Ideology in which the division between mental and manual labor is posited as a founding division that makes possible ideology and the state as an instrument of domination existing apart from the community.[127] As soon as mental labor is separated from manual labor "consciousness can really flatter itself that it is something other than consciousness of existing practice."[128] This division and separation frees mental labor from its implication within the quotidian existence of a given community and makes it possible to present itself (to itself as well as to others) as "mental labor" in general, as thought. This makes possible the substitution of particular interests—the interests of this or that class—for the general interest of the community. It is a materialist explanation of ideology, not simply insofar as it gives the material conditions for ideology—the division of labor—but also the material effects of ideology.[129] These effects include the generation of the state, which, contrary to what Hegel believed, is not the institutional instantiation of the universal, but the instrument of a particular class: "an illusory communal life."

Without attempting to produce an entire genealogy of the problematic of the division between mental and manual labor in Marx, in terms of its emergence and history, it is possible to underline one basic consequence of its emergence: For Marx the division between mental and manual labor, and thus the entire relation between knowledge and work, is never simply a technical matter, it is always a political relation. Balibar has argued that Marx's insistence on a political concept of machinery in *Capital* has as its correlate at least a metaphorics that posits the state as a machine.[130] From *The German Ideology* through the later works, the machine and the state are related to the same origin and process of formation. In each case there is a process of separation (knowledge from the workers and the political community from itself), automation or "autonomization" (this knowledge is incorporated into a mechanism, in the case of machinery, or in a bureaucracy in the case of the state), and conflict (once this knowledge is separated and rendered autonomous, and seemingly neutral, it turns back upon its conditions of possibility as an antagonistic force).[131] Thus, when Marx develops this theme in the analysis of manufacture and handicrafts in *Capital*, it is not a simple matter of describing the technological transformation of working conditions—these technological conditions are always already political. Moreover, we could say that they concern what is for Marx the very problem of the political: the creation of hierarchical forces of "command" over and above the immanent forces of cooperation.[132] Marx writes with respect to the increasing emergence of technological knowledge in production:

> The knowledge, judgement and will which, even though to a small extent, are exercised by the independent peasant or handicraftsman, in the same way as the savage makes the whole art of war consist in the exercise of his personal cunning, are faculties now required only for the workshop as a whole. The possibility of an intelligent direction of production expands in one direction, because it vanishes in many others. What is lost by the specialized workers is concentrated in capital which confronts them. It is a result of the division of labor in manufacture that the worker is brought face to face with the intellectual potentialities [*geistige Potenzen*] of material process of production as the property of another and a power which rules over him. This

process of separation starts in simple cooperation, where the capitalist represents to the individual workers the unity and will of the whole body of social labor. It is developed in manufacture, which mutilates the worker, turning him into a fragment of himself. (CI 482/382)

The working conditions and the very subjectivity of workers is transformed: Skilled artisans are transformed into hobbled fragments of a labor process beyond their control. Marx often describes the transformation with a sort of Dickensian attention to the crippling effects of labor reduced to pure repetitive activity, producing what he refers to as an "industrial pathology" (CI 484/384). It is with the development of machines, the transfer of the mental skills and physical exertions, into the body of the machine that abstract labor is effectively produced. Capital at this point is at least potentially indifferent to the skill, background, gender, and age of the bodies put to work. Moreover, this transformation of abstract labor, its production by and incorporation into machinery, makes possible a different strategy for the production of surplus value: Surplus value is no longer produced simply by extending the working day beyond the necessary time to reproduce labor power but through an intensification of labor, speeding up the machines, making labor more productive.

The displacement of the power relation between worker and capitalist onto a division between mental and manual labor and the materialization of this division and relation into the machine illustrates what I have referred to as a "transversal" conception of power. The conflict between collective labor and collective capitalist is displaced onto the division between mental and manual labor altering the power relation. One consequence of this is that the history of technology, of technological invention, cannot be separated from the relations of power that in part determine and condition this development. This fundamentally changes how one views the history of technological developments: Marx tells Engels in a letter that the clock, which is perhaps a relatively minor achievement compared to something like the steam engine, is important because it is immediately applied to practical social relations.[133]

In a similar vein Foucault's examination of the "technology of power" relations entails as a correlate a transformation, a reexamination, of technology proper. In thinking disciplinary power as a technology Foucault often posits it as causally intermeshed with technology itself. Disciplinary power is formed along with and after such technological inventions as the "repeating rifle" and the development of industrial machinery.[134] As Foucault argues, the repeating rifle necessitates a transformation in the training, discipline, and subjectivity of soldiers: Every soldier must become a functioning and independent part of the unit. Just as in Marx, machinery and large-scale industry demand a working subject that is trained to its regime of repetition. Technological developments cannot be understood outside of or prior to the power relations that they condition or condition them.[135] The mode of production, or what Deleuze and Guattari call a "social machine," is the ensemble that organizes and orders the particular technological developments of production.[136] *Organization* is perhaps a misleading term because it implies stability, or even an agent or force that does the stabilizing: Thus any organization is only a moment artificially isolated in a conflictual process of transformation.[137] Although there is a primacy of the mode of production, or social machine, over the technical machine, there is ultimately a primacy of the conflictual relations over the social machine.

Even though Marx focuses on the more concrete delimited space of the factory or workshop in the bulk of the first volume of *Capital* (leaving a few remarks toward a somewhat different perspective, the perspective of "social capital" in the second volume), this direction of analysis is continually set against the transformations of the larger sense of the capitalist mode of production: the transition from absolute to relative surplus value as a transformation that encompasses the entirety of social relations. As Marx writes:

> The production of absolute surplus-value turns exclusively on the length of the working day, whereas the production of relative surplus-value completely revolutionizes the technical process of labor and the groupings into which society is divided. . . . It therefore requires a specifically capitalist mode of production, a mode of production which, along with its methods, means and conditions, arises and develops spontaneously on the basis of the formal subsumption of labor under capital. This formal subsumption is then replaced by a real subsumption. (CI 645/533)

Placing the development of machinery and large-scale industry within the transition from absolute to relative surplus value interrupts the assumed linear progression, a progression of capitalism perfecting itself, that underlies the former. Rather than simply assuming the progression of technology from handicrafts to the industrial factory, or taking for granted the increasing perfection of capital as it revolutionizes the productive process, Marx poses a modest but important question, Why did absolute surplus value exhaust itself as a strategy for valorization? The answer is the struggle over the working day. It is more correct to say that the answer would be the struggle to shorten the working day because Marx never actually poses this question but places the results of an immense historical analysis of this struggle at the end of the section on absolute surplus value. This struggle, one over the legal limits of the working day, is a particular struggle carried out in England, however, Marx argues that its lessons hold true for all of capitalism. As Marx writes, "Nothing characterizes the spirit of capital better than the history of the English factory legislation from 1833 to 1864" (CI 390/295). The philosophical and political implications of Marx's question thus are lost on any reading that proceeds from a rigid division between conceptual and historical content. This analysis of struggle interrupts the linear progression from relative to absolute surplus value. In discussing the struggle over the working day Marx foregrounds the fact that the relation between the capitalist class and worker is initially, and at its core, a relation of force.

> There is here therefore an antinomy, of right against right, both equally bearing the seal of the law of exchange. Between equal rights, force [*Gewalt*] decides. Hence, in the his-

tory of capitalist production, the establishment of a norm for the working day presents itself as a struggle over the limits of that day, a struggle between collective capital, i.e. the class of capitalist, and collective labor, i.e. the working class. (CI 344/249)

From this force relation Marx indicates the limitations that collective labor power places on the "collective capitalist": It is the encounter between two tendencies: the tendency for capital to reduce labor to a pure commodity and the tendency for labor power to assert its needs and its collective power against capital. The conflict of these tendencies results in a more or less protracted and concealed "civil war" over the length of the working day (CI 412/316). As Negri writes, stressing the general philosophical importance of this conclusion, "The strong result of Marx's analyses of the struggles around the length of the working day and the Factory Acts consists thus in indicating a new constitutive process, not inside but outside the dialectic of capital and situated in the autonomy of cooperation, that is, in the subjectivity of the working class."[138]

This "process" is constitutive in that the antagonism is not just some unfortunate conflict tacked on to the existing order of things, rather, it makes the existing legal, political, and social order. In the struggle over the working day in England there is a victory of sorts: the working day is shortened, and moreover the working class is recognized both as a political force and institutionalized in law. The struggle over the working day puts an end to one form of exploitation, that founded on the simple extension of the working day, and necessarily gives rise to another form of exploitation: an intensive exploitation, based on rendering labor more productive. It is with this second form, relative surplus value, that there is a massive investment in the technological transformation of the labor process. Tronti writes that "the struggle for the normal working day necessarily precedes, conditions, and provokes, a modification of the form of surplus value."[139] First, collective labor imposes on the capitalist enterprise its assumption of disciplinary power. Then, once this labor is organized into a collective force, it imposes continually on capital the demand for technological innovation. As Marx famously wrote: "[I]t would be possible to write a whole history of the inventions made since 1830 for the sole purpose of providing capital with weapons against working class revolt" (CI 563/459). Antagonism—the demands of living labor for more time—has its effects on the capitalist mode of production, profoundly altering it, but these effects are not the same ones intended. Living labor makes the capitalist mode of production, it makes dead labor, but never in its own image.

Balibar argues that despite a long history in Marxist thought the historical and social narrative at the center of *Capital* (parts 3, 4, and 5) cannot be unified under the concept of proletarianization. The term *proletarianization* designates a tendency, or the overlapping of tendencies, which continually transform artisan production into commodity production, skilled labor into de-skilled labor, and continually subject work to increased domination, while subjecting workers to an increased instability and "precariousization." What Balibar takes issue with here is not the respective elements of this tendency but their interweaving in a single concept, as if they were all effects of a single cause.[140] In contrast to such a reading of *Capital*, a reading that has exhausted itself historically and philosophically, Balibar presents a "structural history," which unweaves the components of proletarianization into their component elements.[141] The relation of different tendencies—the de-skilling of labor—and the increasing antagonism between mental and manual labor—the heightened surveillance and control of labor—and the increasing informalization of labor are not always already guaranteed by an economic process. These different tendencies, or structures, are only related through the interplay of conflictual and antagonistic strategies. As Balibar puts it, "What seems very clear, then, if one looks at the actual text of Marx's analysis, is not that there is a predetermined linking of forms, but rather an interplay of antagonistic strategies, strategies of exploitation, domination and resistance continually being displaced and renewed as a consequence of their own effects."[142] As Negri writes, "Every constitution of a new structure is the constitution of antagonism."[143] Without this thought of the displacement of antagonism onto different practices and relations—legal, technological, and social—the assertion of antagonism risks becoming a metaphysical assertion—its presence and identity would be guaranteed in advance.[144]

THE PRODUCTION OF SUBJECTIVITY

The interlocking effects of the conflict between living and abstract labor, which is also the transformation of the capitalist mode of production, cannot be unified under any one tendency. Neither proletarianization, the tendency to de-skill and simplify labor and reduce the desires and demands of labor power to the bare minimum, nor socialization, the tendency to extensively and intensively extend the cooperative relations internal to the productive process, are ultimately dominant. In part because these two tendencies are not necessarily opposed, at least on a large scale, they in fact complement each other insofar as proletarianization of one sector of the labor process often has as its effect or presupposition the socialization of other sectors and relations.[145] More important, it cannot be presented under any one tendency because each of these respective tendencies are not constituted by a pre-given unity of elements—technological, legal, and political—but by the continual displacement and condensation of antagonisms.[146] This antagonistic logic of displacement is riddled with unintended effects, the central example of which is the immense struggle over the working day that has prompted the technological development of the "specifically capitalist mode of production." The assertion of the needs and desires of living labor and the demands of capitalist valorization continually impose themselves on each other, determining and transforming the other, but this transformation is never univocal, it is always affected and altered by the antagonistic struggle.[147] Mario Tronti contends that "there are never decisive defeats nor victories in the contemporary class struggle."[148]

Within this logic of struggle transforming itself and displacing itself—constituting new structures, new terrains—subjectivity and the production of subjectivity plays an increasingly determinant role. However, this role is ambiguous; it is not

turned toward either the needs of living labor or the demands of capitalist valorization. Marx recognized the emergence of the capitalist mode of production as a fundamental transformation of subjectivity. This transformation is, in the first place,
the emergence of an abstract material potential. In the second place, it is also the
emergence of a new mode of subjection. In Deleuze and Guattari's terms the difference between these different modes of subjection is the difference between "machinic enslavement," into which the human being is incorporated in the productive
process as another element of fixed capital under the direction of a "higher unity,"
and "social subjection" in which the worker is no longer a component of the machinery, but a user, whose control is interiorized.[149] In an unpublished chapter of
Capital Marx illustrates this difference bodly and crudely, distinguishing between
the subjectivity of the slave and the free worker.

> In contrast to the slave, this labor becomes more productive because more intensive,
> since the slave only works under the spur of external fear but not *for his existence*
> which is *guaranteed* even though it does not belong to him. The free worker, how-
> ever, is impelled by his wants. The consciousness (or better: the *idea* [*vorstellung*]) of
> free self-determination, of liberty, makes a much better worker of the one than of the
> other, as does the related feeling (sense) of *responsibility,* since he like any seller of
> wares, is responsible for the goods he delivers and for the quality which he must pro-
> vide, he must strive to ensure that he is not driven from the field by other sellers of
> the same type as himself. (R 1031/101)

The same conditions that make the abstract subjective potential of labor unruly—
its liberation from any determinate sphere of need and from any presupposed political relation—are also the conditions of its subjection. There is a fundamental
undecidability at the intersection of the production of subjectivity and capital.

The wage is the precondition for both a struggle over the limitations of needs
and desire and for new forms of subjection and control, which bloodlessly produce
a docile worker. The very appearance of the wage, that one is paid for a day's or an
hour's work, conceals exploitation. "The wage form thus extinguishes every trace of
the division of the working day into necessary labor and surplus labor, into paid
labor and unpaid labor" (CI 680/562). Marx argues that the illusion of the wage, as
a just and equal exchange between buyer and seller, is at the base of all the "mystifications of the capitalist mode of production." Such a formulation reverses the
conventional understanding of mystification, or ideology, which argues that mystification requires a distance from practical life to be effective, as in the case of religion. With the wage "the maximum efficiency of the ideological is found at the
closest point to social contradiction."[150] The wage is situated at the site of exploitation, obscuring the crucial matter of who gets the lion's share of the surplus produced. At the same time, the form of the wage, its abstract indifference as money, is
also the mediation and condition of the needs and desires of the working class.[151]
It is an abstract, or open, condition of reproduction; that is, it does not delineate a
sphere of needs, which is given to workers, separate from a sphere of desires, but is

the formal condition of any need. Thus the wage, combined with the tendency of the capitalist mode of production to produce new needs and desires, opens up the space for an infinite and interminable struggle over the quantitative amount of the wage. The limitation of the wage, the limitation that defines "necessary labor," is articulated through the antagonistic relation of a struggle and counter-struggle.[152] *The wage is a paradoxical and antagonistic element of the capitalist mode of production: Its form is both the basis for subjection and for subversion.* It is perhaps due to the intensity of this paradox that the "book on the wage" was never completed by Marx.[153]

Negri asserts, "The ontological aspects of subjectivity are produced *in different* (or, rather, *antagonistic*) ways."[154] There is a production of subjectivity for capital—docile, individual, flexible and productive—and there is the counterproduction of another subjectivity. This counter-subjectivity is also produced in some sense for capital in that it is a necessary element of the valorization of capital, but it contains a supplement irreducible to the demands of capitalist valorization. With respect to the first production, the production of subjectivity for capital, one of the most powerful instruments along with the wage, is the labor contract itself. Marx indicates that the legal fiction of the contract takes the worker as an isolated individual free to dispose of his or her labor power, thereby excluding the material and social conditions that constrain and force this exchange as well as the power and productivity of the necessarily collective laboring subject implicated in this exchange.[155] It presents and sustains the "idea" of a free exchange between equals. This free exchange is actually a condition of the workers' subordination, because the worker cannot but sell his or her labor power to survive—a condition that conceals the fact that it is always a collective laboring power which capital puts to work.[156] It does not only conceal this fact but actively works against it insofar as the labor contract is inseparable from the competitive market of labor. This market subordinates the freedom and flexibility of the worker of abstract/living labor to competition and precariousness.[157]

A second instrument of this production is the division between mental and manual labor and the entire technical division of labor. This division has already been discussed insofar as it is inseparable from a power relation: from the distribution of tasks of surveillance and control throughout the workplace.[158] Coinciding with this power relation is the idea, or ideology, of a purely technical division of labor—a division and hierarchy that is grounded in the purely technical demands of the mode production rather than in the needs of the capitalist mode of production which constitutes a powerful "mask"—concealing and justifying this relation.[159] Negri argues that these instruments, like abstract labor whose rule they reinforce, are both imaginary, entailing a particular representation of the social, and actually produced in the power relations that traverse the social. Negri's insistence on the simultaneous conjunction of an "appearance" and a power relation is similar to the logic we have already recognized in Marx.

> As we have seen previously (and it is something which applies both in reality and to our method) strategies that run through the social are both rooted in the social and

related to the sphere of ideology. Their reality is always and in every case bivocal. To put it in Marxist terms, these strategies belong both to the structure and the super-structure; and they are involved in the combination of relationships through mechanisms of causation which are very articulated and complex.[160]

Thus if one is committed to thinking in terms of base and superstructure as the topological spaces of the mode of production and the mode of subjection, or more abstractly, the inside and outside of the mode of production, then one would have to include that the mode of subjection is both internal and external to the mode of production. Or, as Althusser claims, its "exteriority" to the mode of production, its fundamental difference in terms of goals and objectives, is necessarily and for the most part carried out in the heart of the mode of production itself.[161]

There cannot be an exhaustive account of the "instruments" that produce subjectivity for capital, in part, because the instruments and apparatuses of the production of subjectivity are continually changing along with the mode of production. These transformations are in part responses to the production of an alternative subjectivity, what Negri calls a "worker" or "proletarian" subjectivity.[162] These terms do not designate any specific content to this subjectivity, in fact, the content would necessarily have to change according to the historical transformations of the mode of production. Rather, they designate a direction, a point of view that is affirmed: the point of view of living labor and of the expansion of its needs and desires. Negri writes:

> These social formations can be seen as being simultaneously singular in the accumulation of individual aspects, ideological thresholds and machines. . . . Now these alternatives become molar, dualistic, and antagonistic when the conflict is focused on essential aspects of the relationship—i.e. when the conflict is focused on those aspects which force major decisions concerning the existence and tempo of social intercourse. In the present case this means that the alternatives become molar, dualistic and antagonistic when what is at issue is *the problem of the expropriation of laboring cooperation*.[163]

Cooperation, the element of worker subjectivity produced and assembled by the productive process itself, is at the heart of this "antagonistic" production of subjectivity. Cooperation constitutes both the material conditions of its production and the object of its desires. At the heart of the capitalist mode of production there are relations of cooperation, which are not only productive for capital but productive of the material possibility of relations that exceed those reinforced by the competitive market of labor and the hierarchy of the technological division of labor. It is this power—the possibility of these relations—that must be continually contained by these instruments and strategies. Tronti writes that "the socialization of production will always be in advance of the organization of society. The historical margin separating these two moments constitutes a formidable form of political domination that capital has utilized in its favor."[164] The cooperative and collective possibilities of the labor process are contained by the social forces and relations that are their condition, necessarily passing through them.

Marx's writings on "Pre-Capitalist Economic Formations" and the formation of capitalism assert in a general way the intersection between the mode of production and the production of subjectivity. In Marx's critique of capital this general problem takes on specific form: Capitalism is dependent on an abstract subjective potential, which is found at the intersection of abstract and living labor, which it must simultaneously develop and control. At the foundation of the capitalist mode of production is the production of subjectivity in both senses of the genitive: the constitution of subjectivity, of a particular subjective comportment (a working class which is both skilled and docile), and in turn the productive power of subjectivity, its capacity to produce wealth. These two senses of "the production of subjectivity" do not or have not coincided in the history of capitalism. In fact it is because they do not coincide that capitalism has a history as the struggles produce legal, technical, and political transformations.[165] Thus, as the capitalist mode of production develops, the problem of subjectivity in the capitalist mode of production develops as well, becoming more central as capital encompasses more of social life in what Marx calls "real subsumption."

THREE

THE REAL SUBSUMPTION OF
SUBJECTIVITY BY CAPITAL

Mass intellectuality is at the center of quite an instructive paradox. One can locate its main characteristics in different functions within labor, but above all at the level of metropolitan habits, in linguistic usages, in cultural consumption. Nonetheless, it is precisely when production no longer seems to offer an identity that it projects itself onto each and every aspect of experience, that it beats into submission linguistic abilities, ethical propensities, and the nuances of subjectivity . . . [Mass intellectuality] demands, thus, a noneconomic critique of political economy.

—Paolo Virno, "Notes on the General Intellect"

REAL SUBSUMPTION

In the discarded draft of the sixth section of *Capital* entitled "Results of the Immediate Process of Production" two problems appear in close proximity, which can be described broadly as follows: first, an investigation into the subjective conditions and effects of the development of the capitalist mode of production, and second, the tendency or development of the capitalist mode of production, its internal historicity. Even though these two problems appear together, their relation is not explicitly thematized or developed. This is due in part to the fact that while the latter constitutes the specific problem of the text the former is only developed in a series of divergent problems and allusions (a point that will be returned to later). Thus this draft, left out of the final published version of the first volume of *Capital*, proves useful for this book in the way that it presents together the historical development of the capitalist mode of production and the problem of the immanent relation of the mode of production to subjectivity.

From a cursory reading of this text it is possible to arrive at two different conclusions with respect to the relation between subjectivity and the development of the capitalist mode of production. First, what Marx calls "real subsumption"—the restructuring of social relations according to the demands of capitalist valorization—is identified by an increasing mystification of the capitalist relation. As capital puts to work science, technology, and the embodied knowledges of the collective, it increasingly appears as if capital itself is productive. Thus subjectivity, at least in the sense of the subjective beliefs and perceptions regarding the constitution of society and the formation of wealth, what I referred to in chapter 1 as "the society effect," would seem to be entirely fashioned by capital. At the same time, Marx argues that as the cooperative and social powers of labor develop the capitalist mode of production becomes increasingly dependent on social knowledge, cooperation, and communication. Wealth is no longer produced by bodies put to work in the closed spaces of the factory but by knowledge, communication, and interactions throughout society. This simultaneous recognition of subjectivity as pure "subjection" and subjectivity as collective power, combined with the fact that all of this is developed in an abandoned draft, would seem to suggest that we are at a, if not the, "limit" of Karl Marx's thought.

This is the limit of futurity, the point at which an analysis based on an examination of existing tendencies attempts to project the course of those tendencies and finds itself caught in the undecidable tension between tendencies: The simple fact that all divergent and contradictory tendencies cannot be realized at the same time.[1] (Contrary to what many maintain today, Marx's relation to teleology is much more complex than a simple proclamation regarding the imminent demise of capitalism.) This limit (I am referring specifically to the relation between the historical development of capitalism and subjectivity) is the position from which we approach Marx. What for Marx was the tension between two different tendencies, which may or may not realize themselves in the future, are for us, and those who come after Marx, elements of the present. This imposes a particular task on reading Marx that is more complex than simply distinguishing between correct and incorrect prophesy, as if Marx was some sort of nineteenth-century Nostradamus looking into the future for the shape of things to come. The problem with such a strategy of reading is that it takes its bearings from the hubris of the present, the idea that history reaches its end point with us.[2] Rather, the difficult task is to recognize the specific way in which various tendencies have realized themselves, or failed to, in the history of capitalism, while at the same time maintaining some element of the tendential, the nonactualized, and the conflictual, which as Marx understood are the conditions for a future different from the past.[3] The present is not a privileged point from which to settle all accounts but is itself a moment in a series of conflicting tendencies.

The tendency that Marx is explicitly concerned with in "Results" is the self-transformation of capital: the manner in which capital acts on and transforms its historical conditions. As Marx writes, capital proceeds from certain preconditions, from commodity production; as it develops, these preconditions are posited once again as results and effects "of the immediate process of production." There is a circular structure of the capitalist mode of production, all of the elements of the capitalist mode of production, commodity, money, and capital, are the starting point and end point of the process, which is not to suggest that this circle is the eternal repetition of the same. There is a fundamental difference between the commodity form at the emergence of capital and the commodity form in its maturity—a difference between the isolated commodities exchanged on the markets of mercantile capitalism and the planned and designed commodities of contemporary (or what used to be called "late") capitalism. The capitalist mode of production, unlike precapitalist modes of production, does not preserve its presuppositions but transforms them. This transformation of the fundamental elements of the capitalist mode of production is also a transformation of the capitalist social relation itself; this is in part what Marx means by the transition from formal to real subsumption.

Formal subsumption is the imposition of the basic forms of the capitalist mode of production—commodity production and wage labor—on preexistent technical and social organizations of production. As such it corresponds to a particular manner of extracting surplus value: what Marx called "absolute surplus value," surplus value produced by the extension of the working day. Capital takes the existing labor practices, the existing technological conditions, as it finds them. The only thing that changes is that production is now production for the market, and the hours are dictated by the demands of surplus value. The definition of formal subsumption would seem to be abstract and minimal; after all it only requires that labor be reduced to wage labor and that all things are produced as commodities, as exchange values. As I demonstrated in the previous chapter, the "formal" dimension of formal subsumption, abstract labor, the wage, and the commodity form, are not simply indifferent to their specific content. Rather, formal subsumption produces a content that it can be indifferent to. Abstraction is inseparable from its material conditions and effects. The abstract and formal conditions of capital must destroy any legal or social order that would stand in their way; that is, anything that would tie labor to particular qualities and skills or production to particular ends or goals.[4] The specific and determinate relations of tradition, power, and authority that exist between master and apprentice, peasant and lord, and slave and master all dissolve into the relation of capitalist and worker.

> Before the process of production they all confront each other as commodity owners and their relations involve nothing but *money; within* the process of production they meet as its components personified; the capitalist as "capital," the immediate producer as "labor," and their relations are determined by labor as a mere constituent of capital which is valorizing itself. (R 1020/92)

Marx's definition of formal subsumption in this chapter pivots around the power relation internal to production. What distinguishes formal subsumption from all precapitalist relations is that in the former the power relation in production is no longer "coded," or subordinated to political or religious ends. "In consequence the process of exploitation is stripped of every patriarchal, political or even religious cloak. It remains true, of course, that the *relations of production* themselves create a new relation of *supremacy and subordination* (and this also produces [*producirt*] its own political expression)" (translation modified, R1027/98). Paradoxically, Marx would seem to define formal subsumption as a purely economic form of subordination: The old political ties and relations are dissolved into relations of buying and selling, the axioms of the labor market. This is paradoxical because as it turns out there is nothing purely economic about formal subsumption: The economic relation is always already contaminated by a political relation, a relation of power. This relation of power does not just manifest itself in a relation of pure force but constitutes a particular type of subjection or production of subjectivity.[5] Thus, Marx's definition of formal subsumption begins from the fundamental intuition that what would seem to apply strictly to the economy, and thus a limited sphere of activity, is inseparable from its effects that necessarily spill over into other social relations. Even in the nascent emergence of the capitalist mode of production one finds a transversal relation of power.

The power relation intrinsic to formal subsumption is brought to light in the "colonies" or America. As Marx observes, the newly settled lands of America are constituted by an openness, an abundance of land at least for the white settlers. Thus every wage laborer is also potentially a farmer, an independent producer. Without the workers' dependency on selling their labor for survival there can be no exploitation of wage labor. This dependency already exists in Europe, created in part by the process of primitive accumulation and more directly by the simple absence of alternatives or frontiers. It does not yet exist in America, forcing the capitalist to employ different means to extract surplus value. "In the old civilized countries the worker, although free, is by a law of nature dependent on the capitalist; in the colonies this dependence must be created by artificial means" (CI 937/798). For Marx the "colonies" represent the truth of capitalist exploitation.

In contrasting formal subsumption to precapitalist or specifically feudal relations the terms *economic* and *political* prove themselves to be totally inadequate descriptions of the difference, because there is in each of the specific modes of production a transversal relation that cuts across the supposed self-identity of the political and economic. (Étienne Balibar argues that in Feudalism political relations are determined as dominant by the economy.) In the *Grundrisse*, reflecting on emergent elements of formal subsumption—namely, money and the wage relation—Marx uses the terms *personal* and *impersonal* to distinguish between the modality of power in the two modes of production.

> In the money relation, in the developed system of exchange . . . the ties of personal dependence, of distinctions of blood, education, etc. are in fact exploded, ripped up (at least, personal ties all appear as *personal* relations); and individuals *seem* independent . . . free to collide with another and to engage in exchange within this freedom;

but they appear thus only for someone who abstracts from the *conditions*, the conditions *of existence* within which these individuals enter into contact (and these conditions, in turn, are independent of the individuals and although created by society, appear as if they were *natural conditions,* not controllable by individuals). The definedness of individuals, which in the former case appears as a personal restriction of the individual by another, appears in the latter case as developed into an objective restriction of the individual by relations independent of him and sufficient unto themselves. . . . These external relations are very far from being an abolition of "relations of dependence"; they are rather the dissolution of these relations into a general form; they are merely the elaboration and emergence of the general *foundation* of the relations of personal dependence. (G 164/97)

Even the terms *personal* and *impersonal* prove inadequate to express the transformation between the different modes of production. It is inaccurate to suggest that in feudalism all power relations—the maintenance of the elaborate hierarchies—could ultimately be reduced to personal and immediate relations. Marx contends that even in this mode of production, in which it is possible to describe political and economic relations through the persons of feudal lord and vassal, landlord and serf, and so on, these seemingly interpersonal relations of subordination are supported by structures and institutions that necessarily exceed intersubjectivity (G 165/98).[6] These terminological difficulties—the inadequacy of the terms *economic* and *political* or *personal* and *objective* to describe power relations—point to the novelty of the problematic of the mode of production (or, more precisely, the intersection of the mode of production and the production of subjectivity).

This novelty, which can briefly be described as an attentiveness to not only the historical production of subjectivity but also the historicity of the relation between subjectivity and its material conditions, often proceeds "without concept," as Louis Althusser would say. The definition of formal subsumption proceeds through a series of paradoxes (paradoxes that illustrate Balibar's "short circuit" of the economic and the political): Formal subsumption both is and is not merely formal (since its forms, such as abstract labor, have their own specific materiality); it both is and is not merely economic (since the economic is inseparable from a political relation); and it both is and is not impersonal (since it is inseparable from its own production of subjectivity). More to the point, however, is the fact that when Marx develops a theory of the internal periodization of the capitalist mode of production, distinguishing between formal and real subsumption, he returns to the epochal distinction between capitalism and precapitalist economic formations—developing the unstable distinction of the materiality of power in each mode of production, which is to suggest that the issue of power is central to the distinction between formal and real subsumption.

For Marx formal subsumption is the stage of capitalism at its emergence as well as a possible modality of capitalism that may exist alongside more developed forms. The concept of 'formal subsumption' serves not only a roughly retrospective function—indicating the specific difference that separates capitalist relations from feudal relations—but it also indicates a process continuing toward the future.

Formal subsumption is the capitalist mode of production extending itself to other regions of the world. Examples of formal subsumption can be found in those parts of the world in which the capitalist mode of production has not yet reached its full dominance. Marx even goes as far as to suggest that these forms coexist and reproduce themselves alongside the "specifically capitalist mode of production" (or real subsumption) suggesting a thought of the complex and differential articulation of a "world market" (R 1023/95).[7] Formal subsumption is not simply the early stage of what would eventually become the "specifically capitalist mode of production," nor is it simply the seed of capitalism as it spreads across the globe. It is a specific articulation of the fundamental elements of the capitalist mode of production against an alien terrain. Formal subsumption is capital at the interstices of other modes of production.

There is perhaps a contradiction of sorts in the initial definition of formal subsumption. The maximum extension of the concept suggests that the minimum conditions of wage labor and commodity production contain within them a specific power relation and a specific production of subjectivity. Thus already implied within the concept of formal subsumption is the destruction of previous modes of production and the instantiation of the capitalist mode of production as a totality—totality at least in the sense that the capitalist mode of production must stand alone and can tolerate no other master. In contrast to this, the minimum extension of the concept of formal subsumption implies its articulation within elements of other modes of production. At the center of this contradiction is a problem that is not resolved, or even posed: the differential articulation of the instances of the social. If formal subsumption can be an element of capitalism against a noncapitalist environment (as in the case of early mercantilism or limited commodity production), then what is required is another concept to explain the articulation of these divergent elements. (It is in response to this problem that Althusser has suggested the term *social formation* as the complex articulation of multiple modes of production—one dominant, the others dominated—in a particular historical period.)[8] Marx does not provide this concept, only a series of observations regarding the uneven relations between the capitalist mode of production and the modes of production that precede it and follow it.[9]

Turning to the major focus of this chapter, the transition from formal to real subsumption, the problem of the homogeneity of the social becomes even more glaring. The tension at work between formal subsumption as totality and formal subsumption as an interstitial element of other modes of production is tilted entirely to one side when Marx addresses the question of its historical development. When Marx poses the question as to what precipitates the transformation from formal to real subsumption, the answer would seem to already imply that formal subsumption constitutes a totality.

> The way in which even the merely formal subsumption of labor under capital begins to become differentiated within itself—and does so increasingly as time goes on, even on the basis of the old, traditional model of labor—is in terms of the scale of

production. That is to say, differences appear later in the volume of the means of production invested, and in the number of workers under the command of a single employer. . . . This enlargement of *scale* constitutes the real foundation on which the specifically capitalist mode of production can arise if the historical circumstances are otherwise favorable, as they were for instance in the sixteenth century. Of course, it may also occur sporadically, as something which does not dominate society, at isolated points within earlier social formations. (R 1022/94)

The necessary and sufficient conditions of the transition from formal to real subsumption are already given in the expansion of formal subsumption. As formal subsumption increases the scale of production, bringing more and more workers into the space of production, it begins to transform the social and technological conditions of production. The collective conditions of labor make possible a transformation of the social organization and technological conditions of labor: workers working side by side makes it possible to alter the division of labor, while the increased size and differentiated tasks also make possible investments in productive machinery. Although the last sentences in the quote just cited allude to the contingent nature of this encounter, the overall thrust of this assertion is that real subsumption—the qualitative transformation of the capitalist mode of production—unfolds almost naturally from the quantitative expansion of formal subsumption. It is a classical transition from quantity to quality; once enough labor and wealth has been formally subsumed, the qualitative transformations of real subsumption inevitably follow. What is significant here is that the transition from formal to real subsumption does not meet any resistance either in the legal, political, and social structures of the precapitalist modes of production or in the workers whose existence must be totally transformed in the process.[10] The transition from formal to real subsumption appears then to be a simple matter of capitalism positing its own presuppositions, creating its own social and technical conditions.

In "Results of the Immediate Process of Production" Marx also demonstrates the way in which the transition from formal to real subsumption is also an intensification of the "mystification" immanent in the capitalist mode of production. At the level of formal subsumption the mystification inherent in the capitalist mode of production stems from the apparent invisibility of the division between "surplus" and "necessary" labor. There is no division in time or space between the point at which the worker ceases working for his or her own sustenance and begins to produce value for capital, and there is no palpable reminder in the form of a lord to reinforce this division. All labor appears to be necessary; the extraction of surplus takes place out of sight. Or, more to the point, since the capitalist or the firm supplies the conditions for work—the means of production—all work appears to be given by the capitalist. "The mystification inherent in the *capital-relation* emerges at this point. The value-sustaining power of labor appears as the self-supporting power of capital; the value creating power of labor as the self-valorizing power of capital and, in general, in accordance with its concept, *living* labor appears to be put to work by *objectified labor*" (R 1021/93). The intensification of this mystification in real subsumption follows this same logic: In each case the productive power of living labor—its ability to create value—is presented as an attribute of capital. The "socius" (capital) appears to preexist the determinant activity and labor that produces it. In real subsumption, this mystification follows the contours of the new technical and social organization of labor. In real subsumption labor is social labor not simply in the sense that it is undertaken collectively and is necessarily cooperative in the factory but because it involves the products of social activity in general, science, language, and so forth.[11]

> This entire development of the productive forces of *socialized labor* (in contrast to the more or less isolated labor of individuals), and together with it the *uses of science* (the general product of social development), *in the immediate process of production*, takes the form [*stellt sich dar*] of the productive power of capital. It does not appear as the productive power of labor, or even of that part of it that is identical with capital. And least of all does it appear as the productive power either of the individual workers or of the workers joined together in the process of production. (R 1024/95)

The intensification of the mystification inherent in the capitalist relation encompasses all of social activity, which is immediately present as the productive power of capital.[12] Thus there is a qualitative change in this intensification. At first mystification applied to the relation between capital and worker—inverting the relation of priority between product and production—now it applies to all of society, making it appear as if all of society has been produced by capital.

There is a point of contact between the account of the transition between formal and real subsumption and the intense mystification of social relations at the heart of real subsumption. This point of contact can be crudely framed by the following question: Has not Marx fallen into the same mystification he criticized in presenting the social and political transformation of real subsumption as a transformation produced by and for capital? Of course it is not exactly the same thing. When Marx addresses the mystification at the heart of capital, he is concerned with a fairly specific problem—the production of value and the displacement of the source of this productivity from the networks of living labor to capital—while in the case of the transformation and development of the specifically capitalist mode of production we are speaking of production in a much looser sense: the production of new social structures and relations. However, these two senses are always intertwined for Marx who sought to examine not only how capitalism produces but how it is itself produced as a social relation. "The production of capitalists and wage laborers is thus a chief product [*Hauptprodukt*] of capital's realization process. Ordinary economics, which looks only at the things produced, forgets this completely" (G 512/419).

As I have demonstrated with respect to a reading of the *Grundrisse* in chapter 1, Marx's concept of a mode of production entails an expanded sense of production, a production of subjectivity and social relations rather than simply of things. Thus, we can extend Marx's criticism of mystification to include this second sense of production: production as the production of ways of life and subjectivity necessary for the production of value. As I argued in the previous chapter the technological and social transformations of the capitalist mode of production are neither the pure product of capitalism nor of resistance to capitalism but rather are formed by the antagonistic interplay of the competing strategies: capitalist strategies to expand surplus value and the workers' strategies to expand needs and desires. Thus there is a mystification not only of the production of value but also of the production and transformation of social relations.

Marx's treatment of the development of capital from formal to real subsumption in *Capital* would seem to have at least implicitly acknowledged this problem. In the difference between "Results of the Immediate Process of Production" and *Capital* it is possible to see some of the conditions that may have caused Marx to leave the concepts of formal and real subsumption largely in the draft. In *Capital* the concepts of formal and real subsumption are linked to the concepts of 'absolute and relative surplus value' (in fact, the former pair appear only as elements of the definition of the latter).

> The production of absolute surplus-value turns exclusively on the length of the working day, whereas the production of relative surplus-value completely revolutionizes the technical process of labor and the groupings into which society is divided. . . . It therefore requires a specifically capitalist mode of production, a mode of production which, along with its methods, means and conditions, arises and develops spontaneously on the basis of the formal subsumption of labor under capital. This formal subsumption is then replaced by a real subsumption. (CI 645/533)

Even though this passage participates in part in the mystification of social transformation by referring to the development from formal to real subsumption as a "spontaneous" development, ultimately the interlinking of the two conceptual transitions contains elements of antagonism and conflict absent in "Results." In *Capital,* absolute and relative surplus value are given a linear definition that roughly follows that of formal and real subsumption. Absolute surplus value leaves the technological and social conditions—the intensity of labor—untouched; it is based on the simple extension of the working day that increases the amount of surplus produced, while relative surplus value alters the intensity and organization of labor within the constraints of a fixed working day. However, Marx is quick to add that this distinction is somewhat relative: Absolute surplus value presupposes a given intensity and duration of labor—an intensity that is historically produced. In other words both absolute and relative surplus value presuppose the simple fact that labor power is super-adequate to its own reproduction; that is, absolute and relative surplus value both presuppose a surplus and are simply two different ways of organizing this surplus.

What then constitutes the distinction between the two ways of producing surplus value? Marx's response obliquely refers to the material constraints that the different strategies for extracting value encounter. "But if we keep in mind the movement of

surplus value, this semblance of identity vanishes. Once the capitalist mode of production has become the established and universal mode of production, the difference
between absolute and relative surplus value makes itself felt [*fühlbar*] whenever there
is a question of raising the rate of surplus value" (CI 646/534). The question then is,
What makes this distinction felt, that is, produces the distinction between absolute
and relative surplus value as different strategies for creating surplus value? The answer
would obviously cross a series of complex conditions including the conditions under
which the introduction of technological transformations is profitable. However, if
one wanted to look for the limit of absolute surplus value—what makes it impossible to produce value from the simple extension of the working day—then the answer
would have to include the struggle over the length of the working day and the corresponding ten hours bill (discussed in the previous chapter). It is the irreversibility
of this struggle—an irreversibility grounded not only in the law that is passed but
also the struggle that produces this law—that makes necessary the transition from
absolute to relative surplus value. "The establishment of a normal working day is the
result of centuries of struggle between the capitalist and the worker" (CI 382/287).
Once the working day has been shortened, in this case reduced to ten hours, that
amount of time functions as a limit and constraint of capitalist accumulation. It becomes necessary to extract value another way: to intensify labor power by altering
its technological and social conditions—in short, it becomes necessary to pass from
formal to real subsumption.

As I argued in the previous chapter, Marx's documentation of the struggle over
the length of the working day in *Capital* (close to fifty pages) is not just an example of capitalism in one particular country, illustrating an otherwise dry and conceptual articulation, nor is it simply a residue of Marx's own particular political
biases (that he was for the workers and against capital). It is not just an example
because without it there is no adequate explanation of the transformation of capitalism: It is quite possible that capitalism could have continued profiting from
twelve-, fourteen-, and sixteen-hour working days of formal subsumption. The
struggle over the working day is an integral element of the antagonistic constitution of the capitalist mode of production, its irreducibility to a single strategy, intention, or logic. The struggle over the working day is a contingent event, an
encounter, as such it indicates what Althusser calls the "necessity of contingency"
in the formation and development of the capitalist mode of production.[13]

What is important now is the light that this "antagonistic constitution" casts on
the concept of real subsumption. Real subsumption at times appears as the complete and total self-production of the capitalist mode of production, capital producing its own social and technological conditions without an "outside" or any
limitations. It is presented as a reorganization of technological legal and social
space by capital for the production of capital. Marx writes that "*capitalist production* now establishes itself as a mode of production *sui generis*, and brings into
being a new mode of material production" (R 1035/105). This aspect of the concept is in some respect useful in that it poses the problem of developments and
transformations internal to the capitalist mode of production. It breaks up the

large epochal divisions—feudalism, capitalism, and communism drawing attention to the transformations internal to the capitalist mode of production. No one
would deny the manner in which capital has migrated into new social spaces and
relations, setting up industries and services within formerly private terrains of
reproduction—the quotidian matters of food and rest—and in formerly state-
controlled enterprises. These transformations are often recognized, but often as
simply being a simple quantitative extension of the capitalist mode of production.
It is often argued that capital is by definition imperialist, searching for new markets. Thus the more things change, the more they stay the same. (This difficulty in
recognizing the new unfortunately has a defining element of Marxist thinking—
an ironic fate for a mode of thought that has as its starting point the effectivity of
history.) The concept of real subsumption, however, insofar as it foregrounds the fact
that this extension is the subsumption of society by capital, and thus a transformation of social relationships, of the knowledges, desires, and practices constitutive of
social relations, posits a qualitative change, a new form of capitalism.

The disadvantages of the concept are equally clear. Real subsumption is presented as qualitative transformation with only a single cause, a single logic. It is the
reshaping of all social relationships according to the dictates of capital; that is, according to the demands of relative surplus value, all social relations are reshaped
according to the overall goal of making labor more intense, more productive. The
social becomes a smooth space for the flow of capital. Marx's criticisms of the mystification immanent to the capitalist mode of production and the historically
dense genealogy of the struggle over the working day all begin to point to the necessity of exploding the concept. Exploding the concept is not the same as doing
away with it but, rather, breaking open its unity and self-identity to expose the
complexity and antagonism internal to it. As Antonio Negri writes, describing the
possibilities and limitations of the term:

> Furthermore, we analyzed the above-mentioned evolution in the forms of control
> of the labor-process, within the conceptual framework of a *transition from "formal
> subsumption" to "real subsumption"*: Marx, as is clear at various points in his work,
> foresaw this transition and described it as the achievement of the subjection by the
> capitalist mode of production, of the whole of society. I believe that this theoreti-
> cal framework will withstand scrutiny. It might then be asked: "So why so much
> political excitement about (and literary dramatization in the description of) a pe-
> riod that was thought to be already well understood?" The answer—as is obvious—
> is that there is something which, while pertaining to the inner nature of this
> transformation, at the same time hails it as the radical innovation that it is, and
> which had not been sufficiently explained. Here we wish, above all, to emphasize
> this hidden something.[14]

Explaining this "hidden something" means examining the extent to which the real
subsumption of society by capital must also be a qualitative transformation of "living labor," of the cooperative networks of living labor. This entails taking up the
second broken thread that runs throughout "Results of the Immediate Process of

Production"—the investigation of subjectivity and the contradictory incorporation, or subsumption, of subjectivity by capital—and extending it beyond the limits of this text to the point at which it begins to outline the contours of the present.

THE FRAGMENT ON MACHINES

Refiguring the concept of real subsumption involves an interrogation of just what
is meant by the real subsumption of society by capital. What sort of process is designated by this idea of subsumption? What sort of power relation does it entail?
How does real subsumption alter or transform the relationship between living and
abstract labor, as well as the antagonistic articulation of capitalism, outlined in the
previous chapter? Answering these questions will involve passing through and reworking Marx's central conceptual pairs of living labor and dead labor, production
and consumption, and production and reproduction, as well as the ontological
commitments that inform and underlie such concepts.

Real subsumption is the transformation of the technical and social conditions
of the labor process: A transformation in which what is originally outside of capital, the social and technical conditions of labor, becomes internalized. They become a functional element of the process. To risk the obvious, real subsumption is
the interlinking or rather the inseparability of a technical and social transformation—the technical conditions of labor are changed at the same time that living
labor is transformed becoming intensified. Thus at the center of the concept is a
transformation of machinery, one that I have claimed is always a political transformation. (Of course it remains to be seen in what way the technological, social,
and political combine in real subsumption.) Placing technological change, or more
exactly, the relationship between technological change and social transformation,
at the center of the concept of real subsumption raises some difficult and seemingly irresolvable questions, for example, the question of the determining element
in the relation between "forces" (roughly understood as technology) and "relations" (roughly understood as social relations) of production. At the same time it
also expands the textual grounds for discussing real subsumption beyond the relationship between "Results of the Immediate Process of Production" and the fin-
ished volume of *Capital* to include other texts, which develop and problematize
the relationship between forces and relations of production, most notably the
notebooks known as "The Fragment on Machines" in the *Grundrisse*.

In chapter 2 I argued that the development of the technological conditions of
labor is inseparable from a political transformation of the social condition of
labor. Political relations of control, surveillance, and discipline are immanent to
the development of machinery. The primary goal of technological development
in the factory under capital is, after all, the intensification of the labor process.
Technological development also entails a mutation of the social, anthropological,
and ultimately ontological grounding of labor. In chapter 7 of *Capital*, Marx outlines the basic schema of the labor process "independent of any specific social
formation." According to this schema, every labor process involves three compo-

nent elements: work or purposeful activity; the object being worked on; and the instrument, or means, of production. This definition is, for the most part, anthropological; that is, it provides the invariants that are posited as the limits of the human condition within which historical change operates. Marx contends that it is primarily through the mediating term, the instrument as simultaneously product and element of the process, that history enters into the schema. "Relics of bygone instruments of labor possess the same importance for the investigation of extinct economic formations of society as do fossil bones for the determination of extinct species of animals" (CI 286/194). What the instrument indicates is not simply the technological development of the social formation, rather something of the social relations within the mode of production. As such the instrument as indicator of a social sign is ambiguously poised. It is unclear whether the instrument, or technology, indicates the "economic formation" because it is the determining instance or if it functions as only a sign of a complex social formation. Mutation of the instrument does not simply alter what can be produced, or how, but it falls back on the process, transforming the producer himself or herself. The production of things is also always an autopoieis, a production of the one producing—a production of subjectivity. As Marx writes with respect to the laborer, "Through this movement he acts upon external nature and changes it, and in this way he simultaneously changes his own nature" (CI 283/192).

Marx's chapter on the labor process, a brief anthropological speculation in the midst of the overarching critique of political economy, would seem to proceed through a series of undecidable theoretical alternatives. The chapter vacillates between ascribing the determinant role to forces or relations of production—at times leaning toward a technological determinism and at times implying that technology is only an effect or a sign of a larger social process.[15] The chapter would also seem to be equally ambiguous with respect to the question of human nature, outlining a fundamentally anthropological schema of the transcendental conditions of any process of production, while at the same time arguing that the transformation of the object is also always a transformation of the subject, transformation of the very "nature" of the subject.

Despite Marx's assertion that the schema of the labor process applies to any social formation of labor, it is precisely this schema that is disrupted in his analysis of the development of capitalism from handicrafts through manufacture to large-scale industry in the later chapters of *Capital*. In these later chapters Marx is dealing primarily with the limited sense of the mode of production, mode of production as a particular technical and social manner of producing. However, these chapters also sketch out a tendency regarding the relationship between living labor, machinery, and science that will be integral to the definition of real subsumption. As Marx focuses on the mode of production in its limited sense, he sketches a picture not only of the factory as a social space but also its effects on the tempo and organization of all social relations.

Marx's understanding of the history of the technological division of labor traces the displacement of the organizing principle of production: from the commodity as individual product to the commodity as social product. Handicrafts, the techno-logical and social division of labor that exists prior to capitalism (and is formally subsumed by capital), has as its organizing principle the skill and talents of the worker. This principle acts as a limit to the technical and social division of labor; the tasks and aspects of producing a specific commodity can be broken down only in-sofar as they constitute separate handicrafts. Manufacture does not so much chal-lenge this principle as it pushes it to its limit. Its operation is both analytic and synthetic: It breaks each of the handicrafts down into its component elements (from the assembly of carriages as a handicraft to woodworkers, leatherworkers, and so forth), while at the same time unifying these workers under one roof or within the same process. "The commodity, from being the individual product of an in-dependent craftsman, becomes the social product of a union of craftsmen, each of whom performs one, and only one, of the constituent partial operations" (CI 457/358). The principle of handicraft remained intact. It is still the knowledge of an individual worker, the skill and talents of one person, that dictate how labor is divided. Similarly, Claude Lefort writes with respect to manufacture, "A corporeal schema continued to determine how the workshop was structured."[16] For Marx the break is not between handicrafts and manufacture but between both of these labor processes, which are organized around the unity of the worker and the means of labor, and large-scale industry that is organized around a different unity—the unity of the means and object of labor. It is no longer the skill of the worker that organizes the process of production but the demands of the commodity.

The machine makes possible the break with the worker as organizing unity of production. For Marx the characteristic that distinguishes a machine from a tool is not motive power—the transition from manual power to an external source of power—but the latter's capacity to exceed the anthropological limit of handicrafts.

> From the moment that the tool proper is taken from man and fitted into a mecha-nism, a machine takes the place of a mere implement. The difference strikes one at once, even in those cases where man himself continues to be the prime mover. The number of implements that he himself can use simultaneously is limited by the number of his own natural instruments, i.e. his own bodily organs. (CI 495/394)

With the machine, labor is not limited to a human scale; the organic limits of the human (two arms, two eyes, and so on) no longer dictate how work is to be done. Although the limits established by the handicrafts rest ultimately on the human body, the limits are social as much as they are biological because they also include the tendency to divide work into trades: positions that can be occupied for life. Just as there is no natural need, or use value, underlying the conservative nature of precapitalist modes of production, no purely natural schema of the body un-derlies the principle of handicrafts. The social practices of the guilds and handi-crafts continually produce and reproduce the very idea of the natural productive body as governing unity.[17] This body is already a social body. Underneath the ap-parent historical continuity of the division of labor, which can trace its philosophical origins back to Plato's *Republic*, lies a real difference: between a division governed by human capacities and their limits and a division governed by the technical capacities of machinery.[18] Liberated from the schema of the human being, the division and organization of labor can be subject to not only the technical demands of machinery but also ultimately, the demands of capitalist valorization.

> [The] subjective principle of the division of labor no longer exists in production by machinery. Here the total process is examined objectively, viewed in and for itself, and analyzed into its constitutive phases. The problem of how to execute each particular process, and to bind the different partial processes together into a whole, is solved by the aid of machines, chemistry, etc. But of course, in this case too, the theoretical conception must be perfected by accumulated experience on a large scale. (CI 502/401)

The machine, or system of machines, is inseparable from a displacement of labor power. First, living labor no longer occupies the central and organizing place within the labor process; it is displaced, positioned, as an adjacent element to a massive structure of machines. In Marx's words, workers become merely "conscious organs [*bewußte Organe*] of the automaton" (CI 544)/442).[19] This displacement is made possible by the incorporation of science, chemistry, and even what Marx refers to as "accumulated experience on a larger scale": the experiences and observations collected from the shop floor and from other sites of production. Machinery has rendered impossible the thought of labor as the activity of an isolated subject or even as a group of workers operating under the same roof. All labor is socialized labor; cooperation is no longer restricted to the factory floor but encompasses all of the social processes (scientific research, transportation, coordination, and perhaps even advertising) necessary for the coordination of the laboring process. "There are laborers in this cooperation who are not present at the workplace."[20] In describing a transformation of the mode of production in the limited sense—the particular technological organization of labor—Marx's description opens onto what was described in the last chapter as the larger sense of the mode of production, the immanent relations of the entire social field.

The historical mutation of labor from handicrafts to large-scale industry is not only a displacement of the schema of labor from the human body to the machine, it also entails a fundamental transformation of the organization of knowledge. In the case of handicrafts the knowledge and skills necessary to perform work were closely guarded and handed down to members of a trade.

> It is characteristic of this situation that, right down to the eighteenth century, the different trades were called "mysteries," into whose secrets none but those initiated by their profession and their practical experience could penetrate. Large-scale industry tore aside the veil that concealed from men their own social process of production and turned the various spontaneously divided branches of production into riddles, not only to outsiders but even to the initiated. Its principle, which is to view each process of production in and for itself, and to resolve it into its constitutive elements without

looking first at the ability of the human hand to perform the new processes, brought into existence the whole of the modern science of technology. (CI 616/510)

Knowledge is "deterritorialized"—separated from the human hand, from tradition, from a way of life—in the same way that labor is deterritorialized—freed from its moorings in the community to become more productive for capital.[21] The sphere and domain of what constitutes productive labor is fundamentally redefined by this deterritorialization. "In order to work productively, it is no longer necessary for the individual himself to put his hand to the object; it is sufficient for him to be an organ of the collective laborer, and to perform any one of its subordinate functions" (CI 664/549). Technology under capitalism simultaneously limits and extends the role of labor, limiting labor in the factory to an adjacent part of an "automaton," while at the same time putting to work science and the collected knowledge of all of the cooperative multitude. This simultaneous extension and delimitation of the role of labor in the productive process is an effect, or rather a concrete development, of the contradictory tendency of proletarianization and socialization. In the first case, living labor is reduced to abstract labor, to an interchangeable, mechanical, and precarious process, while at the same time other activities, which are perhaps irreducible to wage labor such as research and science, are made productive for capital.

The notes in the *Grundrisse* known collectively as "The Fragment on Machines" provide a sketch of the end point of this contradictory process, a sketch that is also offered as a definition, at least implicitly, of real subsumption. In the fragment we see elements of what will become the analysis of machinery in *Capital* (the breakdown of the anthropological schema and the increasing importance of scientific knowledge) put to somewhat different philosophical and political uses. These tendencies of machinery are presented not simply as elements of the existing factory system but as constitutive elements of real subsumption or, as Marx refers to it in the fragment, the specifically capitalist mode of production. Moreover, and somewhat paradoxically, Marx presents the tendency toward the development of machinery as the dissolution of capitalism and as a materialist foundation of communism. The dissolution of capital and corresponding remarks on the foundation of communism given in this section are fundamentally different than those found in Marx's other writings.[22] To give a sketch of this difference, one could say that in Marx's most famous texts (*The Communist Manifesto, The German Ideology*, and even parts of *Capital*) capitalism dies of proletarianization (the production of a proletariat as a destitute mass with nothing to lose but their chains), whereas in "Fragment" capitalism dies of socialization (the production of a cooperative and knowledgeable labor force). Of course, these are not entirely separable because each tendency is immersed in the same antagonistic logic. Although Marx's different texts may focus on either the socialization or proletarianization of labor power as the dominant tendency of the capitalist mode of production, neither of these tendencies are given in pure form entirely apart from the other. The difference is really only a difference of emphasis. What is perhaps more useful for our purpose here is the light the fragment sheds on a different contradiction: the contradiction of real subsumption, which is a contradiction between the total subjection of sociality and subjectivity to capital and the concomitant development of a subjective and social power irreducible to abstract labor.

Marx's statements in "Fragment" follow the same logic as that developed in *Capital*. As in *Capital*, Marx identifies the emergence of machinery with the destruction of skill as the basis for production. Even though a tool is always dependent on the virtuosity of the worker, the incorporation of knowledge into the machine in terms of its design and ability to mimic and duplicate activities that were performed by workers makes it so the machine itself is the "virtuoso." As the skill, technical know-how, and science is made into a physical attribute of the machine itself, it is no longer necessary for the worker to know what is going on. "The science which compels the inanimate limbs of the machinery, by their construction, to act purposefully, as an automaton, does not exist in the worker's consciousness [*Bewußtsein*] but rather acts upon him through the machine as an alien power, as the power of the machine itself" (G 693/593). The development of machinery—a development driven by the demand to extract more relative surplus value, to intensify the productivity of labor—actually tends to reduce the need for labor in the productive process.

> Labor no longer appears so much to be included within the production process; rather, the human being comes to relate more as watchman and regulator to the production process itself. (What holds for machinery holds likewise for the combination of human activities and the development of human intercourse.) No longer does the worker insert a modified natural thing [*Naturgegenstand*] as a middle link between the object and himself; rather he inserts the process of nature, transformed into an industrial process, as means between himself and inorganic nature, mastering it. He steps to the side of the production process instead of being its chief actor. (*G* 705/601)

The "anthropological schema" of a relation to nature mediated by an object, which is a product of history, is completely shattered as living labor takes a subordinate role in the process of production. It is no longer labor power at the basis of production but rather the powers of the intellect objectified.

> Nature builds no machines, no locomotives, railways, electric telegraphs, self-acting mules etc. These are the products of human industry; natural material transformed into organs of the human will over nature, or of human participation in nature. They are *organs of the human brain, created by the human hand*; the power of knowledge objectified [*vergegenständlichte Wissenskraft*]. The development of fixed capital indicates to what degree general social knowledge has become a *direct force of production,* and to what degree, hence, the conditions of the process of social life itself have come under the control of the general intellect and been transformed in accordance with it. (G 706/602)[23]

Capitalism can do without the anthropological schema fragmenting the body into parts of a massive automaton. What is potentially devastating, however, is that labor time—the time of abstract labor—is a necessary condition for capitalist valorization, for the production of exchange and surplus value. By displacing the skill and strength of labor power into the machine, capital undoes its own basis as a mode of production founded on the exploitation of labor power. "Capital itself is the moving contradiction, [in] that it presses to reduce labor time to a minimum, while it posits labor time, on the other side, as sole measure and source of wealth" (G 706/602). Capital destroys its own foundation rendering itself superfluous.[24]

Up to this point Marx's understanding of the historical tendency of machinery in capitalism, or of technology as the dominant element of the real subsumption of society by capital, would seem to be an unrealized, even utopian tendency. As Paolo Virno argues in his consideration of the different interpretations of this fragment, "What jumps to one's attention now, in fact is the full *factual realization* of the tendencies described in the *Grundrisse*, without, however, any emancipatory—or even merely conflictual—reversal."[25] Technology and knowledge have become directly productive, but this has done nothing to threaten capitalism. Of course this possibility is accounted for in Marx's text: It is possible for capitalism to measure the gigantic social forces thus created at the rate of labor time (G 706/602). Despite the fact that the source of productivity lies elsewhere—in the knowledge incorporated into machinery—it is still possible for labor time to serve as the criteria for wages, for the distribution of needs and desires. It is possible for the labor time, for the exchange value of labor, to live on as a measure, as a political standard, long after it has ceased to function as a measure of productivity. Value outlives its death. "Labor time is the unit of measure *in force*, but it is no longer the *true* unit."[26] Thus, in registering the difference that separates Marx's "Fragment" from the present it is not sufficient to simply point to the conclusion because this conclusion already possesses an ambiguous character. Although its critical stance toward the capitalist organization of production is clear, "Fragment" has a somewhat equivocal relationship to its own teleological conclusion. It posits the grounds for the dissolution of capitalism, as well as the possibility for a mode of production not founded on the exploitation of labor time, while at the same time accounting for the possibility that capital can outlive itself—lingering on zombielike. What does, however, seem to date this fragment is that Marx conceives of the real subsumption of society almost exclusively as the incorporation of social knowledge, or the general intellect, into machinery, into fixed capital. As Virno states, "Marx completely identified the general intellect (or, knowledge as the principle productive force) with fixed capital, thus neglecting the instance when that same general intellect manifests itself on the contrary as *living labor*."[27]

In "Fragment" Marx focuses primarily on the limitation of labor, its reduction to a conscious organ, excluding for the most part the other side of the contradictory process of real subsumption—the extension of labor, of living labor, to dimensions of social life that were previously nonproductive and outside of capitalist valorization. However, Marx alludes to, without necessarily conceptualizing, the other side of the process.[28] Even though Virno is correct in identifying the overall character of "Fragment," and in arguing that there is no explicit conceptual articulation of the relationship between the general intellect and living labor, he perhaps overlooks the insistent presence of this other dimension. Reading Marx for the intersection of the general intellect and living labor is not a matter of rescuing "Fragment" from its own excesses and limitations. The goal is not to turn these ten short pages into an adequate representation of the present, rather, it is to engage with the problem of real subsumption, the simultaneous incorporation of all social relations into capital and the development of new productive force irreducible to abstract labor power. It is a question of that which cannot be measured or controlled by capital but is nonetheless essential to its functioning. We have seen that Marx gives many names to this immeasurable excess—primitive accumulation, living labor, and now the general intellect—names corresponding to different phases different problems in the history of capital. In thinking this problem as a problem the gaps or difficulty of its articulation are as important as the concepts.

When Marx describes the process by which capitalism reduces the centrality of labor time he does gesture toward a dimension of this process that exceeds the incorporation of knowledge and power into the machine.

> On the one side, then, [capital] calls to life all of the powers of science and of nature, as of social combination and social intercourse [*gesellschaftlichen Verkehrs*], in order to make the creation of wealth independent (relatively) of the labor time employed on it. On the other side, it wants to use labor time as the measuring rod for the giant social forces thereby created, and to confine them within the limits required to maintain the already created value as value. Forces of production and social relations [*gesellschaftlichen Beziehungen*]—two different sides of the development of the social individual—appear to capital as mere means, and are merely means for it to produce on its limited foundation. (G 706/602)

The repetition of the word *social*, and specifically the juxtaposition of social relations or intercourse alongside science and the forces of production as two different sides of the same process, would seem to indicate an aspect of real subsumption that is irreducible to the displacement of labor by science and technology. A similar reference can be found in a previous passage regarding labor as watchman. Marx writes that labor stands watchman over the independent process of machinery and "likewise for the combination of human activities and the development of human intercourse." This would seem to imply that labor—abstract labor measured by time and subject to a wage—stands as watchman and regulator not only to the knowledge incorporated in machinery but also to the social forces that exceed it. There is the implication that just as the machine is productive without being subject to the wage or value as a measure, the productive power of social relations, or the social individual, is simultaneously productive and without measure. What is put to work in real subsumption are not only the powers of nature contained in the machine but also the power of sociality, of social relations, that make possible the machine but are also ultimately not reducible to the machine.

In real subsumption living labor mediates living labor insofar as it is not simply an instrument that is poised between the worker and the object but rather other labors, or the knowledge accumulated through labors. A thought of the general intellect, as something other than its incorporation into machinery, entails rethinking the relation between different workers, between different sites of production, a relation that exceeds cooperation. In cooperation the primary relation is between the mass of assembled workers under one roof, in one factory, and the capitalist control of the labor process, manifested either in the capitalist owner, management, or the plan. The relation between workers is only one of the intensifications of the labor of relatively isolated and independent individuals. In real subsumption it is no longer possible to identify production within the limited space of the factory—every act of production incorporates knowledge, instruments, discoveries, and social relations that are not present in the limited space or time of the factory. The factory becomes a social factory.[29] This social factory entails a relation between different labors, different workers, that is not limited to their simultaneous subjection to the same capitalist or the same design, nor can it be adequately expressed by the inchoate sociality of cooperation. It is a relation of the mediation of living labor by living labor in which not only machines but labor as it is performed in different sites extends and transforms the power of labor. Just as this transformation cannot be understood through the limited spatial instance of the factory, it also cannot be understood simply through production, at least in the limited sense. Since this relation exceeds the factory, it must also include the relations of circulation and consumption. Or rather, returning to the reading of the "1857 Introduction" in the first chapter it must include circulation and consumption insofar as they are also productive.

IMMATERIAL LABOR

Negri states that Marx's method in the *Grundrisse* is a continual interplay between research [*Forschung*] and presentation [*Darstellung*] in which the results of one determinate area of research, or series of notebooks, is presented as the starting point for another area of research.[30] This is not a simple linear progression in which the different researches are added up but an open movement of crisis and displacement. This conceptual movement is an attempt to trace the progression of the fundamental contradictions and antagonisms of the capitalist mode of production.[31] In this movement the fundamental categories of Marx's research are shifted, seen from different angles, problematized, and even placed onto different conceptual and ontological grounds. In the last section we saw how labor was initially given an anthropological grounding only to have the rug pulled out from under it, as it were, by the development of the technological and social powers of labor. The entire "Fragment" seems to move in this direction—problematizing and redefining the concepts of value, fixed capital, and circulating capital. Thus it is possible to read it not only as another account of the imminent demise of the capitalist mode of production, or even as an account of real subsumption, but as reworking some of the fundamental categories of Marx's writing in light of the social transformation that is real subsumption. Negri asserts that the high point of this process of reworking can be found in a passage that redefines both consumption and fixed capital in order to grasp the role of subjectivity in real subsumption.[32]

> The capability to consume is a condition of consumption, hence its primary means, and this capability is the development of an individual potential, a force of production. The saving of labor time is equal to an increase of free time, i.e. time for the full development of the individual, which in turn reacts back upon the productive power of labor as itself the greatest productive power. From the standpoint of the direct production process it can be regarded as the production of *fixed capital,* this fixed capital being man himself. It goes without saying, by the way, that direct labor time itself cannot remain in the abstract antithesis to free time in which it appears from the perspective of bourgeois economy. Labor cannot become play, as [Charles] Fourier would like, although it remains his great contribution to have expressed the suspension not of distribution, but of the mode of production itself, in a higher form, as the ultimate object. Free time—which is both idle time and time for higher activity—has naturally transformed its possessor into a different subject, and he then enters into the direct production process as this different subject. This process is then both discipline, as regards the human being in the process of becoming; and at the same time, practice [*Ausübung*], experimental science, materially creative and objectifying science, as regards the human being who has become, in whose head exists the accumulated knowledge of society. (G 712/607)

This passage repeats, in a fundamentally different way, what Marx identified earlier as a fundamental difference between precapitalism and capitalism. Whereas in precapitalism subjectivity is reproduced, along with the community and its corresponding relations of domination and subordination, as an integral element of the mode of production, in capitalism subjective potentials, desires, and needs are continually mutating along with the needs of the capitalist mode of production. Here this process of self-transformation and experimentation is presented not as the epochal difference between capitalism and what came before but as constitutive of a new form of fixed capital: subjectivity as fixed capital. Knowledge and social relations are incorporated not only into fixed capital as machinery but also as human subjectivity. This new subject is produced during "free time," outside of the time of wage labor—it is produced in and through consumption.

In the *Grundrisse* the production of a new individual, a new subjectivity, is often presented as foundation of the critical perspective. Thus the *Grundrisse* continues a theme that is most forcefully articulated in the *1844 Manuscripts* a critique of the present from the possibilities latent within it.

> We have seen the significance, given socialism, the *wealth* of human needs has, and what significance, therefore, both a *new mode of production* and a new *object* of production have: a new manifestation of the forces of *human* nature and a new enrichment of *human* nature. Under private property their significance is reversed: every person speculates on creating a *new* need in another, so as to drive him to fresh sacrifice, to place him in a new dependence and to seduce him into a new mode of gratification and therefore economic ruin. (147)

In the *1844 Manuscripts* the production of new needs, of a new subject, is presented as a fundamental contradiction of capitalism, a fundamental element of the alienation intrinsic to capitalism. "This estrangement manifests itself in part in that it produces sophistication of needs and of their means on the one hand, and a bestial barbarization, a complete, unrefined, abstract simplicity of need, on the other" (148). The wealth of capital is contrasted to the poverty of the worker. The generation of new sensibilities, and a new humanity, within the emerging sphere of consumption is contrasted to the subhuman conditions of production: the factory in which air, light, rest, and food are nonexistent or reduced to the minimum necessary for survival. The critical and political task, then, is overcoming such a contradiction by overcoming private property.

In the *Grundrisse* the opposition cannot be rendered so neatly. The production of new needs, of a new subjectivity, does not stand on one side, within the sphere of consumption against the deprivation of needs in production, nor does it characterize the decadence of the bourgeoisie against the poverty of the proletariat. Moreover, in the *1844 Manuscripts* the production of a new humanity was an effect of the production of things: The development of new objects through industry, music, art, and science produce a subject capable of enjoying them. In *Grundrisse* the production of a new sensibility, a new humanity, becomes integral to production without the necessary mediation of the object. (As I will argue in the next section, an important aspect of real subsumption is the direct production of subjectivity, of affects and knowledge, through services.) The rhetorical force of the earlier contradiction between the demands of capitalist consumption and capitalist production is lost. However, to say that it becomes integral to production does not automatically mean that it simply becomes a functioning element of the system, as if all antagonistic force is lost. The reference to Fourier's utopian vision of a society founded on play rather than work in a previous passage indicates that for Marx the production of a new individual through consumption cannot simply be reduced to the transformation of all human capacities and powers to human (fixed) capital. It cannot be separated from the question of the ultimate grounds of the capitalist mode of production. The production of subjectivity as fixed capital, and the productive and transformative nature of free time is given, as a possible foundation of revolution.

If this passage breaks with some of the most famous statements and logics of Marx's political writings—logics that are often thought to contain and govern the entirety of Marx's writing—then it is no less significant that it breaks with Marx's conception of labor. We have seen how the machine, or large-scale industry, significantly ruptures the anthropological schema: transforming the instrument from an object through which man relates to nature and the world to a mechanism, or mechanized nature, within which man has the status of "conscious organ." It would now seem that the other side of real subsumption—the development of a socialized individual, of new subjective powers—also breaks with the anthropological schema of the labor process. Whereas the former challenged the relation between the subject and instrument of labor, demonstrating how the subject can become subordinated to the instrument, the latter challenges the very definition of productive labor insofar as it posits the existence of labor in which "the product is inseparable from the act of producing." It is a model of labor in which the effect on social relations, on subjectivity, is not a byproduct of a more primary transformation of things as in the schema of the labor process but is directly produced by labor itself—labor becomes autopoetic.

As we have seen, Marx argues that in real subsumption "it is no longer necessary for the individual himself to put his hand to the object; it is sufficient for him to be an organ of the collective laborer, and to perform any one of its subordinate functions" (CI 644/532). Thus substantially changing the definition of productive labor from direct interaction with an object to any of the social process and support functions in contemporary capitalism. Despite this radical redefinition of productive labor, the model of direct interaction with the object—an instrumental relation—seems to dominate Marx's thinking. Thus the question of productive labor is a vexed question for Marx. In "Results of the Immediate Process of Production" Marx proposes a rigorously nominalist definition of productive work. There is no content or specific quality that would identify labor as productive. Productive labor is labor that produces capital, any wage labor that produces surplus value. Thus Marx argues that many forms of what are often called today "cultural production" can be considered productive.

> For instance, [John] Milton, who wrote *Paradise Lost*, was an unproductive worker. On the other hand, a writer who turns out work for his publisher in factory style is a productive worker. Milton produced *Paradise Lost* as a silkworm produces silk, as the activation of *his own* nature. . . . A singer who sings like a bird is an unproductive worker. If she sells her song for money, she is to that extent a wage-laborer or merchant. But if the same singer is engaged by an entrepreneur who makes her sing to make money, then she becomes a productive worker, since she produces capital directly. A schoolmaster who instructs others is not a productive worker. But a schoolmaster who works for wages in an institution along with others, using his own labor to increase the money of the entrepreneur who owns the knowledge-mongering institution, is a productive worker. But for the most part, work of this sort has scarcely reached the stage of being subsumed even formally under capital, and belongs essentially to a transitional stage. (R 1044/113)

What is significant in these examples is the implication of subjectivity in this redefinition of productive labor. In the case of the singer, it is her intimate talents and capacities that produce surplus value, while in the case of the schoolmaster, teaching, the development of new knowledges, skills, and capacities, new subjective potential, is rendered productive for capital. This is done directly insofar as the school is made into a profitable business, producing capital, but also indirectly insofar as the subjects produced become part of human fixed capital. In each of these cases what is produced and what is productive is subjectivity itself: In the first case the talent to sing is harnessed for the production of surplus value; in the second the school produces knowing (and also obedient) subjects. These two types of productive labor can be extended to a virtual point of intersection at which the production of subjective capacities in one area or industry becomes the ground for a new production in a different area—the production of what Marx calls "the social individual." Despite this possible point of intersection Marx relegates this sort of production—a production of production—to "microscopic significance when compared with the mass of capitalist production" (R1045/114).

There are of course historical reasons for this near dismissal, the most obvious being the historical development of the capitalist mode of production itself. Marx was writing at a time in which even the definition of real subsumption, of the factory as the dominant technological mode of production, were themselves projections, possible tendencies within a much more conflictual and uneven mode of production. Without necessarily examining all of the historical material, it is possible to concede that Marx's marginalization of the production of subjectivity by subjectivity follows some of the historical tendencies of his time. Most notably, it follows the incomplete subsumption of many activities and practices, cultural production such as writing and teaching, but also services other productive activities that leave no object and disappear in the act of producing. Despite Marx's argument that capitalism reduces all activities "from the prostitute to king" to wage labor, at the time of his writing, these activities, what we today call "cultural production or services," were for the most part not productive of surplus value. Moreover, as items to be consumed, cultural products and services—from artistic performances to the services of waiters, butlers, and other precursors of the service economy—are often consumed by capitalists and not by wage laborers. The money spent on these luxuries is profit: capital that is spent unproductively rather than reinvested into the productive apparatus. Thus this sort of production, the production of subjects or of social relations, was primarily outside the sphere of capitalist production or reproduction.

Even though Marx seems capable of fully entertaining the possibility that the production of cultural objects, such as books and artworks, will ultimately become subject to the laws of capitalist valorization, services, or relations of service seem doomed to occupy a marginal place in the capitalist mode of production. For Marx the latter are examples of luxury spending, money that is spent without producing capital. Services, products that disappear in the act of producing, are "wage labor that is not at the same time productive labor" (R 1045/112). Rather than recognize a possible future of capitalist valorization in these relations, Marx relegates them to the past. They are attempts on the part of the bourgeoisie to enjoy the expenditure and thus the prestige and "service" that one associates with feudalism. As Leopoldina Fortunati indicates, Marx understands service to belong entirely to a precapitalist economy of prestige, thus he cannot recognize the relations of service constitutive of capitalism in the form of housework.[33] Since capitalism is by definition the replacement of personal relations of dependence, such as exist between master and lord, with impersonal and abstract relations of dependence, there is no place, or only a marginal place, it would seem for relations of service.[34]

These marginal elements of production—cultural and service work—move to the forefront in real subsumption. Although they occupy a place of ambiguous centrality in Marx's theoretical account of real subsumption, alluded to through the references to the production of a social individual and the productive powers of social relations, it is possible to make a stronger argument for their existence in the present, in what we could call "actually existing real subsumption." Maurizio Lazzarato argues that the contemporary capitalist mode of production can be identified by the centrality of what he calls "immaterial labor."

> The concept of immaterial labor refers to *two different aspects* of labor. On the one hand, as regards the "informational content" of the commodity, it refers directly to the changes taking place in workers' labor processes in big companies in the industrial and tertiary sectors, where the skills involved in direct labor are increasingly skills involving cybernetics and computer control (and horizontal and vertical communication). On the other hand, as regards the activity that produces the "cultural content" of the commodity, immaterial labor involves a series of activities that are not normally recognized as "work"—in other words, the kinds of activities involved in defining and fixing cultural and artistic standards, fashions, tastes, consumer norms, and more strategically, public opinion.[35]

To argue that immaterial labor is central is not to suggest that other forms of labor—factory production, for example—no longer exist. Such a claim would be ludicrous. Rather, it is to suggest that there is an articulation, a relation of relations, that asserts the dominance of immaterial labor over other forms of production. In *Capital* Marx demonstrates that the factory system as a specific technological and social mode of production is dominant by showing how it intersects with other modes of production—handicrafts and agriculture—determining the rate and conditions of their production. These other technical and social modes of production either appropriate the factory model internally, assuming its discipline, technology, and structure, or they adapt to it externally, producing for the expanded urban population of factory society. To say that the factory is dominant is to argue that it is hegemonic over other forms of production.[36]

A similar argument can be made for immaterial labor. There is an internal adoption of the dense communicational and relational interfaces into industrial production. In these cases production is still the production of material commodities, but the mute production of things is drowned out by continual interrelations of communication—communication between factories and retailers as well as communication between workers and management.[37] More significant, there is an "external" incorporation of immaterial labor into production. Production continues according to the technological and social demands of preexisting modes of production—factory or handicrafts—but every product must pass through immaterial labor. Every commodity produced must have an image, a lifestyle, and an immaterial "halo" that accompanies it to the market. These images are not simply produced by the dictates of advertising executives; rather, they draw from existing cultural practices and ways of life. "The process of social communication (and its principal content, the production of subjectivity) becomes here directly productive because in a certain way it "produces" production.[38]

One possible objection to the concept of 'immaterial labor' is that it would appear to eclipse the contradictory tendencies of labor within capital: the overlapping tendencies toward socialization and proletarianization of the labor force. Immaterial labor would seem to be a highly "socialized" form of labor—cooperative, skilled, and intellectual—without a corresponding proletarianization. Thus the dual tendencies of capitalism offer something of a precaution. It is important not to confuse immaterial labor as a general tendency of the capitalist mode of production with the specific figure of the highly paid computer programmer or advertising executive. Immaterial labor also includes "affective labor." Affective labor includes all forms of labor that produce and circulate states of being, feelings of well-being, desire, ease, and passion.[39] Types of affective labor run the gambit from advertising executive to "care worker" in the health-care or day-care industries. At the bottom of the ladder of affective labor thus is a sector of the workforce (primarily female) that is not socialized in the sense of trained or invested with skills. The bottom rung of affective labor there is "degree zero sociality": the simple capacities to care, communicate, or interact. It is this capacity that is then exploited. It is necessary to point out that this degree zero sociality is not some residue of nature at the heart of culture. As Mariarosa Dalla Costa indicates, it has been constituted, produced, by a long history that has kept the family, and reproductive work, isolated from the cooperative networks and technological transformations of production.[40] The degree zero of sociality is itself historically produced through the constitution of certain activities—such as caring for children and housework as "natural," and it is for this reason that such relations prove ripe for exploitation.

Although the concept of proletarianization entailed the reduction of a subject with a high degree of cooperation and skill (the handicrafts and artisans of precapitalist production) to an interchangeable unit of abstract labor time, the degree zero sociality of affective labor entails the exploitation of the minimal and most common aspect of social relations. In the first case there is a reduction of subjectivity to abstract labor power, while the second can best be described as a "social" primitive accumulation: an accumulation of the very capacity to be social or to interact—a capacity that exists prior to and outside of capital.[41] In each case, however, there is the constitution of a hierarchy of labor powers, one that has as its basis a degree zero of human potentiality: the potential to work or to communicate. Moreover, just as it is possible to locate something of an analogue of proletarianization in the lowest paid forms of affective labor there is also a generalized possibility for proletarianization in all forms of immaterial labor. Immaterial labor is often labor off the clock: It is not measured by the workday or week but by the "project." The irregularity of work, and with it the irregularity of pay, becomes an aspect of control and exploitation.[42] Immaterial labor is not opposed to proletarianization, as was socialization, rather, it is inseparable from a transformation of the very conditions of proletarianization.

Returning to Marx from the perspective of immaterial labor, there is a tension between Marx's tendency to place the social relations that extend beyond the factory and the production of a new social individual at the heart of real subsumption, on the one hand, and the persistence of a model of the cycle of capitalist production that takes the production of commodities, and the factory, as its dominant image, on the other hand. It is a tension between a tendency projected into the future and the model used to imagine that tendency. The situation with respect to immaterial labor can be productively compared to the displacement of the anthropological schema of the labor process by the development of machinery. In that case Marx posited a three-part schema of subject, instrument, and object and then proceeded to show how this schema unravels through the transformation of the middle term. Once the machine replaces the tool it is no longer possible to think of labor as the activity of an isolated individual on an object. The historical tendency completely transforms the model. This transformation is not only a change at the level of work, or in the isolated space of labor; in fact in the case of the machine, it is a total transformation of political and social space—affecting the relations of knowledge and power. It is perhaps necessary to chart a similar deterritorialization with respect to immaterial labor. This deterritorialization would perhaps begin not with the mutation of the instrument in the aforementioned schema but with the object—the object of production is no longer a commodity, a thing, but a social relation. As in the case with the development of machinery, the transformation of one of the terms is inseparable from a mutation of the entire schema and the anthropology underlying it. Moreover, as with the deterritorialization of the instrument, the effects of this transformation are not isolated to the schema governing labor. The effects are inseparable from a radical transformation of social space and social relations. Along with this transformation—the transformation of real subsumption—there is a "deconstruction" of some of Marx's fundamental concepts and conceptual divisions, including the relationship between fixed and circulating capital, as well as the triad of production, consumption, and circulation.

The overlapping schemas and cycles of production in Marx's corpus identify the instrument as the entry point of history into the process. It is the instrument, tool, or machine, which in capitalism becomes fixed capital, that changes with time. This change can be as simple as wearing out or it can include the incorporation of science and knowledge into the machine. Of course this transformation of fixed capital is caused by other social and political transformations—as Marx argues it is the struggle over the working day that in part provokes the development of machinery—and consequently the transformation has effects on the other elements of the labor process. The displacement of skill and knowledge from the worker to the machine makes possible the proletarianization of the labor force. What does not change in this history is that fixed capital is owned by and controlled by the capitalist, or collective capitalist, and that it requires variable capital in order to be put to work producing value. Living labor is necessary to animate dead labor. These two aspects of fixed capital delineate much of the conflict within capitalism. With immaterial labor it is no longer possible to simply identify fixed capital with the machine. According to Marx, with real subsumption the production of new sensibilities and relations within the worker, a production that often takes place in and through free time and consumption, produces fixed capital not as machinery but in the subjectivity of the worker. Fixed capital can no longer be simply identified with capital itself, because it exists and is produced outside of the temporal and spatial control of the capitalist.

For Marx consumption was always productive. As I argued in chapter 1, Marx replaces the static anthropology of political economy in which consumption figures only as the natural end point of the process with an ontology of production in which consumption is productive, producing the conditions and desires of production.

> Consumption creates the motive for production; it also creates the object which is active in production as its determinant aim. If it is clear that production offers consumption its external object, it is therefore equally clear that consumption *ideally posits* the object of production as an internal image, as a need, as drive and as purpose. It creates the objects of production in a still subjective form. No production without a need. But consumption reproduces the need. (G 92/27)

There is a tension in this passage where on the one hand consumption is presented as the active constitution of drive and need, as creating something new, and on the other hand, this creation would seem to be placed within a closed circle of reproduction, as if it only returned a drive to the same needs. With immaterial labor the circle is cracked open on two sides. All consumption becomes a condition for further production.[43] "Immaterial workers (those who work in advertising, fashion, marketing, television cybernetics and so forth) satisfy a demand by the consumer and at the same time establish that demand."[44] The creative constitutive side of consumption is unhinged from reproduction, as it becomes a labor process in its own right. Consumption produces both the conditions for further consumption, in the constitution of new desires, and the constitution of new production, in the creation of new subjective potentials as fixed capital.

There are at least two different ways of thinking about this incredibly catachrestic use of the term *fixed capital* to consider the production of subjectivity. Catachrestic because as much as the subjective potentials of living labor must occupy the function of fixed capital, as prerequisite of production, they are neither temporally nor spatially fixed. From the point of view of "productive" labor— labor operating on objects—it is machinery that occupies the place of fixed capital. With real subsumption it is the city or social space itself that occupies the place of fixed capital. Negri draws this analogy:

> Society thus offers itself to work in the same way that, in the factory, a single machine, several machines and the entire system of machinery offered themselves to the labor force: namely, as a *system of preconditions*. The machines are preconditions in the sense that they represent accumulated labor, or concentrated labor power, which only further labor power can reactivate and in so doing, draw off further strands of value,

know-how and wealth. . . . In advanced capitalism, society is an ontologically fixed technological system of enormous potentialities. It is inherently equipped to absorb vitalizing labor and as consequence, to activate the system of reproduction.[45]

If one focuses on the dimension of immaterial labor that provides the cultural content of commodity—not only the style of packaging, designing, and deploying commodities but also the lifestyle that each commodity is associated with—it is possible to argue that social space, specifically the city, can be seen as an immense archive of immaterial labor.[46] This archive exists in the official form of museums, libraries, universities, and cultural centers and in the more subterranean form of countercultures and artistic circles. This archive contains knowledge, images, sounds, and ways of relating capable of being used to market and produce commodities. Given the marginalization of abstract labor in the production of wealth—a marginalization that makes it difficult to measure value—and the centrality of spatial territories in the production process, it is perhaps more accurate to think in terms of "cartographies of value" rather than measures of value.[47] Cartographies of value draw out the social spaces that are exploited by capital. The cartography of value does not simply draw lines between public and private, factories and homes, since the reservoirs of immaterial labor are often outside of capital. It marks out the territories, which, with their corresponding cultures and spaces, have become productive for capital.

Not all immaterial labor is localized in these territories, nor is immaterial labor only solidified in the archive: It travels in and through the various epistemic, aesthetic, and affective models that structure social communication. Virno asserts that these include "artificial languages," theorems of formal logic, theories of information and systems, epistemological paradigms, certain segments of the metaphysical tradition, linguistic games, and images of the world.[48] For Virno the general intellect is the series of "conceptual constellations" that are communicated through manuals, videos, and training sessions. They are embedded in the heads and minds of workers as little productive machines, without necessarily originating from them.[49] Virno thus retains Marx's distinction between the consciousness of the worker, or the worker as conscious organ, and the automaton that operates outside of consciousness, only now this distinction is "interiorized." The person is not simply a conscious organ of the machine, but consciousness becomes occupied and animated by little machines, by programs and rules. This is in part why Donna Haraway argues for the "cyborg," part human part machine, as the figure of subjectivity in contemporary capitalism.[50]

For Marx, fixed capital in formal subsumption—fixed capital as machinery—led to definite political confusions not only on the part of radical workers, bourgeois political, economy, but also Marx himself.[51] Without following all of the areas of this confusion, it is at least useful to reiterate how the very concept of fixed capital is inseparable from certain questions of the appearance of the social, of the society effect, to trace how this question is repeated and transformed with respect to subjectivity as fixed capital. First, as the long history of the Luddites in

England attest to it is difficult to distinguish between the machine and its use by capital. In the machine, the independence or the alienation of the productive process from the worker takes on a material and palpable form—it is the concrete instance of a general social antagonism. Furthermore, machines are utilized by capital to respond to the provocations and resistances of living labor, from the struggle over the working day onward. "It would be possible to write a whole history of the inventions made since 1830 for the sole purpose of providing capital with weapons against working-class revolt" (CI 563/459). Moreover, fixed capital as machinery is a crucial element of the mystification immanent to the capital relation: They not only make it appear as if capital itself is productive without labor and social relations, but they also make capitalism appear as a necessary condition of technological development.

Machinery, fixed capital as machinery, is the very definition of reification. With machinery, a social relation—capitalist control over production—appears as a necessary attribute of things.[52] A similar mystification is perhaps at work in subjectivity as fixed capital, albeit in a fundamentally different way. In the first case, what fixed capital effaces is the difference between technology and the social order, between capital as the accumulated technological means of production and capital as a mode of production. In the second, however, what is effaced is perhaps nothing less than the presence of the antagonistic force of living labor in real subsumption. The effacement of the difference between machinery and capital becomes the effacement of the difference between subjectivity and capital. If machinery as fixed capital provides the very model for reification, then subjectivity as fixed capital would seem to be reification taken to its extreme conclusion. As Georg Lukács writes:

> The specialized "virtuoso," the vendor of his objectified and reified faculties does not just become the [passive] observer of society; he also lapses into a contemplative attitude *vis-à-vis* the workers of his own objectified and reified faculties. . . . This phenomenon can be seen at its most grotesque in journalism. Here it is precisely subjectivity itself, knowledge, temperament, and powers of expression that are reduced to an abstract mechanism functioning autonomously and divorced both from the personality of their "owner" and from the material and concrete nature of the subject matter in hand.[53]

Extending the term *fixed capital* to include the subjective capacities or reservoirs of subjectivity necessary for immaterial labor moves in two opposite directions. Initially, it would seem to underscore a dramatic difference: Unlike the fixed capital of machinery, subjectivity is either outside of direct control of capital, as in the city, or is disseminated across social space. Subjectivity as fixed capital is entirely outside of capital: It is no longer owned by capital or contained within the spaces of the factory. At the same time, however, subjectivity as fixed capital would seem to be entirely interior to capital—produced by capital as a functional component. Thus, subjectivity as fixed capital completely eclipses not only any antagonism but also any ground for antagonism. By examining subjectivity as fixed capital we see how it is produced, but not how it is productive; that is, we do not see how its production exceeds production for capital, how it ultimately produces new social relations and antagonisms.

The ambiguous position of subjectivity, or subjectivity as fixed capital, as both inside and outside of capital attests to two things: First, it indicates the limitation of the very figure of the inside and the outside as descriptions of capitalism.[54] Formal subsumption is, by definition, the encounter between capitalism and its outside. With formal subsumption capital confronts a technical and social exteriority in the form of the preexisting structures and relations of the labor process. It is also possible to add that since formal subsumption is often named as the relation between the capitalist mode of production and other modes, it is also an encounter with the world, or the world market, as exteriority. Real subsumption entails not only the elimination of the first of these, with the formation of a "specifically capitalist" social and technical mode of production, but also perhaps the latter. Real subsumption is inseparable from the movement by which capital covers the globe: It is a process of social endo-colonization, the transformation of all social relations into relations for capital, which follows the process of exo-colonization. There is nothing, no place or relation, that can be considered outside of capitalism. At the same time, as real subsumption penetrates all social relations, it also increasingly puts to work forms of social knowledge that it neither owns nor directly controls. *Thus it is possible to say, paraphrasing Althusser, that with real subsumption capital has no outside, and at the same time, it is nothing but outside.* The second ramification is that as suggestive as the concept of fixed capital is for thinking about the role of subjectivity in real subsumption it is not in itself adequate, nor could it be, to the presentation of real subsumption. This is made clear by the fact that fixed capital leaves the question of antagonism completely undetermined in that fixed capital appears to be entirely outside of capital, and entirely functional to it.

Virno argues that the mobile dimension of the general intellect—its extension through various conceptual models across social space—is perhaps more adequately understood as a real abstraction than fixed capital. Virno's presentation has an advantage over fixed capital in that the very concept of "real abstraction" is inseparable from an antagonistic force that is both immanent and artificial.

> Inasmuch as it effectively organizes production and the world of everyday life, the general intellect is indeed an abstraction, but a *real abstraction,* equipped with a material operability. In addition, because it consists of paradigms, codes, procedures, axioms—in short, because it consists of the objective concretizations of knowledge—the general intellect is distinguished in the most peremptory way by the "real abstractions" typical of modernity, by those abstractions that give form to the principle of equivalence. Whereas money, the "universal equivalent" itself incarnates in its independent existence the commensurability of products, jobs, and subjects, the general intellect instead stabilizes the analytic premises of every type of practice. Models of social knowledge do not equate the various activities of labor, but rather present themselves as the "immediate forces of production."[55]

Marx focuses on the real abstractions of money and abstract labor. Virno calls these real abstractions typical of modernity. It might be more accurate to refer to them as the real abstractions of formal subsumption because they relate to the two constitutive dimensions of capitalism: the flow of money and the flow of labor power. These abstractions are real in that they are not merely mental generalizations, concepts, but are continually produced through social practices. Abstract labor is produced through the norms and disciplinary apparatuses that render the labor of different bodies and individuals equivalent. Money is nothing other than the general figure of equivalence.

As I argued in the previous chapter, each of these general equivalents is inseparable from an antagonist dimension. Abstract labor is inseparable from cooperation, from the intensification of the force of living labor. The flexibility and mobility of abstract labor, its capacity to be utterly indifferent to the content of its work, has as its necessary correlate the subjective power of living labor. Money, or money in the form of the wage, unhinges desire from a desire for a particular form of life, for determinate conditions of reproduction. With money there are no qualitative limits on the demands of the working class. With money it becomes possible to demand anything. The antagonistic dimension is also the intersection with subjectivity: The real abstractions constitute the desires and potentials of subjectivity. Thus if the real abstractions of formal subsumption are immediately intertwined with the conditions of antagonism, it is possible that the new conditions of antagonism are intertwined with the real abstractions of real subsumption. The real abstractions of formal subsumption assert in different ways a principle of equivalence: Abstract labor is the materialist correlate to the idea of abstract humanity, and money equalizes all desires rendering them equally attainable or at least potentially attainable. Despite the very real inequalities and exploitations of capitalism, the real abstractions of capital are inseparable from a utopian movement. "The principle of equivalence, which stands at the foundation of the most rigid hierarchies and the most ferocious inequalities, guarantees nonetheless a certain visibility of social connections, a commensurability, a system of proportionate convertibility."[56] The general intellect, in that it is directly productive, does not assert the equivalence of different activities, rather, it asserts the interchangeability of diverse and heterogeneous practices. An individual is often called upon to adopt multiple languages, communicative models, and styles in the course of a single day and job. It is for this reason—the flexibility and indifference of different practices—that Virno sees in the general intellect the contemporary figure of the cynic; that is, an indifference and a resignation to "whatever" rules and tasks may come his or her way.[57]

If one keeps in mind that these aspects of the general intellect are not solely produced by capital, but traverse the entirety of lived space and time, produced across the urban networks and through all the time of life, then it is possible to argue that the critical potential of the real abstractions of real subsumption is not the principle of equivalence but the relation between capital and life.[58] To follow the critical potential of the new real abstractions, and the new relation between capital and life that is at stake in them, it is necessary to follow the overturning, or

deconstruction, of another conceptual opposition: the relationship between reproduction and production.

SUBJECTIVITY: FROM REPRODUCTION
TO PRODUCTION

In chapter 1, through a reading of primitive accumulation and "Pre-Capitalist
Economic Formations," I argued that Marx's general theory of the mode of production necessarily entails the production of subjectivity. Every mode of production necessarily presupposes and reproduces particular forms of sociality and
subjectivity. In chapter 2, I argued that the capitalist mode of production has at its
foundation and emergence abstract subjective potentiality. The dynamic of the
capitalist mode of production entails the contradictory simultaneous development
of this potential—an increase of its collective power—and its disciplinary subjugation to the demands of capitalist valorization. If the real subsumption of subjectivity by capital designates something other than a simple repetition of these
two points, of the immanence of subjectivity to the mode of production, in general, and the immanence of abstract subjectivity to the capitalist mode of production, in particular, then it will be necessary to grasp the particularity of the relation
between capital and subjectivity in real subsumption.

Marx understood precapitalist modes of production to be essentially conservative: They necessarily repeat or reproduce their initial technical, social, and subjective presuppositions. In contrast to this, the capitalist mode of production is a
mode of production proper—its aim is the continual production of surplus value,
and thus the perpetual transformation of its presuppositions. As Marx argues, underneath the limited bourgeois form—the subordination of all productive activity to capitalist valorization—capital is nothing other than the unfettered forces of
production, including the production of subjectivity. In Capitalism "[humanity]
does not reproduce [him]self in one specificity, but produces his totality? Strives
not to remain something [s]he has become, but is in the absolute movement of becoming?" (G 488/396). The epochal difference between precapitalist modes of
production and the capitalist mode of production can be crudely described as a
difference between modes of reproduction and modes of production. Crudely because, as I argued in the first chapter, despite Marx's remarks regarding the primacy
of use values in precapitalist modes of production (and thus reproduction as the
supposed reproduction of natural needs) precapitalist modes of production are not
without surplus and domination.[59] In these modes of production there is production, and a surplus of production, not just reproduction of use values. Moreover,
capitalism cannot be identified entirely with an unfettered development of production, it too must reproduce particular economic, legal, and social conditions,
what Marx refers to as its "bourgeois limitations."[60] The reproduction of these
conditions is necessary to the production of surplus value.

It is from the recognition of the role of reproduction in production that we can
distinguish between the role of subjectivity in formal and real subsumption. The

best way to articulate this difference is to proceed from another epochal division, this time between the role of subjectivity in formal and real subsumption. Like the division between precapitalist and capitalist modes of production, this distinction will at first appear to be crude and static and thus will later need to be problematized and rendered mobile. *In formal subsumption the production of subjectivity is linked primarily to reproduction, while in real subsumption the production of subjectivity itself becomes productive for capital.* At first glance this distinction seems to be at least paradoxical if not wrong. Is it not true that capitalism has at its foundation an abstract subjective power, the indifferent capacity for any labor whatsoever? It is perhaps necessary to distinguish between the abstract subjective potential (as abstract and living labor) underlying the capitalist mode of production, and the constitution of determinate modes of subjection. The fact that capital proceeds from abstract labor, from a necessary equivalence of diverse bodies and actions, means that on one level it must be indifferent to the particular subjective backgrounds and abilities. Marx argues that with capitalism arrives the ideal of abstract humanity. Although it is necessary to add that, as with formal subsumption, indifference does not designate an absolute indifference—a freedom to let a thousand flowers bloom—such that capital can tolerate any specific "coding" of subjective abilities; rather, indifference is produced by social apparatuses that reduce qualitative diversity to quantitative equivalences, as in the case of the norm of abstract labor time. The axioms of capital necessarily destroy any traditions, customs, or codes that would stand in the way of the development of abstract labor power. Those which are not destroyed are rendered irrelevant and private. As Gilles Deleuze and Félix Guattari write:

> The person has become "private" in reality, insofar as he derives from abstract quantities and becomes concrete in the becoming-concrete of these same quantities. It is these quantities that are marked, no longer the persons themselves: *your capital or your labor capacity,* the rest is not important, we'll always find a place for you within the expanded limits of the system, even if an axiom has to be created just for you.[61]

Thus capital, at least at the stage of formal subsumption, does not render determinate subjectivities, or subjects, productive but the abstract potential of any subjectivity whatsoever. This abstract subjective potential is, as we have seen, fundamentally indeterminate: It can always work for or against capitalist accumulation. The real abstractions of formal subsumption—money and abstract labor power—are capable of constituting insurgencies against capital as much as they are capable of being rendered productive for capital. Thus a necessary correlate of the development of abstract subjective potential, of living labor, is the engagement of the capitalist mode of production with subjectivity at the level of reproduction. Reproduction is reproduction of the biological, technological, and social conditions of production, conditions that include the reproduction of subjectivity as subjectivity productive for capital. The capitalist mode of production must fetter this abstract subjective potential by tying it to particular modes of subjection, particular ways of living. As Deleuze and Guattari argue, these modes of subjection often take the form of archaisms: feudal and traditional forms of identity revived for the purpose of social and political control.[62] Thus in formal subsumption it is primarily at the level of reproduction that capital engages with determinate subjectivities or modes of subjection.[63]

Althusser investigated, or really was the first to propose, the crucial relation between reproduction, subjectivity, and capitalism in his essay "Ideology and Ideological State Apparatuses" and the manuscript *Sur la reproduction* (from which the former was drawn). Before turning to Althusser's analysis it is necessary to note the ambiguity of Althusser's position historically vis-à-vis the distinction between formal and real subsumption I have mentioned. Althusser's investigations were written in the period between 1968 and 1970, a period that many would argue was transitional in the passage from formal to real subsumption.[64] Althusser's position on such a period of transition could be understood as the twilight flight of the "Owl of Minerva," in which the constitutive elements of a mode of production become apparent as they pass out of existence. However, Althusser's writing was provoked in part by the "events of May," which among many things were revolts against the restructuring of the educational system, one that would serve to integrate the educational system into capitalist production.[65] Bill Readings argues, for example, that part of the struggle in May was a refusal on the part of the students of both the antiquated elitist French University and its modernization into a modern university geared toward the need of capital.[66] Thus Althusser's reflections are not simply situated in the passive transition from formal to real subsumption but are provoked by the active struggles that precipitate this transformation.[67] Althusser's historical position, in the interstices of a process of transition, is reflected in the way in which his essay straddles elements of what I will argue are constitutive of the role of subjectivity in formal and real subsumption. Insofar as Althusser focuses on the ideological production of subjectivity as an aspect of the reproduction of the relations of production, and thus as an element of political control that is a necessary supplement to capitalist production, his essay would seem to be situated within formal subsumption. However, insofar as the essay both specifically presents the educational institution as the dominant "Ideological State Apparatus" and in general focuses on a subject who actively participates in subjection, thus positing an intellectual and active subject, it would seem to prefigure elements of real subsumption.[68]

In *Capital* Marx argues that the reproduction of the labor force is a necessary aspect of the perpetuation of the capitalist mode of production: "The maintenance and reproduction of the working class remains a necessary condition for the reproduction of capital" (CI 718/597). Althusser's own investigation into the connection between reproduction and ideology takes its bearings from this point. Even though both Marx and Althusser argue that any mode of production necessarily must reproduce its subjective and objective conditions, in *Capital* Marx primarily stresses the physical and biological dimension of the reproduction of subjectivity—the physical reproduction of the working class—and only marginally addresses the political and social dimension of reproduction.[69] Before immediately rushing to conclude that Althusser's analysis is superior, since it includes in the reproduction of the relations of production the obedience and subjectification of the worker, it is necessary to pause over Marx's examination of the biological dimension of reproduction. Necessary, because as Althusser claims reproduction is always overdetermined, it encompasses the reproduction of the worker as a biological being, as a skilled and trained worker, and as a docile and obedient subject.[70] The combination of these diverse practices—from the biological demand to consume sufficient food to the reproduction of ideological environments—under the same term would make the term seem hopelessly confused and monolithic, prompting many to reject it. Rather than reject the term *reproduction* almost in advance, it would seem to make more sense to construct its specific problematic from the diverse senses of the term: biological, technical, and political.[71] From this reconstruction it is possible to expose the limits of the term, as well as its specific historicity.

Marx argues that for the most part capital can leave reproduction to the "worker's drives for self-preservation and propagation" (CI 718/597). For Marx the reproduction of the biological existence of the worker is not examined as a process but posited as a fact. It explains, poorly one might add, why the worker shows up for work. It does not answer the question as to why these same drives for self-preservation do not lead to revolt or insurrection. Moreover, Marx's treatment of reproduction leaves the entire relation between reproductive labor—the work of care and housework—and productive labor—labor performed indirectly for capital—for the most part completely outside of his analysis.[72] Furthermore, by framing the biological reproduction of the working class as the brute confrontation of the workers' drive for self-preservation and the capitalists' drive for profits, it would appear that class struggle is an almost biological and ahistorical struggle for survival.[73] Thus, in considering the dynamic of capitalist reproduction, Marx lapses behind his critique of the supposed natural ground of need underlying classical political economy in the *Grundrisse* and the recognition of the need and desire as a conflictual terrain, framed by the simultaneous demand of the capitalist mode of production to produce new needs and to reduce the cost of labor power in *Capital*. In these later points (covered in the previous chapters) Marx does not reduce history to the interaction of natural laws but recognizes that nature is thoroughly historical and history is thoroughly natural.[74] This interrelation of nature and history as it relates to the reproduction of life is expounded on in *The German Ideology*.

> The production of life, both of one's own in labor and of fresh life in procreation, now appears as a double relationship: on the one hand as natural, on the other as a social relationship. By social we understand the co-operation of several individuals, no matter under what conditions, in what manner and to what end. . . . Thus it is quite obvious from the start that there exists a materialistic connection of men with one another, which is determined by their needs and their mode of production, and which is old as men themselves. This connection is ever taking on new forms, and

thus presents a "history" independently of the existence of any political or religious nonsense which in addition may hold men together.[75]

In light of this assertion it becomes necessary to read against this biological ground of reproduction, not to purge from Marx any reference to the biological dimension of reproduction but to locate in this biological dimension not the simple and ahistorical conflict of the needs of the working class versus the desires of the capitalist but the historical transformation of biological existence—what we could call the "biopolitics of capitalism."

Marx argues that one of the fundamental differences between the capitalist mode of production and precapitalist production is that in the former the conditions of reproduction are mediated by the commodity form and wage rather than directly provided. The capitalist does not feed or care for the worker, at least directly, as in the case of slavery, but provides the abstract conditions for reproduction in the form of a wage. Under formal subsumption, or generalized commodity production, one of the presuppositions of capitalist production is that the conditions for living can and ultimately must be bought in the form of commodities, which is not to argue that there may not be some forms of precapitalist practices of reproduction (such as small gardens, homecooked meals, and children cared for at home) but that the time constraints imposed by commodity production (the working day) as well as the availability of commodified substitutes work to diminish the role of these practices of reproduction in capital.[76] The process of primitive accumulation "frees" the worker from any communal or hierarchical system that would provide for the conditions of existence, exposing him or her as "naked life" on the market.[77] Of course this "freedom" is at best partial, if not wholly illusory because the wage makes possible a new hierarchy between wage work—male work—and the nonwaged work of reproduction—female work. The wage and with it the commodity form become the general condition for life and existence. This means that the conditions of the reproduction of existence are subject to the economic constraints and demands imposed by the commodity form. Specifically, one of the ways to increase relative surplus value is to make the costs of the reproduction of labor—the basic necessities of life—cheaper, increasing the ratio of surplus labor to necessary labor. To be exposed to commodity production for the basic conditions of one's existence is to be ruthlessly exposed to the demand for cheaper commodities.

Marx details, with Dickensian attention to the details of poverty and squalor, the effects this pressure has on basic necessities such as bread, milk, and butter: recounting reports that describe the adulteration of bread with chalk, alum, and soot (CI 358/263). The adulteration of the basic necessities of existence reflects not only the demand to cheapen the cost of labor but also the basic fact that labor power is always replaceable: If one worker dies or is made sick by these products, he or she can always be replaced by the reserve army of labor. "Capital therefore takes no account of the health and the length of the life of the worker, unless society forces it to do so" (CI 381/286). Marx's statements regarding the cruel indifference with which the capitalist confronts the living conditions of the working class are ultimately ambivalent. As much as the capitalist is indifferent to the longevity of this or that specific worker, working him or her to an early grave, in general it is dependent on the reproduction of a healthy and vital working class. This ambiguity is apparent in a footnote to the previous quote in which Marx argues that the "health of the population is an important part of national capital" (CI 381/286). Furthermore, Marx's citations from various state reports and legislation describing, criticizing and ultimately seeking to control the content and conditions of the basic necessities of life would suggest that while there may be indifference to the biological conditions of reproduction at the level of the individual firm there is increased control of these conditions at the level of the state.[78] Even when dealing with simple biological reproduction—the maintenance of a living and able working class—the question of reproduction involves a different point of view on social relations: It involves a recognition of the intersection of the interests of the different capitalist enterprises, what Marx called "total social capital."[79]

Michel Foucault names the involvement of state power into the health and well-being of the population "biopower." As with "disciplinary power" it appears that Foucault has not so much filled in the gaps of Marx's analysis—conceptualizing what otherwise exists in a series of observations and statements—as he has followed the emergence and development of capital to investigate aspects of its formation overlooked by Marx and Marxists, although it should be added that there is a significant difference in the formation of the two concepts. Disciplinary power is a concept in part drawn from Marx's analysis of the power relation internal to the factories; Foucault's concept only names and conceptualizes what was already operative in Marx's text. Biopower does not have the same status. There is in Marx's writing a general assertion regarding the "production of life" as a natural and historical process, as well as an oblique recognition of the relation between commodity production—the demand for labor power—and control over the conditions of existence. However, these remarks do not reach the same level of coherence or theoretical articulation as Marx's remarks toward a theory of disciplinary power. In the latter case there is a true theoretical precursor, while in the former there is only the visible void of a problem not articulated.[80]

In many ways the articulation of the concept of biopower falls outside of Marx's problematic. Foucault argues that biopower predates the emergence of industrial capitalism: "This bio-power was without question an indispensable element in the development of capitalism; the latter would not have been possible without the controlled insertion of bodies into the machinery of production and the adjustment of the phenomenon of population to economic processes."[81] Biopower predates capitalism insofar as the recognition of the relationship between the population as a vital entity and the state dates back to at least early mercantilism, or mercantile capitalism. Population does not simply designate the number of individuals bounded by a territory but the dynamic relations of birth and death, sickness and health, which are vital to a nation politically and economically.[82] It is only later, after the rise of the urban centers of production and the threat of revolution, after the health of the rich and the poor become intertwined, that the state concerns itself not only with the population as a statistical entity but specifically with the health and environment of the working body.[83] What is essential for Foucault is the manner in which the investment of the state into the life and death of the population, the environmental conditions of the cities, and the health and longevity of the working class in each case is a properly political relation forming a biopolitics. In each instance the goals of the intervention are political: Biopolitics functions to increase productivity while at the same time reducing the conditions and causes for revolt. Thus, it is more accurate to say that biopolitics works for both economic and political goals, or better, it is constituted at the point at which political power becomes inseparable from economic power.[84] Biopolitics, like Marx's critique of political economy, short-circuits the division between the economic and the political. Moreover, at the same time as biopolitics functions in the service of political and economic goals, it also works to restructure and transform political and social space, for example, by imposing grids and models drawn from the control of contagions onto the city, models that are always both hygenic and political. It brings with it new models of the partitioning of social space, new forms of knowledge regarding social space, new ways of living and understanding life.[85]

Returning to the problem of reproduction, it would seem that Foucault's concepts of biopower and biopolitics make it possible to dispense with the notion that there is ever anything like a simple biological reproduction that functions as the basis or ground of political reproduction. The biological reproduction of living labor is always already implicated in its political reproduction; the problem of the health of labor is inseparable from the problem of control. Foucault's statement regarding the biopolitics of capitalism can then be added to Althusser's fundamental insight regarding the overdetermined nature of reproduction. In Althusser's essay on ideology he primarily considers this overdetermination along the two primary axes of skill and obedience.

> The reproduction of labor power thus reveals as its *sine qua non* not the reproduction of its "skills" but also the reproduction of its subjection to the ruling ideology or the "practice" of that ideology, with the proviso that it is not enough to say "not only but also," for it is clear that *it is in the forms and under the forms of ideological subjection that provision is made for the reproduction of the skills of labor power.*[86]

It is now possible to add health—the reproduction of a living and healthy body—to the intersection of obedience and skill. It is necessary for the working body to be living, skilled, and docile.

For the most part the firm, factory, or individual capitalist is indifferent to these three constitutive elements of reproduction.[87] Marx's observation, that the individual firm is indifferent to the biological reproduction of the workforce is as much insight as error because the very question of reproduction cannot appear at the level of the firm or factory.[88] Althusser argues that the reproduction of a labor force as living, competent, and docile takes place through other institutions: schools, hospitals, families, and so forth. (The same insistence on looking outside of the factory as the privileged site of social relations runs through Foucault's analysis of biopower.) It is possible to argue, then, following classical Marxist terminology, that reproduction would be the relation, or the articulation of the relation, between base and superstructure.[89]

In formal subsumption, reproduction would designate the relation of social institutions exterior to the capitalist mode of production (such as state, schools, and families) to the mode of production. Just as formal subsumption entails the relation between the minimal conditions of capitalist production—the wage and commodity production—and already existing social and technical conditions of labor, it also entails the relation between capitalist production and social conditions for the reproduction of labor power that are exterior to it. These conditions function all the more for capital in that they are understood to be exterior to it. As Mariaros a Dalla Costa and Leopoldina Fortunati demonstrate, the patriarchal family functions for capital insofar as it is understood to be structured according to fundamentally different rules and relations—according to natural relations of love and desire.[90] As Althusser argues, however, as much as the figure of the social topography (base/superstructure) allows one to pose the question of the relation between divergent social institutions and practices, what he calls their "respective indices of effectivity," it remains purely descriptive—trapping thought in its obviousness. What the figure obscures is that even in formal subsumption reproduction does not always, or even necessarily, entail an exterior institution.

As I have already argued, the technical division of labor, machinery, the labor contract, and the wage—all elements of the labor and valorization process—produce as their afterimages ideological effects. In different and divergent ways these practices obscure the social and antagonistic nature of the capitalist mode of production. As Althusser paradoxically insists, "In other words the exteriority of the superstructure to the infrastructure . . . a thesis without which nothing is intelligible in the structure and functioning of a mode of production, and therefore a social formation, this exteriority is exercised, in very large part, under the form of interiority."[91]

In formal subsumption, labor power is reproduced through the interrelation, the connection and discontinuity, of the different social apparatuses. Interrelation includes, in the first case, the "structural isomorphism" of different institutions—the fact that it is the same strategy or abstract diagram of power that defines the concrete social institutions of factories, prisons, and schools. Second, these disparate institutions of reproduction converge insofar as they establish overlapping points of resonance, what Althusser calls the "society effect."[92] Just as the different components of reproduction, (living, skilled, and docile) intersect in the same practice (e.g., the school as an institution of health, learning, and obedience) the different institutions, or apparatuses, of reproduction intersect at a virtual point—the point of the subject of social subjection/subjectification. At the same time, however, the interrelation of the different apparatuses of reproduction also includes the space between them: points of dissonance and difference. As Eric Alliez and Michel Feher argue, these differences are themselves constitutive of subjectivity/subjection.

> On every level, subjection is related to the independence of a subject: as free worker, as responsible citizen, and finally as consumer who maximizes his utility within the limits imposed by his salary. But reciprocally, this sovereign subjectivity is only actualized by voluntary submission to capitalist conditions of production, consumption, and circulation. More specifically, it is in the very crossing of boundaries between sectors—going to the factory, to school, to the supermarket—that actualizes individuals' freedom while guaranteeing their subjection.[93]

These different institutions and practices of subjectivity intersect through the ideal subject, or rather through the ideal of the individual as self-determining subject. It is this general ideal of the subject that subtends and underscores the specific forms of social subjection or ideological interprellation.[94] Thus in capitalism, at least in the formal subsumption of capitalism, what has to be foreclosed by the ideological production of subjection is collectivity, sociality, altogether. This has to be foreclosed in two senses: First is the fact that the conditions of capitalism—wage labor and exploitation, are collective conditions. More important, however, is the power of collectivity: the power underlying living labor and cooperation.[95] Paradoxically, the production of subjectivity, of a specific individualized subject, is thus leveled against the productive power of collective subjectivity.

It would be wrong to assume that all of these conditions have a uniform effect on the production of subjectivity, that all of these causes pile on top of each other like bricks forming a seamless wall of subjection. Even though the different institutions and practices of the reproduction of subjectivity can be understood to reproduce subjection both in their concord and dissonance—in their overlap at the same virtual point and in the space between them—the heterogeneity of institutions also produces potential discord. The different institutions cannot but produce divergent and often contradictory messages and effects.[96] A somewhat simplistic example of this would be the conflict of the demands of consumption and production—the demand to consume as much as possible—necessary for the realization of surplus value and the demand to live frugally in order to be productive, which is necessary for the production of surplus value. Marx recognized this "schizophrenic" tendency of capitalism as early as 1844; and this contradiction has continued to have effects into the present.[97] The dissonance produces possibilities and conditions for subversion. On a more intimate level there is a potential tension in the fundamental activity intrinsic to subjection/subjectification: It demands that we must participate actively in our own subjection. This active component is constitutive of subjection as a relation distinct from simple domination: Subjection is founded on a relative freedom or at least the idea of freedom. Although subjection is thus perhaps more effective than direct relations of force and domination, which are always recognizable and always produce their own effects of resistance, subjection too produces, or at least makes possible, its own resistances. The production of individual subjects from and within the mass or multitude of laboring bodies may have the paradoxical effect of increasing the power of the multitude.[98] The subjection/subjectification of living labor does not resolve the basic antagonism of living labor but, rather, displaces it.

In the previous chapter I argued that the history of capitalism must be understood according to an antagonistic logic of displacement and condensation. The strongest example of this logic is, of course, the transition from absolute to relative surplus value, a transition that both is technological and social, paving the way for the emerging regime of real subsumption. Marx punctuates this transition with a single example, a single case, the struggle over the working day, indicating something of the role of antagonism in the capitalist mode of production. Antagonism is inscribed in the very heart of capital, in the commodification of labor, but it does not remain there nor does it remain fixed as some kind of essence—it is perpetually displaced, encompassing different technological, political, and social relations. Reproduction is also multivalent. It includes the reproduction of bodies, skills, and obedience, all of which come together in the reproduction of a subject that is living, able, and docile. Whereas in chapter 2 I presented the different components of this antagonistic logic according to an order of presentation that was roughly diachronic, starting with abstract labor and proceeding through cooperation and the socialization of labor, following Marx's presentation, in this chapter I have presented the multiple aspects of reproduction in a manner that is roughly synchronic, stressing the overlapping simultaneity of the reproduction of bodies, skills, and obedience. This difference in part reflects something about both the reproduction of the relations of production and Marx's texts. I have argued against some elements of Marx's texts, which refer to simple biological reproduction, that these three elements are all present at the very beginning of wage labor—through the "spontaneous" ideology of the labor contract. This point regarding the historicity of reproduction is made more complicated in that reproduction is inseparable from what Deleuze and Guattari call "archaisms with a current function." As I argued in chapter 1, the society effect includes the manner in which the preconditions or presuppositions of a given mode of production are both reproduced and presented in the mode of production. So-called primitive accumulation entails a particular ideological presentation of the founding conditions of capitalist accumulation: the flow of labor power and money. A similar point could be made regarding the Asiatic despot in the Asiatic mode of production. In each case an idea or image of the origins, the frugal proto-capitalist or the Asiatic despotic, continues to function in the present as alibi and justification. Reproduction continually exploits the temporal acceleration of the capitalist mode of production—the distance between the technological and social innovations and the demands of capitalist accumulation—to maintain the existing social order.

Although the term *archaisms with a current function* illustrates this temporal dislocation of capital—the combination of ancient modes of belief (at the level of relations of production) and cutting-edge transformations (at the level of forces of production)—it does so in a manner that is potentially misleading. To call such codes *archaisms* is to situate them against the backdrop of a dominant progressive direction of time.[99] It is to assume, as Marx did, that with capitalism "all that is solid melts into air"; that is, it identifies capital with a relentless modernization. What the word *archaism* threatens to efface is the complexity of temporality in capital. It obscures the fact that these residues from the past, from patriarchy to the belief in the moral difference constitutive of capital, are actually fully contemporary to the capitalist mode of production. At the same time the term situates certain beliefs, values, and ideologies against the technological and economic transformation, which is assumed to be dominant. Ultimately, as suggestive as the term is, it does not go far enough in understanding what Althusser calls the "differential" temporality of the capitalist mode of production; that is, the coexistence of different temporalities, for technological, political, and social transformations with no dominant or central time line that can be given in advance.[100]

Within the capitalist mode of production temporality is constituted in part by the tension between the reproduction of social relations and the transformations of the forces of production, which is not to suggest that reproduction can be identified with stasis or simple repetition. Reproduction itself changes with the transformation of the technical, social, and political demands of the capitalist mode of production. The socialization of labor—the development of the intellectual and cooperative dimension of labor—entails an increased demand for the reproduction of the skills and knowledge of living labor. At the same time, a tendency for increased proletarianization of living labor may demand an increase in the reproduction of obedience. Thus, in part, the vicissitudes of reproduction are determined by the antagonistic logic of capital. However, this does not encompass the entirety of the historical transformation of the strategies and institutions that reproduce the relations of production. Reproduction also changes historically as the division between what is merely reproductive for capital, maintaining the existing social and political relations, and what is productive for capital, producing surplus value, continually changes. Spheres of existence—from food and medicine to control and obedience—that primarily had a reproductive function for capital become industries unto themselves that are productive for surplus value. The school ceases to be the privileged site of the ideological reproduction of subjectivity (as in Althusser's essay) and becomes itself the site of both the production of surplus value and the production of subjectivity as fixed capital (As Marx writes in "The Results of the Immediate Process of Production"). Thus the historicity of reproduction is determined by two of the historical tendencies of the capitalist mode of production: the antagonistic struggle over living labor, on one side, and the tendency of capital to venture into new areas and exploit profit, on the other side.

The historical transformation of reproduction arrives at the point at which all the components of the reproduction of living labor, as living, competent, and docile, become directly, or potentially, productive for capital. In some sense the very division between production and reproduction becomes untenable, at least in the sense where the two terms would designate fundamentally different spheres of existence and different logics—as in the division between base and superstructure. However, at the same time as the division between reproduction and production becomes untenable, aspects of what Althusser called the "point of view of reproduction"—the overdetermination of reproduction (life, knowledge, and obedience), the interrelationship between different capitalist enterprises or social capital, production as the production of relations and subjects rather than things, and the centrality of subjectivity in reproduction—become crucial to understanding real subsumption. In real subsumption, as subjectivity becomes directly productive, it is no longer possible to juxtapose production—as a spatially and temporally localized act carried out by subjects—and reproduction—as a social process productive of subjectivity and social relations—for even heuristic reasons.[101] All of the aspects of reproduction are included in production. The divide between an abstract subjective potential—put to work in the factory—and a specific mode of subjection—produced by the various institutions and apparatuses of social existence—is fundamentally blurred as more and more dimensions of subjectivity become productive for capital. Production and reproduction are folded into what Deleuze calls "metaproduction": a production of relations rather than things: "What [capitalism] seeks to sell is services, and what it seeks to buy, activities."[102] As Maurizio Lazzarato writes:

> If production today is directly the production of social relations, then the "raw material" of immaterial labor is subjectivity and the "ideological" environment in which this subjectivity lives and reproduces. The production of subjectivity ceases to be only an instrument of social control (for the reproduction of mercantile relationships) and becomes directly productive, because the goal of our post-industrial society is to construct the consumer/communicator—and to construct it as active.[103]

Since immaterial labor is increasingly dependent on the capacity of living labor to communicate, whether in the workplace, through "service," or through media, it can no longer be relatively indifferent to the subjectivity of living labor. Thus, the new position of subjectivity as productive runs through and rewrites the three aspects of the reproduction of subjectivity, changing not only the institutions and apparatuses that produce them but also what is understood by life, knowledge, and obedience as well.

Foucault uses the term *biopower* to cover in part the power relations immanent in the reproduction of life. However, as much as Foucault proposes a fundamental relationship between biopower and capital this relation was primarily thought of as one of exteriority. The reproduction of life as an external presupposition of capitalist production based on the exploitation of living labor is produced and reproduced in spaces and apparatuses outside of the factory space. Thus, in part Foucault's theorization of the relationship between life and capital was determined by formal subsumption. In *Empire*, Michael Hardt and Antonio Negri expand and transform this concept of biopower, drawing from Foucault as well as Deleuze and Guattari. Hardt and Negri first identify in real subsumption a historical transformation in the relationship between life and capitalism: "Life is no longer produced in the cycles of reproduction that are subordinated to the working day; on the contrary, life is what infuses and dominates all production. . . . The excess of value is determined today in the affects, in the bodies crisscrossed by knowledge, in the intelligence of the mind, and in the sheer power to act."[104] Hardt and Negri's transformation of the term *biopolitical* also expands the contours of what is considered life. Life here does not merely designate those elements that could be putatively identified as biological (reproduction, health, sanitation, and so forth) as in Foucault's conception of biopower but also includes all elements of embodied existence such as the affects and desire. It is not just the necessities of "bare life" that have become productive for capital but styles, desires, communities, and ways of communicating, everything that constitutes a "form of life."[105] Hardt and Negri's term *biopolitical production* is formed at the intersection of two tendencies constitutive of contemporary capitalist society: the transformation of "life" and all of its quotidian needs and capabilities into a terrain for commodification and production and the increasing importance of style and language in the production of commodities. Capital does not subordinate production to the reproduction of a form of life, as in precapitalist modes of production, but must continually exploit and produce new forms of life. As life, the life of living labor ceases to be a precondition of capitalist exploitation that must be reproduced, and it becomes an element of capitalist production when it loses its fixed and limited nature, becoming inseparable from a generalized inventiveness. The limits of life are constantly being overcome and challenged by the invention of new forms of life.

A similar transformation can also be found at the level of the skills and knowledge in the production of subjectivity. Althusser recognized that in the educational state apparatus the reproduction of the required "know-how" is inseparable from not only the ideological conditions of obedience but also a highly selective apparatus of separating, dividing, and hierarchically organizing the mass that enters the doors of the school. It organizes them first according to the time and stage at which they are ejected—a mass is ejected into production immediately after high school, others after college, and so on.

> Each mass ejected *en route* is practically provided with the ideology which suits the role it has to fulfil in class society; the role of the exploited (with a "highly-developed," "professional," "ethical," "civic," "national" and political consciousness); the role of the agent of exploitation (ability to give the workers orders and speak to them: "human relations"), of the agents of repression (ability to give orders and enforce obedience "without discussion," or ability to manipulate the demagogy of a political leader's rhetoric), or of the professional ideologist.[106]

In formal subsumption hierarchy is produced immediately in the institutions that reproduce the know-how of living labor. The results of this process of differentiation—subjects with their corresponding skills and ideologies—enter into preconstituted slots in the social division of labor. As I have already argued the "mass intellectuality" of immaterial labor is not to be confused with the reproduction of the hierarchy of intellectual and manual labor, between conception and execution, which is not to suggest that there is no hierarchy of knowledges and corresponding hierarchy of structures of payment in real subsumption—the hierarchy of immaterial labor runs the gambit from highly paid manipulators of public opinion to hyperexploited care workers. The hierarchy, however, is not preconstituted by the apparatuses that reproduce subjectivity for capital. Immaterial labor does not simply designate a particular region within a division of labor, as in the term *mental labor*, but is diffused across social space and relations—it is the use value of living labor today. Immaterial labor is most visible in the highly trained and qualified workers at the top of the pyramid, but it is not limited to these workers. "In the young worker, however, the 'precarious' worker, and the unemployed youth, we are dealing with a pure virtuality, a capacity that is as yet undetermined but that already shares all the characteristics of postindustrial productive subjectivity."[107] The knowledges and affects necessary for immaterial labor are produced not only by the highly stratified institutions of the school and university system but also by practices of consumption and leisure time. The conditions of immaterial labor are distributed across social space. Consumption produces subjectivity: The new talents and potentials of the subject of immaterial labor are continually being produced by the instruments and tools of leisure. Thus, any hierarchy that exists is produced after the fact, by the enterprises of immaterial labor, which select and determine what affects, knowledges, and languages are most productive.

Just as the potential for immaterial labor is distributed across social space, so are the conditions for its control. As Althusser argued with respect to the ideological production of subjectivity in formal subsumption, or rather at the cusp of the transition from formal to real subsumption, the most effective means of control is one that is inseparable from the activity or agency of subjects. As immaterial labor entails the universal demand to be active, to communicate, and to relate to others, it is inseparable from an imperative to communicate. As Lazzarato writes:

> As it is no longer possible to confine subjectivity merely to tasks of execution, it becomes necessary for the subject's competence in the areas of management, communication, and creativity to be made compatible with the conditions of "production for production's sake." Thus the slogan "become subjects," far from eliminating the antagonism between hierarchy and cooperation, between autonomy and command, actually re-poses the antagonism at a higher level, because it both mobilizes and clashes with the very personality of the individual worker.[108]

The disciplinary regime of abstract labor, as much as it endeavored to produce a subject fully capable of regulating himself or herself, was still dependent on a gap that separated the one watching from the one being watched. This residual distance between the apparatuses productive of subjectivity and the subject (a distance also found in Althusser's interprellation) would seem to dissolve with immaterial labor, along with the distinction between the task, or job, and the subjectivity of the worker. Lazzarato's description comes close to Lukács's account of the intellectual worker, one who is by definition entirely sold and transformed into "human capital." However, Lazzarato insists that the collapse, or rather the interiorization, of the disciplinary structure does not simply do away with antagonism but, rather, repositions it at a higher level.

In continually stressing the active participation of living labor and of cooperative networks, capital begins a process that it cannot necessarily limit or control. It is for this reason that the control in real subsumption has two sides: on one side, an increasing interiorization of control, as the demands of production permeate every pore of subjectivity, and on the other side, an extension of control into every aspect of the production process.[109] Because a great deal of work within immaterial labor involves the temporary assembling of teams of workers, whether for a specific project or, in the case of temp work, within a firm, the entire project is often structured through control.[110] In the case of television shows, multimedia productions, and other instances of immaterial labor, the division of labor serves to separate the different workers into isolated teams and to filter and control the final process of production. The two tendencies of control in immaterial labor—interiorization and dissemination—intersect at the point of the temporary or marginal worker. In the words of Alliez and Feher: "Corporations' massive recourse to subcontracting plays a fundamental role in this to the extent that it turns the workers' desire for independence (inherent in the attentuation of the subjection/subjectification process) into a business spirit which meets capital's growing need for satellites."[111]

In formal subsumption the production of subjectivity is a necessary supplement to the capitalist mode of production. It is necessary to produce, and reproduce, a subject that was healthy, competent, and docile. This production had to meet the counteracting demands of capitalist accumulation: On the one hand, it needed to be a reservoir of power—labor power—but on the other hand, it could not identify with that power. In real subsumption the production of subjectivity ceases to be a supplement to capitalist production, both necessary and exterior; it migrates into the center of production itself.

THE COMMON

As subjectivity, and the different forms of life that produce subjectivity, becomes directly productive in real subsumption the status of the real abstraction changes. As I stated earlier, in real subsumption the general intellect itself becomes the dominant real abstraction. What this means can perhaps be clarified by juxtaposing the two different stages of capital.

The central problem of formal subsumption is the problem of form itself. The two real abstractions of formal subsumption—the wage and the commodity form, the two minimal conditions of capitalist production—impose on all manner of existence an acute conflict between the materiality of the abstract and singularity. This can be seen most vividly in the contradiction between abstract and living labor. Abstract labor is the simultaneous reduction of living labor to an empty and exchangeable unit of time and the intensification of living labor to the point when the hour of labor time is stretched to its maximum productivity. To accomplish this, multiple strategies are employed, including disciplinary power, the division of labor, and surveillance. All of these strategies are structured by the demand to subordinate the singularity of living labor—of a living body and its relations—to the abstract standard of labor time. The reverse of this is the struggle by living labor to subordinate the flexibility and equality of abstract labor to the singularity and sociality of living labor: a struggle to materialize the possibility of species-being—to make the abstract indifference of labor a positive condition for new freedoms and a new sociality. A similar struggle runs through the wage. Capital utilizes the abstraction of the wage—its existence as a unit of measure—to eclipse the difference between necessary and surplus labor. Against this tendency, living labor seeks to subordinate the abstraction of the wage and money form to the needs and demands of living labor. It attempts to make the wage a condition for the actualization of desire, rather than a legitimation of the system.

These real abstractions do not pass away with real subsumption; however, their capacity to measure and mediate the productivity of labor does. Abstract labor and the wage step to the side and take a subordinate role in the face of the massive productive power of sociality. What also passes away is their central place within social conflict. In real subsumption social conflict no longer passes between the singular and the abstract, rather, conflict is immediately over the singular and the common. As singular forms of life become directly productive of capital-producing styles, fashions, tastes, and conditions for more production it is also these singular conditions of existence that become grounds for resistance. As Hardt and Negri contend contemporary social struggles from Tianamen to Los Angeles are radically singular and thus incommunicable. These struggles do not make reference, or seek to appropriate, the real abstractions of formal subsumption—they are not demands for wages nor are they necessarily framed by the image of "human rights" (the correlate of abstract labor power).[112] They are struggles in the name of the singularity of a particular form of life.

The flip side of this struggle of singularity is the struggle over the common itself. At the heart of the general intellect, of all the myriad forms of immaterial labor, is sociality itself—the very possibility to communicate, whether in terms of affects, images, styles, or language. As Giorgio Agamben writes in a provocative commentary on Guy Debord's *The Society of the Spectacle*:

> Today, in the era of the complete triumph of the spectacle, what can be reaped from the heritage of Debord? It is clear that the spectacle is language, the very communicativity or linguistic being of humans. This means that a fuller Marxian analysis should deal with the fact that capitalism (or any other name one wants to give the process that today dominates world history) was directed not only toward the expropriation of productive activity, but also and principally toward the alienation of language itself of the very linguistic and communicative nature of humans, of the logos which one of Heraclitus's fragments identified as the common.[113]

Thus, as Negri argues, communication in real subsumption plays the role of the wage in formal subsumption—it is the simultaneous site of mystification and struggle: "In advanced capitalism, therefore conflict, struggle and diversity are focused on communication, with capital, by means of communication, trying to preconstitute the determinants of life."[114] Capital no longer tries to subordinate the singularity and commonality of social relations to the abstraction of labor time and the wage, but instead tries to directly appropriate the singularity and commonality of existence.[115]

There is no resolution, at least no theoretical resolution, to the problem of antagonism in real subsumption. It is not possible to decide in advance how things will turn out. One can, however, draw out the tensions of the initial contradiction: Real subsumption is both the development of the massive cooperative powers of living labor and the production of subjectivity that is entirely subjected to capital. It is possible to move beyond a particular bad infinity in which this contradiction is repeated again and again in different theoretical languages and registers. The contradiction can be rendered productive; that is, it is possible to simultaneously examine it from different angles and at the same time to chart its progress as it gives birth to new concepts (the general intellect, immaterial labor, and biopower) and transforms and undoes some of the central concepts of Marx's corpus (such as fixed capital, consumption and reproduction). Although it is not possible to produce an antagonistic logic of real subsumption, in part because we do not have as of yet the history of struggles, it is possible to at least map the fundamental difference of antagonism in formal and real subsumption.

CONCLUSION

[T]he truth of a philosophy lies entirely in its effects, while in fact it acts only at a distance from real objects, therefore, in the space of freedom that it opens up to research and action and not in its form of exposition alone. This form could be systematic or not, but in any event it was in itself "dogmatic: to the extent that every philosophy posits, not without reason, but without any possible empirical verification, apparently arbitrary theses, which in reality are not arbitrary, since they are a function of the space of freedom (or servitude) that the philosophy intends by its effects to open up at the heart of the space of theses already posed by existing philosophies within a given theoretical conjuncture."

—Louis Althusser, *"The Only Materialist Tradition, Part 1: Spinoza*

As I have argued the capitalist mode of production is constituted through the violence of primitive accumulation. However, the lessons of primitive accumulation are not limited to a simple reversal of values, replacing the idyllic narrative of the foundation of capital with its bloody origins, rather Karl Marx's treatment of primitive accumulation opens the door to another reading of not only *Capital* but the entire trajectory of Marx's thought. Primitive accumulation is not simply the accumulation of wealth, or a transfer of the means of production from the hands of the artisans and peasantry to the hands of the nascent capitalists, it is also the accumulation of subjectivity, the accumulation of a social power. For capitalism to exist, it is not sufficient to simply do away with the customs and structures of the feudal world nor is it enough to set up the economic conditions for the formation of capital: wage labor and commodity production. It is necessary to produce a subject that can find its place within apparatuses and networks of capital. "The advance of capitalist production develops a working class which by education [*Erziehung*], tradition, and habit [*Gewohnheit*] looks upon the requirements of that mode of production as self evident natural laws" (CI 899/765).

At the foundation of the capitalist mode of production is the production of subjectivity in both senses of the genitive: the constitution of subjectivity, of a particular subjective comportment, and in turn the productive power of subjectivity, its capacity to produce wealth. These two senses of the production of subjectivity do not or have not coincided in the history of capitalism. The production of subjectivity by capital is always simultaneously exceeding and falling short of the demands of capitalist production. There is always a surplus of power, of communication, that extends beyond the space of production. At the same time, the docility, obedience, and normalization necessary for capitalist production often fails to take hold. If these two senses of the production of subjectivity did coincide, there would be no history of capital. The capitalist mode of production would come into existence like Marx's image of the Asiatic despot, completely formed and would remain untouched by the winds of history. There would be no passage from formal to real subsumption, no transformation of the technological, social, and political conditions of the capitalist mode of production. The need to transform, to continually evolve, this is the capitalist mode of production's particular necessity—particular modality of a becoming necessary—imposed by the singularity of the encounter constitutive of capital. The capitalist mode of production may strive toward "the end of history," an ideal state in which subjectivity is produced only to occupy its slot within the networks of production and consumption; but this ideal state is a material impossibility.

There are many ways to interpret this impossibility. One way is to refer to an element of human nature or existence that absolutely resists commodification—this is perhaps what is at stake in certain theories of alienation, or certain theories that place alienation at the basis of Marx's philosophy. Given that I have argued, at least implicitly, against this tendency, insisting on an immanent and productive ontology, one within which the human essence is produced anew within the ensembles and apparatuses of social existence, the question remains, How is it possible to interpret this impossibility without recourse to some vague notion of human nature? The answer to this question lies in the particular concepts/figures explored in the preceding chapters: primitive accumulation and precapitalist economic formations in chapter 1; the relation between abstract and living labor in chapter 2; and immaterial labor in chapter 3. Each of these concepts/figures, or even narratives, engages with that which is necessary to the production and accumulation of capital but is nonetheless irreducible to its measure or functioning—an excess, or "supplement," to risk Jacques Derrida's term. This irreducible remainder has a necessarily collective dimension.

The answer to the question of the impossibility of the production of subjectivity ever being reducible or adequate to the production of capital would have to lie in the collectivity that cuts across both senses of the production of subjectivity. Collectivity is not quite the right word, however, because it would seem to suggest a unified collective standing above the isolated individuals. What is in question here is not the constitution of collective identity—a unified collective subject—but rather the "more than one" of the relation. (It is for similar reasons that Étienne Balibar coined the term *transindividual* as that which resists both an atomistic individualism and the tendency to present any whole or totality as an organic totality. As Balibar argues with respect to Marx it is a matter of recognizing the primacy of struggle, the relation, over class, in any invocation of class struggle.[1]) As much as the production of subjectivity and capitalist production may act on and even produce subjects as individuals through a particular mode of subjection, and we have seen that the various dimensions of the "spontaneous ideology" of capital from the labor contract to the wage produce a subject as individuated and even isolated, these productions necessarily entail and encompass more than one individual. It is this "more than one" that makes them uncontainable. The clearest example of this irreducible antagonistic and aleatory dimension of the collective, what could be called the "materiality of social relations" is Marx's discussion of cooperation in *Capital.* As I have argued, the chapter on cooperation is not an isolated example or demonstration, rather, it is the opening to an integral element of the logic of antagonism that animates Marx's text. From this perspective it is possible to see how the capitalist mode of production continually produces and relies on subjective potentials that it necessarily cannot control.

From this perspective, from the answer to this question, it is possible to arrive at a fundamentally different definition of what Marx called "communism." In *The German Ideology* Marx wrote, "Communism is the real movement which abolishes the present state of things."[2] It might be possible to suggest that this movement is nothing other than the restaged and enlarging conflict between the collective productivity/production of subjectivity and the continual attempt on the part of capital to reduce this production to the valorization of existing capital. In this case communism would not be some embarrassing utopian element to remove from Marx's thought to retrieve some supposedly pure critique of capitalist society, it would be an integral element of the critique. Although at the same time conceived in this light, communism is also not some blueprint of the society to come, it is not a political program, it is nothing other than the insistence of living labor at the heart of capital. It is also the expansion of the collective dimension of capitalist production. This expansion continues in two directions: Extensively, it follows the movement of capital across the globe, and intensively, it follows real subsumption into all dimensions of social existence. Perhaps it would be more accurate to say that it both precedes and follows the movement, because as I have argued with the discussion of formal and real subsumption, it is the resistance of living labor that in part determines and drives the development of capital. Thus, this collective dimension is not some static principle of opposition, some motor of history or prime mover, that acts on the history of capital from outside. Rather, it is continually produced anew and differently by the development and transformation of capital. The terms of struggle of formal subsumption, which cut through the wage and abstract labor, are not the terms of struggle of real subsumption.

The formula regarding the unstable relation between the two senses of the production of subjectivity is not intended as an explanatory formula. It does not explain or predict the movement of history, it is, rather, in infinite need of being explained, fleshed out, and historicized: It determines a problematic. First, it is necessary to differentiate between the production of subjectivity in capital and the production of subjectivity that precedes capital. On one reading Marx would seem to argue that subjectivity is produced only in and through capital, and thus what exists prior to capital is in some sense pre-subjective as a sort of collective or communal consciousness, the community as inorganic body of production, or in its harsher and more Eurocentric formulations an undifferentiated herd mentality.

Marx often ascribes an epochal distinction to subjectivity: "The Roman slave was held by chains; the wage laborer is bound to his owner by invisible threads. The appearance of independence is maintained by a constant change in the person of the individual employer, and by the legal fiction of a contract" (CI 719/599). With capital the physical constraints of enslavement, chains and irons, give away to the techniques of subjection, the contract and the flexibility of the labor relation. Subjection is internalized, lived as a dimension of subjectivity. Thus, subjectivity would take its place alongside other attempts to conceptualize the divide between the West and its others, after such concepts as reason and history. With this necessary caveat regarding Eurocentrism in place, it is possible to at least affirm some version of this statement with certain qualifications. First, we are not discussing subjectivity as such but, rather, certain dimensions of subjectivity, most notably an abstract indifference or potentiality coupled with a reservoir of interiority. As I have shown, Marx argues that the specific power relation in capital produces these dimensions of subjectivity. Abstract indifference to not only the content of activity but also to its particular meaning, its immersion in a particular form of life, with its corresponding code, is produced by capitalism's demand for abstract labor. Labor must be flexible, "free" from a determinate mode of life. The various precapitalist modes of production were characterized not only by the subordination of production to the reproduction of a particular mode of life but also by a palpable division between necessary and surplus labor accompanied by an extra-economic instance of inscription. The feudal lord, despot, or slave driver functioned to enforce the exploitation of labor. In capital this externalized compulsion is replaced by the illusions, or objective appearances, of the wage and the labor contract that produce the interiorized ideal of independence and flexibility, an ideal that is not entirely incorrect. My somewhat unsubstantiated point here is, in part, that if these elements—interiority, abstract universality, and transcendence from any determinate existence or mode of activity—seem to be necessary aspects of any definition of subjectivity, then perhaps the entire philosophical and theoretical tradition through which we think subjectivity is itself internal to the history of capital. This is perhaps another stronger version of Marx's point regarding abstract labor and the idea of an abstract humanity: These two concepts arrive at the same time because they are produced in the same factory. Marx's writing makes it possible to locate in the Western philosophical tradition the distant effects of the struggle between subjection and subjectification in the history of capitalism, and not, as that tradition claims, the discovery of a timeless human essence.

Despite Marx's tendency to think of the relationship between capitalism and what came before along the lines of a sharp division—often framed by the opposition between reproduction and production—this divide is complicated by a series of similarities. The most striking of these similarities would include the points of contact between the capitalist mode of production and its absolute other: the Asiatic mode of production. In both the Asiatic mode of production and the capitalist mode of production, there is a fundamental mis-recognition of the productive capabilities of labor: In the Asiatic mode of production it appears that the despot himself is the precondition of production, rather than an effect, while in capital it appears that money, capital itself, begets money. Marx is not merely positing a rhetorical or polemical identity between capitalism and ancient despotism, locating ancient tyrannies at the heart of modernity; rather, he is arguing that in both cases there is a social and a subjective surplus of labor. It is this surplus that is mystified, appearing to be part of the despot or capital. Whereas in ancient societies this surplus is produced by slavery, in modern society it is produced by the development of the cooperative powers of labor. In each case there is a dimension of labor that exceeds any economic calculation. This excessive dimension is cooperation, collectivity itself, the simple fact that a group of individuals working together will always be capable of more than the sum of their parts. Across the historical divide that separates capitalism and precapitalism, there is the persistence of what I have called, following Louis Althusser, "the society effect." This persistence can be explained synchronically, emphasizing certain structural similarities between the two modes of production, or diachronically, emphasizing the uneven development of capitalism and the persistence of "mystifications" or fetishes that would seem to be relegated to precapitalist modes of production in capitalism.

A second less striking similarity can be found in one of Marx's failures. As I have shown, Marx tends to privilege the production of objects, things, relegating "production which disappears in the act of producing" to a marginal place in the capitalist economy. This is due in part to his belief that relations of service, with their corresponding economies of prestige, are fundamentally feudal or precapitalist and have no place in the abstract impersonal tendencies of capital. However, it is precisely this dimension of production—the production of relations—that comes to the center in contemporary capitalism—in the real subsumption of subjectivity by capital—albeit in a fundamentally different way. Whereas formal subsumption was perhaps content to relegate the production of particular conditions of subjectivity to the ideological state apparatuses, real subsumption puts these particular modes of production—their perceptions, styles, and beliefs—to work. The particular codes and comportments of these modes of subjection, especially as they manifest themselves in the relational dimension of services, have led some to find in contemporary capitalism a return to feudal relations. Thus, if in part Marx's critical strategy was to continually indicate the persistence of the mystifications of the past in the rational present, then it is possible to argue that he did not go far enough in this direction. However, the relational aspect of the production of subjectivity is no longer utilized to conceal the relations of exploitation, as in feudalism, or to reproduce the necessary docility of the laboring subject, as in formal subsumption, but has become directly productive. Thus as much as one can isolate, and render exceptional, capitalism and its corresponding production of subjectivity, it would seem to be inseparable from its own specific differential temporality, its reproduction and repetition of particular dimensions of the past in the present.

As much as it is important to historicize while at the same time qualify the initial emergence of the relationship between capitalism and the mode of production, with respect to antediluvian mists of precapitalist modes of production, it is more important to historicize and qualify this relation in the present. If the production of subjectivity was not an immediately pressing problem for Marx (it is not the subject of a proposed volume of *Capital*), this is not simply due to a theoretical error or oversight, rather, it is because the production of subjectivity is in many respects a contemporary problem, hence the necessity of drawing out this problem through the engagement with contemporary philosophy. The reading, or excavation, of Marx that I have produced here is unapologetically rooted in the present, in the same manner that readings of Marx at the turn of the twentieth century focused on the reproduction schemas of capital to comprehend the dynamics of imperialism, or that readings of Marx in the middle of the twentieth century focused on the newly discovered texts on alienation to oppose both capital and state socialism. My point being in part that in each of these cases a new "Marx" is produced to respond to the exigencies of the present. Thus despite the not entirely unwarranted consensus that would brand Marxism, and thus any interpretation of Marx, with the image of a stale repetition of certain unquestioned and increasingly vacuous dogmas, there has been a subterranean current of theoretical production and even inventiveness within this eternal reproduction of the same.

It is possible to grant this new theoretical production with the sort of retrospective comprehension of the past that Marx summed up with his famous formula: "Human anatomy contains a key to the anatomy of the ape" (G 105/309). Thus one could translate the conflicts and constraints of previous modes of production into conflicts over the production of subjectivity. There are multiple points in Marx from which to begin such a reading: from the discussion of war as the breakdown of the symbolic economy of prestige in the ancient mode of production in "Pre-Capitalist Economic Formations" to the discussion of the factory and cooperation as the production of a new subjectivity that is both unruly and productive in *Capital.* However, it has not been my goal here to stress the continuities, to place the conflict over the production of subjectivity within the same rhetorical space that class struggle occupies in *The Communist Manifesto* as that eternal ("now hidden, now open") conflict. I have attempted to underscore the difference and the novelty of the problem of the production of subjectivity, without at the same time falling into the narcissism of the present that sees itself as totally unique and singular. Thus, although accepting in a general way that the production of subjectivity is a fundamental element of even precapitalist modes of production, I have tried to show how the production of subjectivity has moved to the center of the contemporary capitalist mode of production, or real subsumption. Moreover, I have argued that this transformation did not simply fall from the sky nor has it been imposed by the demands of capital but has itself been produced in and through a history of antagonism. Capital no longer relies on cooperative networks of the reproduction of subjectivity that are exterior to it; instead, it directly produces and profits from the production of subjectivity, and this transformation has been imposed on it in part by the productive powers of subjectivity. If the capitalist mode of production is all pervasive, running through all dimensions of life, then it is precisely because its hold over the subjective power of living labor has been, and continues to be, precarious.

Capital's direct involvement in the production of subjectivity fundamentally transforms the categories and terms used to understand the capitalist mode of production. Most notably it scrambles the division between production, as the production of things, and reproduction, as the reproduction of the relations of production. The reproduction of the worker as healthy, skilled, and docile is no longer left outside the circuits of capitalist production—in the home or the state—but has become directly productive for capital, paving the way for a whole series of new businesses and interests. It is for this reason—the breakdown of the divisions and hierarchies used to grasp the capitalist mode of production—that the problem of the production of subjectivity in real subsumption requires an examination and a transformation of the ontology of production underlying Marx's thought. This ontology is continually split between an anthropological schema that privileges the relationship between a subject, instrument, and object of production, on the one hand, and an expanded sense of production that posits subjectivity and social relations as both produced and productive on the other hand. This first ontology, in that it presents subjectivity as unchanged and natural, underlies both economism and humanism. More important, it is responsible in part for the dominance that the image of the factory maintains over Marxist thought. It is no longer possible to think of production as simply the production of commodities, nor is it possible to maintain the division between production, as an intrinsically instrumental and mute activity, and action, as an engagement with plurality and difference. As Antonio Negri writes, underscoring this ontological transformation:

> No longer are capitalist relations of production exercised solely on a subject characterized through misery and a "predeconstructive" reference to a generic human essence. On the contrary, the exploited subject appearing on this new scene, who must deal with ghosts, is presented rather as a flux, a mobile and flexible reality, a hybrid potential that traverses the spectral movement of production and, in so doing continually reconstitutes itself anew. Today, exploitation, or, rather, capitalist relations of production, concern a laboring subject amassed in intellectually and cooperative force. A new paradigm; most definitely exploited, yet new—a different power, a new consistency of laboring energy, an accumulation of cooperative energy. This is a new—post-deconstructive—ontology.[3]

The contemporary factory is the "social factory," production is disseminated across social space as the production of affects, relations, and desires, and with this mutation it becomes necessary to rethink our received critical vocabulary, ontology, and political imaginary.

In this book I have focused on the first two of these transformations. With respect to the critical vocabulary, I have returned and expanded Althusser's project of symptomatic reading, not to return to the purity of Marx's original intention but to show that Marx's writing continually conflicts with its own internal limits, namely, "economism" and "humanism." Of course these terms are a bit dated, and it is important to know why one should be opposed to them. In each case all of history, all societies, are reduced to a simple cause, the economy or human nature, and its differing effects, that is, in each case what is missed is a rigorous thought of the materiality of social relations. Thus, the strategy of critical reading continually returns to, and expands upon, a critical interrogation of the ontology underlying Marx's thought. The idea of production, of labor, as an unchanging constant, such as Marx's schema of "the labor process" fits within both economism, which only grants history to exchange or the market, and humanism, which can make mankind's self-production an essential attribute. Thus going beyond these two theoretical, or ideological limitations, means going beyond what Negri calls the "predeconstructed" ontology of labor, recognizing the extent to which labor exceeds any such schema to be the production of sociality, of communication and desire, by social relations. The final dimension, the transformation of the "political imaginary" has for the most part been neglected.

In this way I have perhaps mirrored Marx's own error. He became so engaged with his "critique of political economy" and its massive destruction of the existing language (anthropology and ontology) of political economy and political philosophy that he often neglected to propose much with respect to the difficult questions of political organization and struggle. The latter remained pretty much a blank page, left to be filled by the inevitable tendencies of history or by the latter Marxists who produced official "Marxism" and the structure of the party in his name. We know now not to wait for the former, and what a disaster the latter can become. However, it was my intent to focus on the critical vocabulary and ontology, to revitalize the terms of Marx's critique and highlight their contact with the present. At the same time, just as the reworking of the critical vocabulary—the reinterpretation of mode of production, labor, and reproduction—continually worked to transform the ontology underlying these concepts, work in these areas has at least already begun to spell out a political direction, or at least begun to show what a politics would not be from the perspective developed here. First, and foremost, it is clear that such a project would work against the prevailing "realism," or cynicism, which proclaims, triumphantly or nostalgically, that the large-scale political transformations and utopias are a thing of the past. The only political possibilities that exist now, it is said, lie in the minute adjustments and reforms of various laws and statutes against the backdrop of impersonal and unstoppable economic laws. Such a point of view cannot see anything other than the "society effect," or socius of capital, that is, it only sees in the present the auto-production of capital, and not the antagonistic force sustaining and subverting this production. The perspective of the production of subjectivity, of the productive power of living labor, inverts this perspective, demonstrating that the future is not predestined by unavoidable laws but is open to the contingency and antagonistic force of the multitude of desires, labors, and needs constituting the present. Moreover, at the same time that the perspective developed here works against the prevailing pessimism of the present, it also undermines any revolutionary nostalgia. If Marx's attentiveness to history means anything, it means that the possibilities for resistance and revolution are constituted by and constitutive of the current development of the capitalist mode of production. There is no return to the factory or to the revolutionary models produced from within its belly. It is necessary to pose the question as to what kind of mode of organization, what kind of subversion, is adequate to the contemporary structures of not only capital, but to the "working class" of immaterial labor.[4] It is not so much that the old models are bankrupt but that there are new possibilities, new political structures and subjectivities underlying the present, waiting to produce the future.

These two directions—against the complacency of the present and against any nostalgia for the past—are admittedly broad outlines, which is to say that they are open. There are multiple directions, for not only politics but for other areas of research, sketched out here. Thus, I have attempted to reread Marx, to return to the prehistory of our present, not to rescue the past (in this case the Marxist tradition) unscathed, as if nothing had changed, but to undermine the limitations, complacency, and pessimism of the present, to produce a present that is different from itself, which is the precondition for a radically different future.

Notes

INTRODUCTION

1. For an illustration of this point of view, see Judith Butler, Ernesto Laclau, and Slavoj Žižek, *Contingency, Hegemony, Universality: Contemporary Dialogues on the Left*.

2. The question of the status of Marx's philosophy occupies a central place in the recent debate over Jacques Derrida's *Specters of Marx: The State of Debt, the Work of Mourning, and the New International*.

3. Étienne Balibar, *The Philosophy of Marx*, 19.

4. Karl Marx, *A Contribution to the Critique of Political Economy*, 20; also published as *Zur Kritik der Politischen Ökonomie*, 13.

5. Louis Althusser, *Sur la reproduction*, 45. In chapter 2, I return to this relation between the expanded and limited sense of the mode of production in a comparison of Marx and Foucault.

6. Michel Foucault, "Questions of Method," 74.

7. Maurizio Lazzarato, "Le 'cycle' de la production immatériel," 115.

8. Antonio Negri, "Notes on the Evolution of the Thought of the Later Althusser," 58.

9. Louis Althusser, "The Object of *Capital*," 189; originally published as "L'objet du 'Capital,'" 405. Hereafter cited as "Object" with English and French pagination.

10. Étienne Balibar, "The Infinite Contradiction," 160.

11. As Althusser writes: "Of course, the material existence of the ideology in an apparatus and its practice does not have the same modality as the material existence of a paving-stone or a rifle. But, at the risk of being taken for a Neo-Aristotelian, I shall say that 'matter is discussed in many senses' [*la matière se dit en plusieurs sens*], or rather that it exists in different modalities, all rooted in the last instance in 'physical' matter." See Althusser, "Ideology and Ideological State Apparatuses: Notes Towards an Investigation," 166; idem., *Sur la reproduction*, 299.

12. Balibar offers the following provocative definition of structuralism. "Structuralism, then—provided, however, that we understand it not as a combinative or hierarchical schema for constituting sets or totalities, but, on the contrary, as a problematic of differential identities; an analysis of the double inscription of causes and their excess of productivity within the representation of functionalities; finally, as an infinite topic of the noncontemporaneity of events to themselves." (See Balibar, "The Infinite Contradiction," 161).

13. Antonio Negri, "The Specter's Smile," 5.

14. Gilles Deleuze offers a direct trajectory between Althusser, Foucault, and his own work in his book on Foucault, a trajectory that fills in the absent name of Baruch Spinoza. Deleuze places Foucault's statements regarding power within a general history of the problem of immanent causality, a history that includes Althusser's Spinozistic interpretation of Marx. Deleuze's understanding of immanence in many ways complements Althusser's understanding of immanent causality in that in each case it is a matter of recognizing the differences internal to immanent causality, and not the identity.

> What do we mean here by immanent cause? It is a cause which is realized, integrated and distinguished in its effect. Or rather the immanent cause is realized, integrated and distinguished by its effect. In this way there is a correlation or mutual presupposition between cause and effect, between abstract machine and concrete assemblages (it is for the later that Foucault most often reserves the term "mechanisms" [*dispositif*]). If the effects realize something this is because the relations between forces, or power relations, are merely virtual, potential, unstable, vanishing and molecular, and define only possibilities of interaction, so long as they do not enter into a macroscopic whole capable of giving form to their fluid matter and their diffuse function. But realization is equally an integration, a collection of progressive integrations that are initially local and then become or tend to become global, aligning, homogenizing and summarizing relations between forces (*Foucault*, 37/44–45; English/French pagination).

15. Fredric Jameson, *Postmodernism: Or, the Cultural Logic of Late Capitalism*, ix.

16. Even Foucault's criticism of Marx can be understood as an expansion of the concept of 'production.' This will seem paradoxical or even nonsensical to those who are familiar with the argument Foucault levels against an often unnamed, yet nonetheless central, Freudo–Marxist adversary in *The History of Sexuality*. In that book Foucault criticizes the very assumption that the history of sexuality in modernity is governed by the demands of production—that sex has been repressed to make the body of the working class productive. In this respect Foucault is a critic of the assumption that all cultural and political phenomena can be rendered intelligible from the perspective of economic production. Foucault's criticism, however, can more accurately be described as a criticism of the idea that power can only subtract, limit, or alienate that which is already given (labor power or desire). Power does not repress or negate but produces subjectivity, the world, and being. This production is freed not only from a strictly economic designation but also from instrumentality or teleology. Production, or the productivity of power, is open to the aleatory and antagonistic interplay of strategies, producing effects that cannot be reduced to intention. In his philosophical histories Foucault continually provides subjective figures of these unintended effects, such as the delinquent and the pervert, which are produced by certain power relations only in turn to struggle and produce new relations. For Foucault, production is not the attribute of a subject but a conflictual process that produces and is produced by subjectivity. This ontology and historicity of production is mobilized against anything that would be assumed as natural—neither labor nor desire can be assumed to be the "concrete essence of man." Foucault displaces the Marxist insistence on economic production, with its attendant anthropology of the production of man by man, by extending the concept of production to include the conflictual and aleatory productivity of power.

17. Deleuze and Guattari's two-volume *Capitalism and Schizophrenia* remains a significant exception to thinking in terms of any such division between Marxism and poststructuralism. Deleuze and Guattari maintain a complex relation with a version of Marx's

concepts of the mode of production and labor (or living labor) as well as the Marxist problematic in general. As Deleuze states in a conversation with Negri, "I think Felix Guattari and I have remained Marxists in our two different ways perhaps, but both of us. You see, we think any political philosophy must turn on the analysis of capitalism and the ways it has developed." (see *Negotiations:. 1972–1990*, 171)

18. Michael Hardt and Antonio Negri, *Empire*, 260–280.

19. Antonio Negri, *Marx Beyond Marx: Lessons on the* Grundrisse, 56.

CHAPTER ONE

1. "Object," 158/363.

2. Karl Marx, *Capital: A Critique of Political Economy, Volume 1*, 873; also published as *Karl Marx Friedrich Engels Werke Band 23*, 741. Hereafter cited in the text as CI with English and German pagination.

3. Étienne Balibar, "The Basic Concepts of Historical Materialism," 283; originally published as "Concepts fondamentaux du matérialisme historique," 535. Hereafter cited as "Basic Concepts" with English and French pagination.

4. The sentence I am referring to here is the famous sentence from *The Eighteenth Brumaire*: "Hegel remarks somewhere that all facts and personages of great importance in world history occur, as it were, twice. He forgot to add: the first time as tragedy, the second as farce" (Karl Marx, *The Eighteenth Brumaire of Louis Bonaparte*, 15).

5. As Marx writes drawing the parallel between the miser and the capitalist: "This boundless drive for enrichment, this passionate chase after value, is common to the capitalist and the miser; but while the miser is merely a capitalist gone mad, the capitalist is a rational miser. The ceaseless augmentation of value, which the miser seeks to attain by saving his money from circulation, is achieved by the more acute capitalist by means of throwing his money again into circulation" (CI 255/161). Gilles Deleuze and Félix Guattari explicitly pose the question of the formation of the capitalist mode of production in terms of the actualization of desire in *Anti-Oedipus: Capitalism and Schizophrenia*.

6. "Basic Concepts," 215/440.

7. Louis Althusser, *For Marx*, 111.

8. Karl Marx, "Theses on Feuerbach," 122.

9. Étienne Balibar, *The Philosophy of Marx*, 30.

10. As early as the *1844 Manuscripts* Marx recognized in political economy a self-contradictory moral discourse on the values of thrift and spending, which he perceived to be something of a reflection of the contradictory tendencies of reducing "necessary labor" while selling more commodities. See his *The Economic and Philosophical Manuscripts of 1844*, 150.

11. It should be clear given these particulars that Marx, following the political economists he is critiquing, is primarily concerned with Western Europe, particularly England, and to a lesser extent North America.

12. "Basic Concepts," 281/531.

13. Louis Althusser calls this process by which the effects of a particular process are seized and turned to other purpose and other ends *"détournement"*: "This 'detouring' is the mark of the non-teleology of the process and the inscription of its result in a process which has rendered it possible and which was totally alien to it." See his "Le courant souterrain du matérialisme de la rencontre," 572 (translation mine: hereafter cited as "Rencontre").

14. Karl Marx, *Grundrisse: Foundations of the Critique of Political Economy*, 736; also published as *Karl Marx Friedrich Engels Werke Band 42*, 631. Hereafter cited in the text as G with English and German pagination.

15. Despite a discrepancy in terms of the precise dates and mechanism of the process (the fifteenth century and laws against vagabondage in the case of Marx, as opposed to the late eighteenth century and the formation of the penal system in the case of Michel Foucault) it is possible to place Marx's analysis of "bloody legislation" and Foucault's analysis of the punitive society within the same political problem: of converting a mobile mass into a determinate class of producers.

16. Althusser has argued, in a point that I will return to, that it cannot be the same capitalist, or same bourgeois, that destroys the feudal mode of production and is constituted by the capitalist mode of production. He argues that Marx's terminology—his use of the terms *capital* and *capitalist* to apply to both merchant and usury capital in precapitalist modes of production as well as capitalism proper—makes it possible to conceive of the capitalist class as a kind of subject of history ("Rencontre," 574).

17. Massimo De Angelis, "Marx and Primitive Accumulation: The Continuous Character of Capital's 'enclosures,'" 5.

18. Roman Rosdolsky, *The Making of Marx's "Capital,"* 279.

19. Michael Hardt and Antonio Negri, *Empire*, 238.

20. Gilles Deleuze and Félix Guattari, *A Thousand Plateaus*, 447; originally published as *Mille Plateau*, 558.

21. Michel Foucault, *Discipline and Punish: The Birth of Prison*, 85.

22. Antonio Negri, *Insurgencies: Constituent Power and the Modern State*, 254.

23. The concept of lawmaking violence, the violence that instantiates a new legal order, as well as the distinction between lawmaking and law-preserving violence, the violence that maintains an existing order, is drawn from Walter Benjamin's essay "The Critique of Violence," 280.

24. "The immediate violence of the exploitation and the juridical superstructure becomes a mediated violence and a structure internal to the productive process. The law—or really, the form of violence—becomes a machine, or really, a permanent procedure [of] its constant innovation and its rigid discipline" (Negri, *Insurgencies*, 257). Negri goes on to argue that this transformation entails the passage form "the world of sovereign violence" to the "world of discipline" following Foucault's argument regarding the different periods of sovereign power and disciplinary power. This claim, and the relation between disciplinary power and the capitalist mode of production will be explored in the next chapter.

25. Michael Perelman, *The Invention of Capitalism: Classical Political Economy and the Secret History of Primitive Accumulation*, 196.

26. In a similar manner to Althusser, Theodore Adorno has argued that capital cannot be represented or thought according to one or more of its constitutive elements such as "the profit-motive" but must be represented through a complex "constellation" of elements (*Negative Dialectics*, 166). Despite the rather obvious differences between the two philosophers, Fredric Jameson has suggested a fundamental similarity between Althusser and Adorno around the question of the logic of presentation of capital (*Late Marxism: Adorno, or, the Persistence of the Dialectic*, 244). As a literary and cultural theorist Jameson has repeatedly underscored the problem of the representability of the capitalist mode of production across such diverse practices and media as film, theater, philosophy, and literature. As Jameson argues, one of the difficulties of representing the capitalist mode of production is that it is both more than or less than its constitutive elements; that is, it is not money but the intersection of the point where money becomes more than itself, as capital, and less than itself, as the poverty of workers (*Brecht and Method*, 148). In Althusser this combination of the "more and less" is expressed through the combination of "metonymical" and "immanent" causality.

27. Antonio Negri, *Marx Beyond Marx*, 47.

28. In the first edition of *Lire le Capital* Althusser expanded on the extent to which this idea of *Darstellung* necessarily intersected with the problems of representation, and aesthetic representation through a comparison/etymology of the terms *Darstellung* and *Vorstellung*. As Althusser writes, "In *Vorstellung,* one certainly has to do with a position, but one which is presented *out front,* which thus supposes something which is kept *behind* this pre-position, something which is *represented* by that which is kept out in front [represented] by its emissary: the *Vorstellung. In Darstellung on the contrary, there is nothing behind:* the very thing is there, 'da' presented in the position of presence." (*Lire le Capital*, 646). For this point regarding the significance of the concept of structure/Darstellung and its history in Althusser's thought, I am indebted to Michael Sprinker whose translation of the passage from Althusser I have relied on here (*Imaginary Relations: Aesthetics and Ideology in the Theory of Historical Materialism*, 291).

29. In his contribution Althusser seems to refer to this relation as that between the regional mode of production and the global mode of production ("Object," 183/397), in a sense giving the term *mode of production*, at the global level, a larger more inclusive sense that goes beyond the economic proper, which would seem to be a regional mode of production. It is this distinction that would justify Jameson's claim, "If therefore one whishes to characterize Althusser's Marxism as a structuralism, one must complete the characterization with the essential provision that it is a structuralism for which only *one* structure exists: namely the mode of production itself, or the synchronic system of social relations as a whole" (*The Political Unconscious: Narrative as a Socially Symbolic Act*, 36). In a latter text Althusser seems to move away from this expansive definition on the grounds that every social formation is composed of at least two modes of production in the limited and quasi-economic sense (*Sur la Reproduction*, 45).

30. "Object," 191/405.

31. Ibid, 193/411. As Warren Montag makes clear, in the first edition of *Lire le Capital*, this metaphor of the theater moves in two directions: First as a purely immanent process without subject, an authorless theater in which there is no hierarchy between the script and its taking place. However, in a passage removed from the later editions of *Reading Capital* Althusser writes, "[W]e know that it is the presence of a completed whole which lives in

each moment and in each character and in all the relations between characters given in their personal presence, only to be grasped, however, as the presence of the whole, as the latent structure of the whole, in the whole and only felt in each element and each role" (*Lire le Capital*, 646). As Montag argues, this final sentence would seem to deviate from the general product of immanent causality in suggesting a "latent structure," a behind the scenes running the show ("Althusser's Nominalism," 71).

32. It is through the analysis of the commodity form that Marx develops the famous thought of commodity fetishism as a figure and a theory of the phenomenal appearance of social relations. Given the discussion of so-called primitive accumulation, and the manner in which it entails a particular appearance of the capitalist mode of production, as ahistorical, it may be possible to draw a direct line linking the two, perhaps utilizing Georg Lukacs's theory of reification. However, in line with Althusser's thought of Darstellung I would argue that any connection between the disparate and different theories and statements regarding "appearances" in Marx, from ideology through commodity fetishism to the "trinity formula," must be articulated from the ground up as it were, from the specific instances, elements, and examples constituting the theory.

33. While Althusser's earlier text in *Reading Capital* was an attempt to restore and reconstruct a Marxist practice of philosophy that would avoid the pitfalls of Stalinism and humanist Marxism, this later text is primarily concerned with the limits, gaps, and inadequacies of Marx's texts. As such, this later text is very much concerned with the limits and crises of Marxism, a crisis which cannot simply be attributed to this or that deviation from a true and proper Marx (Stalinism, Leninism, existentialism, and so forth) but a crisis that extends to the heart of Marx's corpus itself ("Marx dans se Limites," 363; hereafter cited as "Limites").

34. "Limites," 395.

35. "Object," 138/337.

36. Karl Marx, *A Contribution to the Critique of Political Economy*, 20; *Zur Kritik der Politischen Ökonomie*, 13.

37. "Object," 139/338.

38. "Limites," 397.

39. There is no real discontinuity between the later and the earlier Althusser provided one recognizes that the first assertion of immanent causality was an attempt to locate an internal tension between economism and a more materialist—that is, immanent—conception of social relations. "For whatever may have been claimed, when [Althusser] enjoined us to 'read *Capital*,' it was not in order to restore some hypothetical purity of Marxism, but precisely in order to try to uncover the traces of the ideological class struggle of which Marx's text was itself a site, at the very moment and in the very forms in which Marx established the concepts that made it possible to theorize this struggle for the first time" (Dominique Lecourt, *The Mediocracy: French Philosophy since the Mid-1970s*, 170).

40. Louis Althusser, "The Crisis of Marxism," 233.

41. Ernesto Laclau and Chantal Mouffe argue that the political relations, the relations of power and struggle, necessary to the constitution of labor power, would invalidate any

economism (*Hegemony and Socialist Strategy: Towards a Radical Democratic Politics,* 79). This point will be returned to in the following chapter.

42. Antonio Negri, "Twenty Theses on Marx: Interpretation of the Class Situation Today," 165.

43. Michael Perelman has argued that despite the fact that the early theorists of classical economics focus on the "invisible hand" of market necessity in their theoretical writings, political writings, diaries, and letters they demonstrate a self-conscious attempt to destroy all traditional relations of self reliance, from the commons to noncommodified production (*The Invention of Capitalism*).

44. Negri, *Insurgencies,* 259.

45. Gabriel Albiac, "Spinoza/Marx: le sujet construit," 13.

46. The problem of, and polemics regarding, economism were not entirely absent from Marx's and Frederick Engels's work, the most famous of which is perhaps Engels' letter to Joseph Bloch (September 21, 1890). Which begins as follows: ". . . According to the materialist conception of history, the *ultimately* determining factor in history is the production and reproduction of real life. Neither Marx nor I have ever asserted more than this. Hence if somebody twists this into saying that the economic factor is the *only* determining one, he transforms that proposition into a meaningless, abstract, absurd phrase. The economic situation is the basis, but the various elements of the superstructure-political forms of the class struggle and its results...especially the reflections of all these real struggles in the brains of the participants, political, legal, philosophical theories, religious views and their further development into systems of dogmas-also exercise their influence upon the course of the historical struggles and in many cases determine their *form* in particular." Despite this quotations long history in the battle lines drawn within Marxism, it offers little towards resolving the problems posed here.

47. Claude Lefort, "Marx: From One Vision of History to Another," 142.

48. Negri has argued on a terrain similar, and in opposition to, Althusser's early work on *Capital* that the *Grundrisse* develops a presentation (Darstellung) and logic that is open to the constitutive force of subjectivity and antagonism. As Negri writes, "In the *Grundrisse,* we can follow in all its stages the logical process that takes place between the *Forschung* and the *Darstellung.* Now, if we take account of the preceding indications, we realize very quickly that this process is neither linear nor, even less, unilateral. The dialectic research-presentation is, on the contrary, open on all sides: every conclusion that takes the form of the presentation of the research opens spaces to new research and new presentation" (*Marx Beyond Marx,* 12).

49. The destabilization of this division is itself perhaps a constant throughout Marx's writing, although one that in itself takes different forms and dimensions depending on the tensions and stakes at work in a particular text (Balibar, *The Philosophy of Marx,* 97). I will return to this "destabilization" in the second chapter.

50. "Rencontre," 571.

51. Deleuze and Guattari, *Anti-Oedipus,* 225/266.

52. "C'est-à-dire qu'au lieu de penser la contingence comme modalité ou exception de la nécessité, il faut penser la nécessité comme le devenir-nécessaire de la rencontre de contingents" ("Rencontre," 566; translation mine).

53. Negri, *Marx Beyond Marx*, 45.

54. The term *over-coding* could simply be understood in a loose and figurative sense: in which coding is simply the layering over of an additional or supplemental "meaning" or sense attributed to an existing set of differences, such as the moral coding of the difference between capitalist and worker. However, my use of the term is based on Deleuze and Guattari's development of this concept in *Anti-Oedipus*. Even though Deleuze and Guattari's use of the term *code* or *over-coding* plays of this loose sense, it also draws a specific relation to the problem of Marx's "Pre-capitalist Economic Formations" in which code entails the relation a given mode of production has to its presuppositions. Deleuze and Guattari's thought of over-coding, in which partial or local practices are rewritten or reinterpreted according to a dominant central meaning, is developed from Marx's concept of the relation of the Asiatic despot to the primitive communities that preexist it (194/224). Of course for Deleuze and Guattari code only applies to precapitalist economic formations. Capital is founded on axioms that are purely immanent and do not refer to another level of meaning for explanation, however, Deleuze and Guattari acknowledge the persistence of "re-coding" in capitalism, and I would argue that moral categories continue to function as an important element of re-coding, ascribing moral meaning to the meaningless equations of value.

55. Althusser, *Sur la reproduction*, 20. It almost goes without saying that my insistence on the relation of habits and comportment to the reproduction of a mode of production is very much indebted to Althusser's understanding of ideology as a materialist practice.

56. Althusser's argument of the necessary supplement of the society effect to any historical account of a mode of production is provoked in part by the following statement by Marx: "How, indeed, could the single logical formula of movement, of sequence of time, explain the structure of society, in which all relations coexist simultaneously and support one another?" (*The Poverty of Philosophy*, 110).

57. Louis Althusser "From *Capital* to Marx's Philosophy," 66; originally published as "Du 'Capital' à la philosophie de Marx," 75. Hereafter cited as "Philosophy" with English and French pagination.

58. Ibid.

59. Étienne Balibar, *La Crainte des Masses: Politique et philosophie avante et après Marx*, 30.

60. Deleuze and Guattari's remarks and reading of Marx's text on precapitalist modes of production is heavily indebted to Althusser and Balibar's *Lire le Capital* (*Anti-Oedipus*, 10/16).

61. Karl Marx, *Capital Volume III*, 966.

62. Balibar's distinction between determinant and dominant is founded almost exclusively on the following quote from Marx:

> One thing is clear: the middle ages could not live on Catholicism, nor could the ancient world on politics. On the contrary, it is the manner in which they gained their livelihood [*Die Art und Wiese, wie sie ihr Leben gewannen*] which explains why in one case politics, in the other

case Catholicism, played the chief part [*die Hauptrolle spielte*]. For the rest, one needs no more than a slight acquaintance with, for example the history of the Roman Republic, to be aware that its secret history is the history of landed property. And then there is Don Quixote, who long ago paid the penalty for wrongly imagining that knight errantry was compatible with all economic forms of society. (CI 176/96)

63. "Basic Concepts," 224/454.

64. Ibid., 452/223.

65. Ibid., 218/444.

66. Althusser argues that it is Marx's project, at least in *Capital*, to expound the society effect down to its particular micro-political relations ("Philosophy," 66/75). It is debatable perhaps whether such a goal is ever accomplished. Althusser's *Sur la reproduction* can, given its attentiveness to the complex interrelations of institutionalized and "everyday" (*quotidienne*) forms of ideology, however, be read as an attempt to produce such a theory of the society effect of the capitalist mode of production within a particular conjuncture (*Sur la reproduction*, 211).

67. For a critique of the purely formal nature of such a theory of the society effect, or the mode of appearance as society effect, there is perhaps no better source than Balibar's own self-critique. As he indicates in "Sur la dialectique historique: quelques remarques critiques à propos de *Lire Le Capital*," this formulation has two basic problems: First, such a theory of the structural determination of the subject, or at least the perceptions or consciousness of the subject, has all of the faults of both structuralism and humanism in that it produces a theory of the essentially alienated subject (224). Second, and more important, it limits the production of subjectivity to an effect, one that despite attempts to link it to structural causality acts only as an effect and is attributable to a single element or instance of the mode of production (217).

68. Lefort, "Marx," 149.

69. Maurice Godelier, "La notion de 'mode de production asiatique' et les schemas marxistes d'evolution des societes" 25.

70. The Asiatic mode of production, as Marx has begun to develop it here, poses multiple problems to what has been received and recognized as Marxist theories of the state, political society, ideology, and power. And, of course, all of these problems are above and beyond the initial and unavoidable problem of the fact that this theory seems to have its proper place within a rather sustained Western fantasy, from Aristotle to Montesquieu to Hegel, regarding "Oriental Despotism" rather than in any localizable or datable Asian society. Marx's own statements seem to place the orient in Peru or Mexico as much as he does in India or China (Perry Anderson, *Lineages of the Absolutist State*, 462–472). It is precisely because of these problems, which are problems of both theoretical coherence and historical application, that the Asiatic mode of production has been dropped for the most part from Marxist theory proper. One of the most difficult of the theoretical problems for Marxist orthodoxy is the manner in which the Asiatic mode of production posits a sort of state prior to the reason for a state, namely, class struggle. It is on the grounds of a violation of the official Marxist definition of the state (without class struggle there is no state) that Barry Hindess and Paul Hirst reject the Asiatic Mode of production (*Pre-Capitalist Modes of Production*, 198). At the same time that many have rejected the theory of the Asiatic mode of

production due to its failure to conform with the rudiments of a theory of the state in Marx's work (rudiments generally extracted from *The German Ideology* and *The Communist Manifesto*), others have argued that this drawback, its irreducibility to a theory of a state that sees the state as both an effect and instrument of class struggle, is precisely the strength of the Asiatic mode of production. These projects have been provoked in part by the formation of bureaucratic state socialism in the name of Marx and communism, facts that would seem to attest to an element of state power that actively resisted "withering away." Karl Wittfogel, perhaps the most famous of this second group, has gone so far as to argue that Marxism must necessarily blackout the theory of the Asiatic mode of production because of its embarrassing proximity to the bureaucratic totalitarian socialist state (*Oriental Despotism: A Comparative Study of Total Power*, 411).

71. As Marx writes in *Capital*,

> The simplicity of the productive organism in these self-sufficing communities which constantly reproduce themselves in the same form and, when accidentally destroyed, spring up again on the same spot and with the same name—this simplicity supplies the key to the riddle of the unchangeability of Asiatic societies, which is in such striking contrast with the constant dissolution and refounding of Asiatic states, and their never-ceasing changes of dynasty. The structure of the fundamental economic elements of society remain untouched by the storms which blow up in the cloudy regions of politics." (CI 479/379)

72. Karl Marx and Frederick Engels, *The German Ideology*, 50.

73. Frederick Engels, *The Origin of Family, Private Property, and the State*, 75.

74. Marx and Engels, *The German Ideology*, 51.

75. Engels, *The Origin of Family, Private Property, and the State*, 74.

76. Gayle Rubin, in her influential essay "The Traffic in Women: Notes on the 'Political Economy' of Sex," would seem to implicitly work from this distinction and its articulation in her concept of a "sex/gender system": "A sex/gender system is the set of arrangements by which a society transforms biological sexuality into products of human activity and in which these transformed sexual needs are satisfied" (75).

77. The paradoxical nature of Marx and Engels's treatment of the family, as a historically contingent institution grounded on a natural division, has led in part to the difficulty of developing a relationship between Marxism and Feminism. See Donna J. Haraway, *Simians, Cyborgs, and Women: The Reinvention of Nature*, 131.

78. Engels, *The Origin of the Family*, 152. It is for this reason that Socialist Feminists, such as Iris Young, have suggested that the concept of the 'division of labor' is a suggestive point of intersection between Marxism and Feminism ("Beyond the Unhappy Marriage: A Critique of Dual Systems Theory," 43).

79. Mariarosa Dalla Costa, "Women and the Subversion of Community," 21.

80. Negri has argued that such a passage would seem to reframe the entire question of liberation around the constitution of subjectivity and not the return to some pre-alienated state (*Marx Beyond Marx*, 112).

81. Marx stated reasons for not publishing the introduction were as follows: "A general introduction, which I had drafted, is omitted, since on further consideration it seems to me

confusing to anticipate results which still have to be substantiated, and the reader who really wishes to follow me will have to decide to advance from the particular to the general" (*A Contribution to the Critique of Political Economy*, 18).

82. Jean Baudrillard, *The Mirror of Production*, 25.

83. Althusser argues that this "anthropology" remains out of site in and through the manner in which classical economy assumes "need" as a necessarily preconceptual given that delineates the field of political economy, one that is concerned with material need. Thus this anthropology is at the same time a moral ideology: what it excludes by definition is the determination of the economy by other factors such as power or domination. There is by definition only production for need ("Object," 162/368).

84. Marshall Sahlins, *Culture and Practical Reason*, 154.

85. Slavoj Žižek develops this observation in his contribution to *Contingency, Hegemony, Universality* (by Judith Butler, Ernesto Laclau, and Slavoj Žižek) arguing that this "double inscription" should be applied to the contemporary series of "race, class, gender . . . etc." Class is both one of the terms in the series of identities and the metonymic stand in for the totality of capitalist social relations that constitutes the struggles (96).

86. The definitive, and often dogmatic, version of the relation between forces and relations of production can be found in *A Contribution to the Critique of Political Economy*. As Marx writes in that text, "At a certain stage of development, the material productive forces of society come into conflict with the existing relations of production or—this merely expresses the same thing in legal terms—with the property relations within the framework of which they have operated hitherto. From the forms of development of the productive forces these relations turn into their fetters" (21). As Althusser argues, this relation has primarily been interpreted according to the Hegelian dialectic of the correspondence and noncorrespondence of form and content. Such a dialect leaves no room for class struggle, or subjectivity (*Sur la reproduction*, 246).

87. Sahlins, *Culture and Practical Reason*, 158.

88. Marx, *The Poverty of Philosophy*, 119.

89. "Object," 174/385.

90. Deleuze and Guattari, *Anti-Oedipus*, 4/10.

91. Ibid., 141/165.

92. Deleuze and Guattari's understanding of a code incorporates several elements of Marx's understanding of precapitalist economic formations. Code establishes a relation of inscription between production, or all of the effects of activity in general, and the presuppositions of the precapitalist mode of production, or what Deleuze and Guattari call the "socius," or "full body." Code, for Deleuze and Guattari, is intimately connected with belief and tradition: "[I]t implies a system of collective appraisal and evaluation, and a set of organs of perception, or more precisely of belief, as a condition of existence and survival of the society in question" (Ibid., 247/294). Code establishes a relation between various practices and activities of the social, and the socius or society effect, so that there is no activity that cannot be recognized as social. More important for our purpose, code, in the manner that Deleuze and Guattari propose to understand it here, unifies or brings together the two

sides of determination within the mode of production: social relations and technological development. Code is a system of tradition, of belief, but it bears directly on relations of production, distribution, and exchange. As Deleuze and Guattari indicate, coding establishes a relation or a series of relations between all of the elements of Marx's expansive sense of production, what they call production of production, the productions of recording, and the productions of consumption.

93. Félix Guattari, "Regimes, Pathways, Subjects," 96.

94. For Deleuze and Guattari codes, as the production of subjective dimensions of the mode of production, apply only to precapitalist modes of production; as such they encompass various other aspects of the distinction between precapitalist and capitalist modes of production, from Marx, Althusser, and Balibar. As Deleuze and Guattari argue,

> All these code characteristics—indirect, qualitative, and limited—are sufficient to show that a code is not, and can never be, economic: on the contrary, it expresses the apparent objective movement according to which the economic forces or productive connections are attributed an extra-economic instance as though they emanated from it, an instance that serves as a support and an agent of inscription. That is what Althusser and Balibar show so well: how juridical and political relations are *determined as dominant*—in the case of feudalism, for example because surplus labor as a form of surplus value constitutes a flux that is qualitatively and temporally distinct from that labor, and consequently must enter into a composite that is itself qualitative and implies non-economic factors. . . . In short, there is a code where a full body as an instance of anti-production falls back on the economy that it appropriates. That is why the sign of desire, as an economic sign that consists in producing and breaking flows, is accompanied by a sign of necessarily extra-economic power, although its causes and effects lie within the economy (for example, the sign of alliance in relation to the power of the creditor). Or—what amounts to the same thing—surplus value here is determined as surplus value of code. (*Anti-Oedipus*, 247/294).

95. Engels, *The Origin of the Family*, 26.

96. Despite the fact that Judith Butler locates in Marx's notebooks the rudimentary basis for a theory of the mode of sexual production, in which the culture, sexual identity, and the economy are not seen as separate spheres of existence and political commitment, it would have to be necessary to admit that Marx's notebooks are only suggestive in this regard ("Merely Cultural," 41). Unlike Engels's *The Origin of the Family*, Marx's notebooks do not consider a history of the family.

97. "Rencontre," 573.

98. Lefort, "Marx," 147.

99. Negri, *Marx Beyond Marx*, 108.

100. As Marx argues, "Monetary greed, or mania for wealth, necessarily brings with it the decline and fall of the ancient communities [*Gemeinwesen*]. Hence it is the antithesis to them. It is itself the community [*Gemeinwesen*], and can tolerate none other standing above it," (G 223/150).

101. Negri, *Marx Beyond Marx*, 44.

102. Ibid., 45.

CHAPTER TWO

1. Étienne Balibar, "Plus-value et classes sociales: contribution à la critique de l'économie politique," 108.

2. Karl Marx and Frederick Engels, *Selected Correspondence*, 186.

3. Ibid.

4. A note on the terms *materiality* and *effectivity*. While I would not totally equate these two terms, to make the claim that things are material insofar as they have effects, I do maintain that structural causality allows for an expanded definition of materiality that is based on the different and complex effects that different practices and relations have on each other. Such a thought of materiality is far from a mechanistic causality. On this point, see Louis Althusser, "Is It Simple to Be a Marxist in Philosophy?" (215).

5. Karl Marx, *Critique of Hegel's "Philosophy of Right,"* 18.

6. Karl Marx and Frederick Engels, *The German Ideology*, 67.

7. Ibid., 42. This statement, which suggests a crude opposition between abstract and concrete, is justified only by certain polemical remarks that Marx makes in this early text, and the manner in which those statements have been developed within the history of Marxism to form a positivistic tendency within Marxism. Étienne Balibar has offered a different reading of *The German Ideology*, one more in line with the thought of "ensembles" and the "mode of production" developed here. Balibar's reading stresses the importance of relations in Marx's theory of ideology. As Balibar writes, "The materialist critique of ideology, for its part, corresponds to the analysis of *the real as relation*, as a structure of practical relations" (*Masses, Classes, Ideas: Studies on Politics and Philosophy before and after Marx*, 92).

8. Marx and Engels, *The German Ideology*, 64.

9. Balibar indicates that as much as this latter assertion rigorously follows the opposition between ideality and material existence set out at the beginning of the text, it entails fundamental problems for thinking about politics. Politics, or at least Marxist politics, have had to deal with the complex intermingling between political action and ideology, rather than the division that Marx proposes. It is perhaps for this and other reasons that the term *ideology*, or at least the project of a general theory of ideology, drops from Marx's writing after *The German Ideology* (*Masses, Classes, Ideas*, 97).

10. The term *real abstraction* has received the clearest and most provocative definition from Alfred Sohn-Rethel. For Sohn-Rethel the commodity form, and with it exchange value, is the paradigmatic form of a real abstraction. As Sohn-Rethel writes,

> The essence of commodity abstraction, however, is that it is not thought induced; it does not originate in men's minds but in their actions. And yet this does not give "abstraction" a merely metaphorical meaning. The economic concept of value resulting from it is characterized by a complete absence of quality, a differentiation purely by quantity and by applicability to every kind of commodity and service which can occur on the market. . . . It exists nowhere other than in the human mind but it does not spring from it. Rather it is purely social in character, arising in the spatio-temporal sphere of human interrelations. It is not people who originate these abstractions but their actions. (*Intellectual and Manual Labor. A Critique of Epistemology*, 21)

11. G. W. F. Hegel, *Phenomenology of Spirit*, par. 33.

12. Fredric Jameson has underlined this element of Hegel's thought, Hegel as the first thinker of reification, in the beginning of his essay on Gilles Deleuze ("Marxism and Dualism in Deleuze," 394).

13. Mario Tronti, *Ouvriers et Capital*, 156.

14. David Ricardo, *Principles of Political Economy and Taxation*, 18.

15. This first point is made by Michel Foucault in *The Order of Things: An Archaeology of the Human Sciences* (254). Foucault's argument in this text is to deny that Marx constitutes any sort of break (epistemological or otherwise) with the problems and presuppositions of political economy. In contrast to this argument Deleuze and Guattari turn to the same problem—the connection between subjectivity and value—to find in Marx a recognition of the fact that the problem of capital is the problem of subjectivity (*Anti-Oedipus*, 258/307).

16. *Anti-Oedipus*, 270/322; Karl Marx, *The Economic and Philosophic Manuscripts of 1844*, 128–129.

17. At this point the terms *abstract subjective activity* and *abstract subjective essence*, which Deleuze and Guattari employ in their reading of Marx, are necessarily vague. The component elements of these definitions—the particular sense of abstract, subjective, and essence—are at this point only being developed.

18. *Anti-Oedipus*, 259/308. A note on the concept of deterritorialization. As Fredric Jameson suggests, Deleuze and Guattari's term receives much of its conceptual weight and figurative grounding from Marx (*The Cultural Turn: Selected Writings on the Postmodern*, 152). Deleuze and Guattari develop the term through several different processes discussed by Marx. As they argue the two flows—wealth and labor—constitutive of the capitalist mode of production are formed through deterritorialization,

> [E]ach of these elements brings into play several processes of decoding and deterritorialization having very different origins. For the free worker: the deterritorialization of the soil through privatization; the decoding of the instruments of production through appropriation; the loss of the means of consumption through the dissolution of the family and the corporation; and finally, the decoding of the worker in favor of the work itself or of the machine. And for capital: the deterritorialization of wealth through monetary abstraction; the decoding of the flows of production through merchant capital; the decoding of states through financial capital and public debts; the decoding of the means of production through the formation of industrial capital; and so on. (*Anti-Oedipus*, 225/266)

In each case what is broken down is the intertwining of material conditions with symbols and knowledge. Perhaps the clearest example of this in Marx is Marx's statements regarding the power money has to break down older systems of prestige and belief.

19. *Anti-Oedipus*, 259/308.

20. Tronti argues that Hegel's meditations on abstract labor lack any thought of value as the mediating and differential relation. This can be seen in the Jena philosophy in which Hegel places labor in a dialectical relation of increasing productivity and need. See Tronti, *Ouvriers et Capital*, 166.

21. Michael Hardt, "The Withering Away of Civil Society," 25.

22. G. W. F. Hegel, *Elements of the Philosophy of Right*, par. 198. Hegel's early writings of the Jena period, specifically the 1803/1804 draft of the Phenomenology, ascribe a much more essential role to the tool and machines as instruments of education and discipline. We will see how in a somewhat different manner Marx recognizes that the question of machine is inseparable from questions of power. See G. W. F. Hegel, *System of Ethical Life and First Philosophy of Spirit*, 231.

23. Hegel, *Elements of the Philosophy of Right*, par. 197.

24. Hardt, "The Withering Away of Civil Society," 25.

25. Michel Foucault, *Discipline and Punish: The Birth of the Prison*, 138; originally published as *Surveiller et punir*, 139. Hereafter cited as *Discipline* with English and French pagination.

26. Deleuze has noted this similarity of Foucault and Tronti on the question of counter-power or resistance (*Foucault*, 144 n. 28/96 n. 26).

27. In this passage Marx argues that labor is both "practically true" and is "valid for all forms of society," affirming at once a "historicist" account of labor and an anthropological understanding of labor. Labor totally abstract from any particularity is both a product of the capitalist mode of production and the condition of possibility of understanding prior modes of production.

28. Sohn-Rethel, *Intellectual and Manual Labor*, 21.

29. Tronti, *Ouvriers et Capital*, 154.

30. Lucio Colletti has argued that this interpretation of abstract labor as the product of a mental generalization common throughout many writers of the Second International, such as Edward Bernstein, made possible a purely economistic understanding of capital. What such interpretations miss is that abstract labor is not simply a fiction necessary to the understanding of the economy but constitutive of social power ("Bernstein and the Marxism of the Second International," 80–87).

31. Étienne Balibar, *The Philosophy of Marx*, 60.

32. Sohn-Rethel, *Intellectual and Manual Labor*, 30.

33. Balibar, *The Philosophy of Marx*, 63.

34. Here we see the recognition of the larger sense of production (production of production) indicated in the previous chapter in which exchange and consumption, in the form of the commodity, acts on production itself.

35. Deleuze and Guattari, *Anti-Oedipus*, 248/295.

36. See Jameson, "Marxism and Dualism in Deleuze," 398. Once again Deleuze and Guattari's distinction can be read through not only Marx's text but also Balibar's contribution to *Lire le Capital*. As Balibar argues, in all precapitalist economic formations there is a temporal and spatial distinction between labor and the extraction of surplus. Thus, in precapitalist modes of production the extraction of a surplus is always accompanied by a "noneconomic" instance determined as dominant (politics or religion), which renders visible and palpable the division between necessary and surplus labor; but in the capitalist mode of production this division is in some sense invisible. As Balibar argues, in capitalism

the laborer works in the production process, and its temporality (the working day) and relations (such as the relation between the individual worker and the capitalist) constitute lived experience, while the "valorization" process and its division between necessary and surplus labor never takes place in the lived present. In the capitalist mode of production there is no spatial or temporal division between necessary and surplus labor: thus in some sense, exploitation is invisible, or at least potentially invisible, taking place behind one's back ("Basic Concepts," 223/451).

37. Deleuze and Guattari, *Anti-Oedipus*, 249/296.

38. Ibid., 251/298. According to Deleuze and Guattari, this separation between the functional operations of axiomatics constituting an operative ground and belief explains why capital can be described as a regime of cynicism.

39. "It may be all but impossible to distinguish deterritorialization from reterritorialization, since they are mutually enmeshed, or like opposite faces of one and the same process" (Ibid., 258/306).

40. Slavoj Žižek, *The Sublime Object of Ideology*, 31.

41. As we saw in the first chapter, Deleuze and Guattari argue that every mode of production, every social machine, produces a seemingly ahistorical instance, a socius, which appears to be the precondition and not the result of production. Although Deleuze and Guattari draw this observation from a reading of "Pre-Capitalist Economic Formations," they recognize an important epochal distinction between the way in which the socius functions in capital and precapitalist society. "Hence capital differentiates itself from any other socious or full body, inasmuch as capital itself figures as a directly economic instance, and falls back on production [*se rabat sur*] without interposing extraeconomic factors that would be inscribed in the form of a code. With the advent of capitalism the full body becomes truly naked, as does the worker himself who is attached to this full body" (*Anti-Oedipus*, 249–250/297).

42. Balibar, *The Philosophy of Marx*, 66.

43. Georg Lukács, *History and Class Consciousness: Studies in Marxist Dialects*, 87.

44. Moishe Postone refers to labor as the social synthesis in the capitalist mode of production. He writes, "The character of social relations and the social character of labor in capitalism come to be determined by a social function of labor which replaces that of overt social relations. In other words, labor grounds its own social character in capitalism by virtue of its historically specific function as a socially mediating activity. In that sense, *labor in capital becomes its own social ground*" (*Time, Labor, and Social Domination: A Reinterpretation of Marx's Critical Theory*, 151). Postone's thought of labor as "social synthesis" is similar in some ways to Althusser's society effect. However, Postone argues that in capital labor is the social synthesis, it is the ground of the social relating different practices, while I have argued with respect to Althusser and Deleuze and Guattari that capital must be thought of as the society effect, or socius.

45. Karl Marx, *A Contribution to the Critique of Political Economy*, 30.

46. As Thomas Keenan writes, "Humanity itself arrives with the domination of the commodity form, which it makes possible" (*Fables of Responsibility: Aberrations and Predicaments in Ethics and Politics*, 118).

47. Deleuze and Guattari, *Anti-Oedipus*, 263–264.

48. This is another version of the encounter between the unqualified capacity for labor and the unqualified flows of wealth. As Deleuze and Guattari argue, the abstract potentiality of labor is no longer tied to the production of this or that specific form of wealth or objects but to the commodity as indeterminate or "whatever" object [*un Objet quelconque*] (*A Thousand Plateaus*, 452/565).

49. Heidi Hartmann, "The Unhappy Marriage of Marxism and Feminism: Towards a More Progressive Union," 10.

50. The term *patriarchy* is being used here in a loose sense, simply to denote a fundamental hierarchy grounded on gender differences, or birthright. As such the benefit of such a term is that it foregrounds the fundamentally anachronistic nature of such inequalities, while the risk is that it suggests a universal condition of domination, immune to differences of history, or of its placement in specific modes of production. See Michèle Barrett, *Women's Oppression Today: The Marxist/Feminist Encounter*, 14.

51. For a critical discussion of the history of responses to this problem, see Kathi Weeks, *Constituting Feminist Subjects*, 73–93.

52. Leopoldina Fortunati, *The Arcane of Reproduction: Housework, Prostitution, Labor, and Capital*, 107.

53. Michael Hardt and Antonio Negri, *The Labor of Dionysus: A Critique of the State Form*, 9.

54. Postone, *Time, Labor, and Social Domination*, 146.

55. Marx, *The Economic and Philosophic Manuscripts of 1844*, 141.

56. Lukács's *History and Class Consciousness* and Sohn-Rethel's *Intellectual and Manual Labor*, despite their merits, which I have relied on in this section, are two examples of this tendency.

57. The opening paragraph of Lukács's chapter "Reification and the Consciousness of the Proletariat" in *History and Class Consciousness* reads as a definition of Althusser's concept of expressive causality: "For at this stage in the history of mankind there is no problem that does not ultimately lead back to that question and there is no solution that could not be found in the solution to the riddle of commodity-structure" (83).

58. Marx highlights the precapitalist nature of isolated commodity production in a draft of an unpublished chapter of *Capital*, published as an appendix entitled "Results of the Immediate Process of Production." In this text it is partly Marx's task to elucidate the manner in which capitalism transforms its own conditions. Although the capitalist mode of production necessarily presupposes commodity production (isolated producers exchange goods or the excess of production), it eventually generalizes commodity production, converting both the means of production and labor power into commodities; this generalization has the effective of destroying the earlier basis of commodity production.

59. This separation between exchange as socialization and labor as isolation has led some writers, such as Michel Henry, to locate an underlying commitment to "a philosophy of monadic subjectivity" in Marx (*Marx: A Philosophy of Human Reality*, 194).

60. Postone, *Time, Labor, and Social Domination*, 8.

61. Jean-Marie Vincent, *Abstract Labor: A Critique*, 19.

62. Gayatri Chakravorty Spivak employs the term *super-adequate* to draw our attention to a simple but overlooked element of Marx's thought of labor power: At the basis of this concept is power, the power to exceed the givenness of its condition ("Scattered Speculations on the Question of Value," 154).

63. Postone, *Time, Labor, and Social Domination*, 16.

64. Tronti, *Ouvriers et Capital*, 322.

65. These two tendencies are clearly articulated, on very different grounds, the first by Gérard Granel ("L'ontologie marxiste de 1844 et la question de la 'coupure'") and second by Jacques Rancière ("The Concept of 'Critique' and the 'Critique of Political Economy': From the Manuscripts of 1844 to Capital"). Granel's essay is a direct response to Rancière and the argument of the "break" between the young Marx and the scientific Marx. In citing these essays together I do not mean to suggest a simple balancing of perspectives, or an interpretive indecisiveness, rather, the fact of breaks and tensions in Marx that cannot be fixed by a date.

66. Marx, *The Economic and Philosophic Manuscripts of 1844*, 112; Marx and Engels, *Gesamtausgabe Band 2 März 1843–August 1844*, 369 (translation slightly modified). Spivak has translated the first sentence as "Nature is man's body without organs," drawing out the connections between Marx and Deleuze and Guattari (*A Critique of Colonial Reason*, 328).

67. Marx, *The Economic and Philosophic Manuscripts of 1844*, 113/369.

68. Granel has argued in reading both *The Economic and Philosophic Manuscripts of 1844* and *The German Ideology* that such statements constitute the precondition of a radical rethinking of ontology in Marx ("L'ontologie marxiste de 1844," 294).

69. A note on translation: The translation of *Gattungswesen* as species-being, while not entirely incorrect, tends to ground the term in a biological or anthropological meaning. Although the term, especially as it was inherited from Feuerbach, does entail something of a biological reference, the term itself does not necessarily imply such a meaning. Terminologically, the French translation of Gattungswesen as *la vie générique* (generic life) is perhaps more accurate (Marx, *The Economic and Philosophic Manuscripts of 1844*, 112/369).

70. Ibid., 107/364. As Rancière argues, the terms *value* and *devaluation* have both an economic and an ethical, or anthropological, meaning and in the 1844 Manuscripts it is the second, which ultimately clarifies the first: As workers produce wealth the conditions of workers becomes itself impoverished ("The Concept of 'Critique,'" 87; *Lire le Capital*, 98).

71. Marx, *The Economic and Philosophic Manuscripts of 1844*, 110/367.

72. Marx, "Theses on Feuerbach," 121.

73. The sense of the term *whatever* in relation to abstract labor and species-being is drawn from Giorgio Agamben's meditations on potentiality in such works as *The Coming Community* and *The Idea of Prose*. Without claiming a rigorous parallel of Agamben's concept with that of species-being, in each case it is a matter of a potentiality that cannot be actualized into

a determinate act. As Agamben writes, "If every power is equally the power to be and the power to not-be, the passage to action can only come about by transporting (Aristotle says "saving") in the act its own power to not-be" (*The Coming Community*, 36).

74. Balibar, *The Philosophy of Marx*, 25.

75. Negri, *Insurgencies*, 34.

76. Granel, "L'ontologie marxiste de 1844," 300.

77. Marx and Engels, *The German Ideology*, 53.

78. It is for this reason that this passage has played a foundational role in the theories of Operaismo and Autonomia. See Tronti, *Ouvriers et Capital*, 202–204; Negri, *Marx Beyond Marx*, 69–70.

79. Negri, *Marx Beyond Marx*, 70.

80. It is because living labor is entirely internal to abstract labor, or put otherwise, it is because abstract labor necessarily depends on living labor that Marx's use of terms vacillates. Thus while it would be convenient if abstract labor only referred to the dominating and normalizing aspect of labor and living labor referred to its creative active side, such a terminological separation is impossible.

81. My use of the term *working class* is only meant to designate those whose work, labor, and productivity is directly and indirectly productive of capital. Hardt and Negri offer a similar reworking of the term *proletariat*:

> The fact that under the category of proletariat we understand all those exploited by and subject to capitalist domination should not indicate that the proletariat is a homogeneous or undifferentiated unit. It is indeed cut through in various directions by differences and stratifications. Some labor is waged, some is not; some labor is restricted to within the factory walls, some is dispersed across the unbounded social terrain; some labor is limited to eight hours a day and forty hours a week, some expands to fill the entire time of life; some labor is accorded a minimal value, some is exalted to the pinnacle of the capitalist economy. . . . Our point here is that all of these diverse forms of labor are in some way subject to capitalist discipline and capitalist relations of production. This fact of being within capital and sustaining capital is what defines the proletariat as a class. (*Empire*, 53)

82. Negri, *Insurgencies*, 33.

83. Michael Lebowitz, *Beyond Capital: Marx's Political Economy of the Working Class*, 54.

84. Negri, *Insurgencies*, 264.

85. Lebowitz, *Beyond Capital*, 30.

86. Karl Marx, "Results of the Immediate Process of Production," 1033; also published as Karl Marx-Friedrich Engels, *Gesamtausgabe Band 4 1863–67*, 103. Hereafter cited in the text as R with English and German Pagination.

87. Gayle Rubin argues that patriarchy, the subordination of women to men, is part of this "cultural and moral heritage" that capitalism inherits and exploits ("Traffic in Women: Notes on the 'Political Economy' of Sex," 79).

88. For both Lebowitz and Negri the wage is a central element in defining self-valorization (in Negri) and the political economy of the working class (in Lebowitz). It is for this

reason that the two ascribe a great deal of importance to Marx's early plans to write a book on wage labor and the fragments on the wage in the *Grundrisse*.

89. Negri, *Marx Beyond Marx*, 137.

90. Mariarosa Dalla Costa, "Women and the Subversion of Community," 35.

91. Fortunati, *The Arcane of Reproduction*, 37.

92. Tronti, *Ouvriers et Capital*, 198.

93. Althusser argues that the "bourgeois ideology of labor" is in part founded on the idea of an equivalence, that labor is paid for at its value. The other elements of this ideology include the juridico-moral ideology of the contract and the idea of the neutrality of the technical division of labor (a point that will be returned to) (*Sur la reproduction*, 67). This ideology is "spontaneous" insofar as it is produced by the practices themselves without the necessary imposition of an official ideology. Althusser later clarifies that there is no such thing as a truly spontaneous ideology, an ideology that would be the necessary side effect of a given practice because the different and divergent spontaneous ideologies must come into conflictual relations (ibid., 115).

94. "[T]he ideology of the market is not some supplementary ideational or representational luxury or embellishment that can be removed from the economic problem and then sent over to some cultural or superstructural morgue to be dissected by specialists over there. It is somehow generated by the thing itself, as its objectively necessary afterimage; somehow both dimensions must be registered together, in their identity as well as their difference" (Fredric Jameson, *Postmodernism: Or, the Cultural Logic of Late Capitalism*, 260).

95. "Philosophy," 28–29/22–23.

96. Despite the fact that the sovereign law has only two terms, it is by no means semiotically impoverished. Rather Foucault's analysis of sovereign power reveals it to be a complex economy of signs: The torture and execution of the body of the condemned has as one of its central elements the signification of sovereign power (*Discipline*, 48/52). Foucault's argument regarding the semiotics of sovereign power can be understood as similar to Deleuze and Guattari's argument concerning the centrality of codes in precapitalist society.

97. Ibid., 186/184.

98. Michel Foucault, "Les mailles du pouvoir," 189. Translation mine. Hereafter cited as "Mailles."

99. Ibid., 200. This lecture, which was originally presented in Brazil in 1981, constitutes Foucault's most appreciated estimation of the influence of his relation to Marx. In this lecture not only does Foucault explicitly link the rise of capitalism with disciplinary power, a statement that can be found throughout Foucault's work, but more important, and uncharacteristically, he locates in Marx's work a complex thought of power. This final statement stands in sharp contrast to statements made in *The History of Sexuality* and *Power/Knowledge* in which Foucault argues that Marx, and more important, Marxism remains trapped in a sovereign concept of power in which power is viewed as something that can be possessed rather than a relation.

100. *Discipline*, 85/88.

101. Michel Foucault, "The Punitive Society," 33–34.

102. Michel Foucault, "La vérité et les formes juridiques," 622. In this text Foucault argues quite specifically against a traditional Marxism that understands labor as the concrete essence of man and thus can only understand exploitation as the alienation of this essence and not the production of this relation.

103. Although the term *transversality* is drawn from the work of Félix Guattari (*Molecular Revolution: Psychiatry and Politics*, 17), Foucault himself uses the term to refer to the political struggles after May 1968, which provoked his rethinking of power ("The Subject and Power," 211).

104. "Mailles," 187.

105. Gilles Deleuze, *Foucault*, 75/82.

106. Karl Marx, *Capital: A Critique of Political Economy, Volume III*, 927.

107. Balibar develops this notion of Marx's "short-circuit" in his essay "The Notion of Class Politics in Marx." Balibar writes that

> the work relation (as a relation of exploitation) is *immediately* and *directly* economic and political; and the form of the "economic community" and the State "spring" simultaneously (or concurrently) from this "base." . . . In other words, the relations of the exploitation of labor are both the seed of the market (economic community) and the seed of the state (sovereignty/Servitude). Such a thesis may and must seem blunt and debatable when looked at from a static perspective. . . . However, the thesis can become singularly more explanatory if the notion of "determination" is given a strong sense, that is, if it is considered as the conducting wire to analyze the transformational tendencies of the market and the bourgeois State in the past two centuries or, even better, following the best "concrete analysis of Marxism, to analyze the critical conjunctures which punctuate this tendentious transformation and which precipitate its modifications." (34).

108. Étienne Balibar, "Foucault and Marx: The Question of Nominalism," 51.

109. Michel Foucault, *Power/Knowledge: Selected Interviews and Other Writings, 1972–1977*, 195.

110. Antonio Negri ,"Twenty Theses on Marx: Interpretation of the Class Situation Today," 151.

111. Gilles Deleuze, "Desire and Pleasure," 184.

112. Eric Alliez and Michel Feher draw together Marx and Foucault by stressing the spatial divergences of the different structures while placing them within the same abstract machine.

> Henceforth subjection as a social relation inherent to capitalism permeates all of society : from the subjugation to technical machines (mass producers of goods) that allows the extraction of surplus value, to the subjection to household appliances (mass produced goods) that assures its realization, by way of subjection to public goods that guarantees the continuous functioning of the valorization circuit (or at least its starting up again day after day). On every level, subjection is related to the independence of a subject: as free worker, as responsible citizen, and finally as consumer who maximizes his utility within the limits imposed by his salary. . . . More specifically, it is the very crossing of boundaries between sectors—going to the factory, to school, to the supermarket—that actualizes individuals' freedom while guaranteeing their subjection" ("The Luster of Capital," 345).

113. Here, I am following Balibar's suggestive remarks on antagonism in Marx and agonism in Foucault ("Conjunctures and Conjectures," 33).

114. Here, I am obviously giving an all-too-short presentation of two very different and complex arguments. However, my point is twofold: first, to point out that proletarianization, or the inevitable simplification of class antagonisms, is not the only narrative underlying the persistence of antagonism in Marx; and second, to begin to indicate a tension, in Marx and in capitalism, between the proletarianization and socialization of labor.

115. This argument is developed forcefully and famously in Foucault's *The History of Sexuality* (94/127). However, in a seminar given the same year as the publication of *The History of Sexuality* entitled "*Il Faut Défendre la Société*" *Coursau Collège de France 1976*, Foucault develops a genealogy of the antagonistic or dualistic conception of society, the myth of class or racial struggle demonstrating the tactical merits and shortcomings of such a presentation of society.

116. Without necessarily affirming all that he says, the following quote from Balibar provides a succinct statement of this difference:

> For Marx, the practice is *par excellence* an *external* production, which produces effects outside itself and consequently also produces effects of subjectification (the conflict which develops in the area of the "means of production"), whilst for Foucault, power is a productive practice which acts in the first place *on bodies* themselves, aiming initially at individualization of subjectification (one might go so far as to say a "practice for the self" or "of the self"), in consequence producing effects of an objective nature, or knowledge. What this comes down to is that Foucault's logic of power relations is underpinned by the idea of a plasticity of life, whilst the Marxist logic of contradiction (which interiorises power relations) cannot be dissociated from its immanence within the structure. ("Foucault and Marx," 53).

117. These are the terms of Deleuze and Guattari's criticism of Foucault (*A Thousand Plateaus*, 531), which is developed along lines that follow a logic similar to that of living labor in Marx, in which the question is not simply one of resistance but of a creative element that is both prior to and constitutive of the structures that control it. However, at times Deleuze will present this not as a criticism but, rather, will attribute to Foucault a thought of resistance prior to domination. "In Foucault, there is an echo of Mario Tronti's interpretation of Marxism as a 'workers' resistance existing *prior* to the strategies of capital" (*Foucault*, 144).

118. Deleuze, *Foucault*, 101/108–109.

119. "Structure" is being used here as a generic placeholder for two divergent concepts: the capitalist mode of production and the dispositif of power.

120. A second and altogether different problem is given in one of the specific ways in which Marx and Foucault converge. The convergence I am referring to here is a virtual point, or even a possible point, located in certain tendencies within Marx's and Foucault's texts and actualized in a history of readings that have located in Marx and Foucault an unavoidable determinism. Of course, if Marx and Foucault arrive at determinism, they do so in fundamentally different ways. As I have already suggested, the tendency toward determinism in Marx is intertwined with the tendency toward economism: The social space is entirely determined and grasped by the "laws" of the economy; while the tendency of determinism in Foucault is different: It can perhaps be described as an increased internalization of power relations to the point at which subjectivity is identical to subjection. As

Foucault writes, "The man described for us, whom we are invited to free, is already in himself the effect of a subjection much more profound than himself" (*Discipline*, 30/34). It is not within the scope of this book to respond to the various works of criticism that have converted these tendencies, which themselves are inseparable from countertendencies, into the supposed truth of their respective texts, making way for a dismissal on the grounds that such texts are impossibly pessimistic (see Warren Montag, "The Soul Is the Prison of the Body: Althusser and Foucault, 1970–1975," 55). Rather, these tendencies highlight the importance and radical nature of the perspective of living labor, as it is developed by Tronti and Negri (implicitly in the first case, explicitly in the latter).

121. Balibar has proposed the term *trans-individuality* to designate Marx's refusal to either posit individuality or collectivity as a methodological or ontological starting point (*The Philosophy of Marx*, 121). See Balibar's *Spinoza: From Individuality to Transindividaulity* for a definition of this term.

122. *Tendency*, a word with an immense baggage of connotations in the Marxist tradition, is not used here to indicate a telos, in the strong sense, or a law of historical development. There is never one tendency, as the paragraph above suggests, and thus a tendency is inseparable from a countertendency.

123. Tronti, *Ouvriers et Capital*, 229/254.

124. In a related but somewhat different point, Balibar has argued for a revival of Marx's argument regarding the polarization of class struggle, not as a teleology leading toward the demise of capitalism but as a tension internal to capitalism. For Balibar this tension is not between proletarianization and socialization, but between proletarianization and "embourgeoisement." Thus, Balibar focuses not on the cooperative dimension of labor but on the extension of social resources and conditions for ideological belonging to a portion of the laboring population—including the production of a racially privileged class.

> The logic of capitalist accumulation involves *two* contradictory aspects here: on the one hand, mobilizing or permanently de-stabilizing the conditions of life and work, in such a way as to ensure competition on the labor market, draw new labor power continually from the "industrial reserve army" and maintain a relative over-population; on the other hand, stabilizing collectivities of workers over long periods (over several generations), to "educate" them for work and "bond" them to companies (and also to bring into play the mechanism of correspondence between a "paternalist" political hegemony and a worker "familialism"). ("Class Racism," 212)

125. As Deleuze writes, "Do not the changes in capitalism find an unexpected 'encounter' [*un 'vis à vis' inattendu*] in the slow emergence of a new self as a center of resistance?" (*Foucault*, 115/123).

126. Tronti, *Ouvriers et Capital*, 267–268.

127. Marx and Engels, *The German Ideology*, 51.

128. Ibid., 52

129. Étienne Balibar, "Sur le concept marxiste de la 'division du travail manuel et du travail intellectuel' et la lutte des classes," 97.

130. See Étienne Balibar "Appareil." As Marx so famously wrote with respect to the state, "All revolutions perfected this machine instead of smashing it" (Karl Marx, *The Eighteenth Brumaire of Louis Bonaparte*, 122).

131. "Limites," 463–464.

132. This is Negri's understanding of the central political question in Marx ("Labor in the Constitution," in Hardt and Negri, *Labor of Dionysus*, 76–77).

133. Marx and Engels, *Selected Correspondence*, 129.

134. As Deleuze writes, "In other words, the machines are social before being technical. Or, rather, there is a human technology which exists before a material technology" (*Foucault*, 39/47).

135. Although Marx makes the political distinction between machines and "its employment by capital" in his criticism of the Luddites, this does not preclude the recognition of an immanent relation between technology and the social forces of the mode of production. Rather, it is because the demands of valorization internal to the capitalist mode of production so thoroughly penetrate existing technological developments that the political act of smashing machinery is ineffective (CI 554–555/452).

136. Deleuze and Guattari, *A Thousand Plateaus*, 398/495. This could just be another, perhaps more precise, way of asserting the primacy of relations of production over forces of production.

137. Tronti, *Ouvriers et Capital*, 250.

138. Negri, *Insurgencies*, 262.

139. Tronti, *Ouvriers et Capital*, 255.

140. Étienne Balibar, "From Class Struggle to Classless Struggle?" 162.

141. Ibid., 179.

142. Ibid., 164.

143. Negri, *Marx Beyond Marx*, 56. This statement is expanded in *Insurgencies*: "One must look carefully at this nucleus of living labor, this creative tension that is at the same time political and economic, productive of civil, social and political structures—in a word, constituent. Cooperative living labor produces a social ontology that is constitutive and innovative, a weaving of forms that touch the economic and the political; living labor produces an indistinct mixture of the political and economic that has a creative figure" (33).

144. Balibar, "Plus-value et classes sociales," 179.

145. Ibid., 143.

146. Louis Althusser, *For Marx*, 211. Althusser also stresses this logic of unintended effects in "Le courant souterrain du matérialisme de la rencontre," 587.

147. This displacement of struggles is given a rather striking form by William Morris: "Men fight and lose the battle, and the thing that they fought for comes about in spite of their defeat, and when it comes turns out not to be what they meant, and other men have to fight for what they meant under another name" (cited in Antonio Negri, *The Politics of Subversion: A Manifesto for the Twenty-First Century*, 34).

148. Tronti, *Ouvriers et Capital*, 256.

149. Deleuze and Guattari, *A Thousand Plateaus*, 457/570.

150. Étienne Balibar, "Marx, the Joker in the Pack (or the included Middle)," 21.

151. Lebowitz, *Beyond Capital*, 55.

152. Negri, *Marx Beyond Marx*, 132.

153. This statement is only meant as a provocative suggestion. For a discussion of the planned book on the wage and the conditions and consequences of its absence, see Negri, *Marx Beyond Marx*; Lebowitz, *Beyond Capital*, and Roman Rosdolsky, *The Making of Marx's "Capital."*

154. Negri, *The Politics of Subversion*, 128.

155. See also Eugenii Pashukanis, *Law and Marxism: A General Theory*, on this point.

156. Tronti, *Ouvriers et Capital*, 254.

157. Balibar, "Plus value et classes sociales," 143.

158. Althusser, *Sur la reproduction*, 64.

159. Negri, *The Politics of Subversion*, 136.

160. Ibid., 137.

161. Althusser, *Sur la reproduction*, 236.

162. Negri, *The Politics of Subversion*, 136.

163. Ibid., 129.

164. Tronti, *Ouvriers et Capital*, 254 (translation mine).

165. Étienne Balibar, *La Crainte des masses: Politique et philosophie avant et après Marx*, 30.

CHAPTER THREE

1. Antonio Negri argues that the "tendency" or viewing the present in light of the future, or possible futures, is as important to Marx's understanding of capitalism as the genealogical element: "The tendency: it is not simply what permits a passive construction of the categories on the basis of a sum of historical acquisitions; it is above all what permits a reading of the present in light of the future, in order to make projects to illuminate the future" (*Marx Beyond Marx*, 49). It is important to remember that this examination of tendencies applies not only to Marx's observations regarding such topics as the world market, real subsumption, and the techno-scientific dimension of labor, which for Marx were obviously projections based on tendencies, but also the dominance of the factory system, which at the time of Marx's writing was also a tendency yet to be realized.

2. Jacques Derrida has indicated the complicity between those who would "have the last word" on Marx and the discourse on "the end of history" in *Specters of Marx: The State of Debt, the Work of Mourning, and the New International*.

3. With respect to the matter of the tendency, it is worth noting that one of the most famous definitions Marx gives of communism is "Communism is the real movement which abolishes the present state of things" (Karl Marx and Frederick Engels, *The German Ideology*, 57). Thus for Marx there is an intimate connection between the methodological selection of

the tendency and the political project. Negri's emphasis on the tendency also entails a collective dimension, or as Negri writes, it is a "communism in method." At this point this may seem entirely circular; the selection of the tendency as a methodological criteria would already seem to prefigure the political conclusion—the cards already stacked toward communism. However, I think it is possible to maintain the link between the methodological and political dimension of the tendency without collapsing the two into a circle if one introduces the "social" dimension of labor—the irreducible sociality of living labor—as the linking term.

4. André Gorz, *Critique of Economic Reason*, 22.

5. In the previous chapter I suggested that the wage relation is itself constitutive of both a particular form of subversion (the demand for abstract needs and desires, for any desire whatsoever) and a particular form of subjection, obliterating any palpable distinction between necessary and surplus labor. The relationship between the wage and the production of subjectivity will be returned to in latter sections of this chapter.

6. Barry Hindess and Paul Hirst argue that Marx's description of feudalism as a relation of personal dependence constitutes a lapse in his thought of a mode of production which, as Louis Althusser argues, is necessarily irreducible to intersubjective relations (*Pre-Capitalist Modes of Production*, 228).

7. These suggestions have paved the way for a massive amount of critical literature on "uneven development" and analysis of the world system. Addressing this area of research is far beyond the scope of this book. However, I will return to the matter of the "uneven articulation" of the capitalist mode of production in a later section of this chapter as both a continuation of the examination of the tendencies of socialization and proletarianization, from the previous chapter, and as an element of the existing conjuncture of capitalism.

8. Althusser writes, "This plurality of modes of production in all social formations, the actual dominance of one mode of production over the others . . . makes it possible to fully render the complexity of the contradictory empirical facts observable in all concrete social formations."(*Sur la reproduction*, 43, translation mine).

9. Given the time of his writing Marx often reflects on the relation between capitalism and modes of production that preexist it (such as feudalism). However, there are a few points where Marx considers elements of the future (communist) mode of production to be already at work in capitalism.

10. E. P. Thompson has demonstrated that these two aspects of inertia or resistance, law, and custom, on one side, and the working class, on the other side, are not actually or necessarily separate. Early forms of worker's resistance to capitalism—Luddites and early unions—often referred back to an earlier legal and social order (*The Making of the English Working Class*).

11. At this point it is not clear how science, knowledge, and information fit in Marx's division between constant and variable capital (machinery and labor power) since they are produced by the latter only to become embedded in the former. This point will be returned to in the following sections.

12. Returning to the discussion of Althusser's concept of the 'society effect' and Gilles Deleuze and Félix Guattari's concept of the 'socius,' we can see that an element of real sub-

sumption, of the incorporation of knowledge into the productive apparatus, was already implied in the later concept.

> Machines and agents cling so closely to capital that their very functioning appears to be miraculated by it. Everything seems to be objectively produced by capital as a quasi-cause. As Marx observes, *in the beginning* capitalists are necessarily conscious of the opposition between capital and labor, and of the use of capital as a means of extorting surplus labor. But a perverted, bewitched world quickly comes into being, as capital increasingly plays the role of a recording surface that falls back on all of production. (Furnishing or realizing surplus value is what establishes recording rights.) . . . Capital thus becomes a very mystic being since all of labor's social productive forces appear to be due to capital, rather than labor as such, and seem to issue from the womb of capital itself." (*Anti-Oedipus*, 11/17)

13. "Philosophy," 45.

14. Antonio Negri, *The Politics of Subversion*, 72.

15. Deleuze and Guattari point to this undecidability: "Nothing is more obscure, as soon as one considers the details, than Marx's propositions concerning productive forces and relations of production. The broad outline is clear enough: from tools to machines, the human means of production imply social relations of production, which however are external to these means and are merely their 'index.' But what is the meaning of index?" ("Balance Sheet Program for Desiring Machines," 131; originally published in *L'Anti-Œdipe: Capitalisme et Schizophrénie*, 481). Deleuze and Guattari continue to develop the latter of the two theoretical possibilities mentioned above—technology as indicator of a larger social assemblage—throughout *Anti-Oedipus* and *A Thousand Plateaus*. As Deleuze writes, "It's easy to set up a correspondence between any society and some kind of machine, which isn't to say that their machines determine different kinds of society but that they express the social forms capable of producing them and making use of them" ("Postcript on Control Societies," 180).

16. Claude Lefort "Marx: From One Vision of History to Another," 159.

17. Didier Deleule and François Guéry, *Le corps productif*, 25.

18. As Marx argues, "With Plato, the division of labor within the community develops from the many-sidedness of the needs of individuals, and the one-sidedness of their capabilities" (CI 487/396). It is a precapitalist argument for the division of labor based on use value and skill.

19. It is interesting to note that this image or idea of the machine breaking up the body, and attaching parts of the body to it, can be found in Henry Ford's autobiography. As Mark Seltzer writes,

> The production of the Model T required 7,882 distinct work operations, but, Ford observed, only twelve percent of these tasks—only 949 operations required "strong, able-bodied, and practically physically perfect men." Of the remainder—and this is certainly what Ford saw as the central achievement of his method of production—"we found that 670 could be filled by legless men, 2,637 by one legged men, two by armless men, 715 by one-armed men and ten by blind men." If from one point of view such a fantasy projects a violent dismemberment of the natural body and an emptying out of human agency, from another it projects a transcendence of the natural body and the extension of human agency through the forms of technology that supplement it." ("Serial Killers," 99)

20. Étienne Balibar, "Basic Concepts," 240/474.

21. "[E]very technical machine presupposes flows of a particular type: *flows of code* that are both interior and exterior to the machine, forming the elements of a technology and even a science. It is these flows that find themselves encoded, coded, or overcoded in the precapitalist societies in such a way that they never achieve any independence (the blacksmith, the astronomer). But the decoding of flows in capitalism has freed, deterritorialized, and decoded the flows of code just as it has the others—to such a degree that the automatic machine has always increasingly internalized them in its body or its structure as a field of forces, while depending on a science and a technology, on a so-called intellectual labor distinct from the manual labor of the worker. . . . In this sense, it is not machines that have created capitalism, but capitalism that creates machines"(*Anti-Oedipus,* 233/277).

22. The unique status of this fragment, as well as its odd prophetic resonance with late capitalism, has accounted for its resent popularity in contemporary critical writing. In France and Italy, Paolo Virno, Maurizio Lazzarato, Antonio Negri, and Jean-Marie Vincent have all offered interpretations of this fragment or employed its terminology in their works. In the United States, Moishe Postone and Nick Dyer-Witheford have made the fragment the central theoretical source for their rereading of Marx's critical theory. These works will be considered in the next few pages.

23. The term *general intellect* is in English in the original. It is not unusual for Marx to slip into English or even French for a word or phrase in the *Grundrisse,* usually in relation to a text he is citing. Thus, there is no immediate conceptual significance to the term. However, the term has been adopted by contemporary French and Italian philosophers as the name of the role of knowledge in the contemporary production process—giving it conceptual significance.

24. Moishe Postone argues that Marx's critical theory in the *Grundisse* is based on a radical distinction between value and wealth. Value is measured by labor time, while wealth is the totality of that which can be produced. Thus, it is capital itself that undoes labor as the measure and mediator of wealth by reducing its significance compared with that of knowledge and science in the productive process (*Time, Labor, and Social Domination: A Reinterpretation of Marx's Critical Theory,* 359).

25. Paolo Virno, "Notes on the General Intellect," 267.

26. Ibid., 268.

27. Ibid., 270.

28. Maurizio Lazzarato and Antonio Negri offer the following description of this tension in Marx's writing:

> The process is the following: on the one side, capital reduces labor power to "fixed capital," while subordinating it more and more in the process of production; on the other side, it demonstrates by this total subordination that the fundamental actor of this social process of production has become now "the socialized general intellect" (either under the form of general scientific knowledge or under the form of the "putting into relation" of social activities: cooperation). ("Travail immatériel et subjectivité," 90; translation mine)

29. Michael Hardt and Antonio Negri describe this transformation as follows:

> The factory can no longer be conceived as the paradigmatic site or the concentration of labor and production; laboring processes have moved outside of the factory walls to invest the

entire society. In other words, the apparent decline of the factory as a site of production does not mean a decline of the regime and discipline of factory production, but means rather that it is no longer limited to a particular site in society. It has insinuated itself throughout all forms of social production, spreading like a virus. All of society is now permeated through and through with the regime of the factory, that is, with the rules of specifically capitalist relations of production (*The Labor of Dionysus: A Critique of the State Form*, 9).

30. Antonio Negri, "Marx et le travail: le chemin de la désutopie," 198.

31. As I argued in the previous chapter, antagonism is not a self-identical relation; that is, in capitalism the supposedly direct antagonism between worker and capitalist is continually displaced onto different practices and relations: legal, technological, and social.

32. Negri, "Marx et le travail," 202.

33. Leopoldina Fortunati, *The Arcane of Reproduction: Housework, Prostitution, Labor, and Capital*, 49.

34. Christian Marazzi argues that the rise of service production in real subsumption can perhaps be best understood through the model of housework. In each case the production of things is entirely embedded in the production of a relation (*La place de chaussettes: le tournant linguistique de l'économie et ses conséquences politiques*, 93).

35. Maurizio Lazzarato, "Immaterial Labor," 133.

36. Objections to this argument regarding the dominance of immaterial labor are often satisfied to point out the existence of the coexistence of other forms of labor—from industrial production to peasant-based agricultural production—often existing outside of and alongside the urban centers of immaterial labor (see Lazzarato and Negri, "Travail immatériel et subjectivité," 97). What these arguments perhaps overlook is the real question of the hegemonic articulation of these different forms of production.

37. This overall transformation is often exemplified by the transition from what is called the "fordist" model to the "Toyota" model. In the first, production is both prior to and autonomous from consumption; a set of relatively identical and standardized commodities are produced for a preexistent market. In the second case, there is constant communication between consumption and production; there is a tendency toward low or zero stock, and commodities are produced according to information produced by markets. (see Marazzi, *La place de chaussettes*, 20–22; Michael Hardt, "Affective Labor," 93).

38. Lazzarato, "Immaterial Labor," 143.

39. Michael Hardt and Antonio Negri, *Empire*, 292.

40. Mariarosa Dalla Costa, "Women and the Subversion of Community," 29.

41. Hardt and Negri, *Empire*, 296.

42. Antonella Corsani, Maurizio Lazzarato, and Antonio Negri, *Le Bassin de Travail Immatériel (BTI) dans la Métropole Parisienne*, 65.

43. Maurizio Lazzarato, "Le 'cycle' de la production immatérielle," 114.

44. Lazzarato, "Immaterial Labor," 143.

45. Negri, *The Politics of Subversion*, 90.

46. Antonella Corsani, Maurizio Lazzarato and Antonio Negri, *Le Bassin de Travail Immatériel (BTI) dans la Métropole Parisienne*, 48.

47. Negri, *The Politics of Subversion*, 68.

48. Paolo Virno, "The Ambivalence of Disenchantment," 23.

49. Marazzi, *La place de chaussettes*, 107.

50. Donna Haraway, *Simians, Cyborgs, and Women: The Reinvention of Nature*, 152.

51. Nick Dyer-Witherford offers a comprehensive survey of not only Marx's ambiguous response to machinery, from "Ludditism" to a technological determinism and utopianism, but also how this ambiguity has its effects in the divergent Marxist philosophies of machinery (*Cyber-Marx: Cycles and Circuits of Struggle in High-Technology Capitalism*, 38–61).

52. Georg Lukács, *History and Class Consciousness: Studies in Marxist Dialectics*, 153.

53. Ibid., 100.

54. Hardt and Negri argue that modern political thought (from Machiavelli through Marx to Foucault) has, in different ways, been conceived of as a dialectic between inside and outside. As Hardt and Negri argue, this is no less true of Marx's understanding of class struggle than it is of liberalism's distinction between public and private.

> For Marx, finally, every liberatory initiative, from wage struggles to political revolutions, proposes the independence of use value against the world of exchange value, against the modalities of capitalist development—but that independence exists only within capitalist development itself. In all these cases the critique of modernity is situated *within* the historical evolution of the forms of power, *an inside that searches for an outside*. Even in the most radical and extreme forms of the call for an outside, the inside is still assumed as foundation—albeit sometimes a negative foundation—of the project. (*Empire*, 185)

Without entering into the larger question as to whether this thumbnail sketch of Marx's critical strategy corresponds to my own attempt to present living labor as the artificial, immanent, and irreducible ground for criticism, I think it is important to at least refer here to Hardt and Negri's argument. They argue that this dialectic ends with real subsumption. In real subsumption there is no outside, no nature, use value, or private sphere that could be maintained against capital. Thus even though the ambiguity of the position of subjectivity as fixed capital above would seem to be instructive, it is both inside and outside of capital because these terms have ceased to really mean anything.

55. Paolo Virno, "The Ambivalence of Disenchantment," 23.

56. Ibid., 23.

57. Following remarks made in the previous chapter regarding axiomatics and cynicism, it is possible to at least draw out in broad strokes, elements for a genealogy of cynicism. For Deleuze and Guattari the axiomatics of capital are purely functional without alibi, they do not ask or demand to be believed. As Deleuze and Guattari write with respect to capitalism, "It is no longer the age of cruelty or the age of terror, but the age of cynicism, accompanied by a strange piety. (The two taken together constitute humanism: cynicism is the physical immanence of the social field, and piety is the maintenance of a spiritualized Urstaat; cynicism is capital as the means of extorting surplus labor, but piety is the same as God-capital,

whence all the forces of labor seem to emanate)" (*Anti-Oedipus*, 225). Virno would seem to follow this in arguing that social knowledge and communication become purely functional, stripped from any precapitalist meaning or even the principle of equivalence, then cynicism increases (The Ambivalence of Disenchantment, 24).

58. Hardt and Negri, *Empire*, 54.

59. there is necessarily production, including the production of surplus, in every mode of production.

> If the worker needs to use all his time to produce the necessary means of subsistence for himself and his family, he has no time left in which to perform unpaid labor for other people. Unless labor has attained a certain level of productivity, the worker will have no such free time at his disposal, and without superfluous time there can be no surplus labor, hence no capitalists, as also no slave-owners, no feudal barons, in a word no class of large scale landed proprietors. (CI 647)

60. *Anti-Oedipus*, 259/308.

61. Ibid., 251/298. Another version of this indifference can be found in Brian Massumi's book on Deleuze and Guattari, as Massumi writes: "You can go anywhere your fancy takes you and be anyone you want to be—as long as your credit is good, and you show for work the next day" (*A User's Guide to Capitalism and Schizophrenia: Deviations from Deleuze and Guattari*, 136).

62. Ibid., 257/306.

63. Deleuze and Guattari's later work, *A Thousand Plateaus,* the abstract axiomatics of capitalism are identified with the international or global dimension of capital, and the constitution of specific modes of subjection are identified with the states: "Capitalism arises as a worldwide enterprise of subjectification by constituting an axiomatic of decoded flows. Social subjection, as the correlate of subjectification, appears much more in the axiomatic's models of realization than in the axiomatic itself. It is within the framework of the nation state, or of natural subjectivities, that processes of subjectification and the corresponding subjections are manifested" (458).

64. Thus, as I have already indicated, there is a distinction between real subsumption as a tendency of the capitalist mode of production and actually existing real subsumption as a sociohistorical description of the present. Of course, since the latter is based on the former, the two uses of the term chart the same phenomena. Both cases entail the restructuring of social and technical relations according to the demands of capitalist valorization, a restructuring that entails the privatization of formerly public relations, the disappearance of a noncapitalist outside, and the commodification of all spheres of existence. However, although Marx primarily projected the distinction between formal and real subsumption according to a dialectical transition from quantity to quality, accounts of actually existing real subsumption stress the overdetermined nature of the transformation, one that includes such things as the transition from fordism to post-fordism in production, the breakdown of the gold standard, and the dismantling of the welfare state (see Eric Alliez and Michel Feher, "The Luster of Capital," 322–341; Hardt and Negri, *Empire*, 260–280; Negri, *The Politics of Subversion*).

65. Althusser offers this historicization of his own writing in a letter written in 1976 (an important year in Althusser's intellectual history: It was the year of Althusser's break with the Communist Party) (cited in Mike Gane "On the ISAs Episode," 467).

66. Bill Readings, *The University in Ruins*, 135.

67. I have already made use of the so-called autonomist hypothesis—the argument initially developed by Mario Tronti that workers' resistance precedes and determines the development of capital—in tracing the transition from absolute to relative surplus value and formal to real subsumption in *Capital*. In *Empire* Hardt and Negri apply this argument to the period of historical transformation from 1968 to 1970—the transition from fordism to post-fordism. This transition could also be considered the actual social transition from formal to real subsumption because it is inseparable from the intensive expansion of capital in two new areas of life. Hardt and Negri argue that the various social struggles of the 1960s were in one way or another assaults on the disciplinary regime of labor, the tendency to reduce all labor to abstract labor (*Empire*, 260–280).

68. Althusser's essay and manuscript can be compared to the introductory chapter of Negri's *The Politics of Subversion*. In the former, Althusser somewhat tentatively advances the idea that there may be something like class struggle in the Ideological State Apparatus, referring to the recent struggles against the French university system ("Ideology and Ideological State Apparatuses: Notes Towards an Investigation," 185). The model of struggle is still the factory. Negri argues that in 1985 due to the increased role of immaterial labor, the factory can no longer be taken as model: "In this way the new intellectual subject is established as a principle element of the definition of the proletariat and is shown to be the supporting structure of the critique and revolt of the entire proletariat. If in 1968 the students sought legitimation of their struggle in the workers' organizations and in the factories, *today it is the workers that look to the students*" (*The Politics of Subversion*, 51).

69. See Althusser, *Sur la reproduction*, 20.

70. Although Althusser does not use the term *overdetermination* in the essay on "Ideology," his insistence on the fundamental inseparability of the transmission of skills and knowledge and ideological indoctrination at the heart of the educational ideological state apparatus would at least suggest the concept ("Ideology and Ideological State Apparatuses," 132–133). In *Sur la reproduction* Althusser is more rigorous in expounding not only the overdetermination of the the general function of reproduction but also the overdetermination of the specific ideological apparatuses.

71. Balibar argues that the term *reproduction* is fundamentally equivocal in Marx's texts and many that have come after. Reproduction is at one and the same time a term designating the simple repetition of the basic elements of the economy and a term that indicates the necessary mediation of superstructural instances such as the state. It is ambivalently poised between the very definition of economism and the opposite of economism ("Sur la dialectique historique: quelque remarques critiques à propos de *Lire le Capital*," 235).

72. Fortunati, *The Arcane of Reproduction*, 58.

73. It is on the basis of this naturalistic dimension of Marx's writing, which is perhaps related to the influence of Charles Darwin, that Hannah Arendt argues that he is guilty of reducing politics and political action to a naturalistic conception of necessity (*On Revolution*, 58).

74. Alfred Schmidt, *The Concept of Nature in Marx*, 49.

75. Marx and Engels, *The German Ideology*, 50.

76. Ernest Mandel gives a brief outline of this extension of capitalist relations, stressing that in order for capitalist production to enter into an existing sphere of life it must in some manner displace the existing processes. It must be cheap enough or save enough time to supplant noncapitalist relations (think of something as simple as fast food) or it must actively destroy existing sustenance economies (*Late Capitalism*, 48).

77. The term *naked life* is drawn in part from the work of Giorgio Agamben, who argues that ancient politics was founded on a division between the simple fact of living—bare or naked life—and the form of life proper to an individual or group, in which it was only the latter that concerned politics. In contrast to this, modern politics founds itself on naked life on the simple fact of living. The best example of this is Thomas Hobbes's *Leviathan*, which makes an argument for sovereignty based on the fact that in the "state of nature" we are all equally exposed to death. Thus, unlike ancient politics, which excluded biological life from political decisions, modern politics erects it into a foundation (*Homo Sacer: Sovereign Power and Bare Life*, 35). Despite the fact that Agamben traces his genealogy in relation to sovereignty, it seems to me that Marx's account of the formation of capital, the casting out of the future workers as *vogelfrei*, can be understood as a related account of bare life.

78. Michel Aglietta has argued that the demand to regulate and guarantee the condition of commodities and thus to reproduce the wage relation is met by the state, which thus constitutes an internal condition of capitalist production, rather than fulfilling a superstructural role, as many maintain (*A Theory of Capitalist Regulation: The U.S. Experience*, 32).

79. In the second volume of *Capital* Marx names the aggregate of capitalist enterprises "social capital," the problem of reproduction—social reproduction—can be studied only from the perspective of social capital (*Capital: A Critique of Political Economy, Volume II*, 468). Balibar argues that the connection between reproduction and total social capital means that reproduction is always something more than, or other than, a simple serial repetition of an act. Moreover, Balibar argues that reproduction fundamentally changes the concept of production: "These are therefore the analyses in which Marx shows us the movement of transition (*but this transition is a rupture*, a radical innovation) from a concept of production as an act, the objectivation of one or more subjects, to concept of production without a subject, which in return determines certain classes as its peculiar functions" ("Basic Concepts," 268).

80. A related question to the genesis of the concept of 'biopower' is the relation between biopower and disciplinary power. Since the latter is virtually derived from Marx and the former is absent this question takes on particular importance in terms of the relation between Foucault and Marx. Foucault often explains the relation between the two concepts, which he argues appear at the same time historically, by stating that biopower takes as its object the population, while disciplinary power operates at the level of individuals, and individual comportments. In "*Il Faut Défendre la Société" Cours au Collège de France 1976*, Foucault elaborates on this distinction indicating that since biopower necessarily acts on large entities it is implicated within the history of the state (223). This would seem to explain its absence from Marx and Marxism. Recognizing biopower requires not only an investigation of the state (which Marx never had time to complete) but also a recognition of the extent to which the state exceeds a superstructural role, directly intervening in economic conditions (which is rare in the history of Marxism).

81. Michel Foucault, *The History of Sexuality*, 141,

82. Michel Foucault, "La naissance de la médecine sociale," 214.

83. Ibid., 224. Foucault's argument, which covers a chronological and spatial development of biopower from Germany where it was concerned with the population to France and the concern with the city to England and the concern over the working class, could be shown to have some parallels with Marx's assertions regarding the conditions of the English working class. Foucault, however, begins his essay explicitly criticizing Marx's assertion that political economy is English, politics is French, and philosophy is German: Foucault argues that it was Germany that first developed the science of "governmentality," (or *Staatswissenshaft*) and thus first began to concern itself with the population as an object.

84. Michel Foucault, "Governmentality," 92.

85. Maurizio Lazzarato, "Du biopouvoir à la biopolitique," 48.

86. Althusser, "Ideology and Ideological State Apparatuses," 133. Althusser's manuscript *Sur la reproduction* extends the list of constitutive dimensions to the overdetermined unity of reproduction to include morality and the entire technological division of labor. For Althusser the very idea of a purely technical division of labor, a division based solely on the demands of machinery rather than the overlapping demands of surveillance and control, is one of the constitutive ideological masks of capitalism (62).

87. Althusser, "Ideology and Ideological State Apparatuses," 130.

88. Ibid., 128.

89. Ibid., 136. Balibar has indicated that Althusser's later work tends toward an immanent conception of subjectivity to the mode of production.

> Instead of adding a theory of the "superstructure" to the existing theory of the structure, he aims at transforming the concept of the structure itself by showing that its process of "production" and "reproduction" *originarily* depends on unconscious ideological conditions. As a consequence a social formation is no longer representable in dualistic terms—a thesis that logically should lead us to abandon the image of the "superstructure." Another concept of historical complexity must be elaborated, with opposite sociological, anthropological, and ontological prerequisites." (Etienne Balibar, "The Non-Contemporaneity of Althusser," 8; originally published as "Le non-contemporain," 105).

90. Dalla Costa, "Women and the Subversion of Community," 21; Fortunati, *The Arcane of Reproduction*, 107.

91. Althusser, *Sur la reproduction*, 236 (translation mine). On this point it is necessary to underscore once more the historical context of Althusser's writing. In many ways his understanding of the "internal superstructure" follows Marx's remarks regarding the spontaneous ideology of the wage and labor contract. As Marx writes, "The Roman slave was held by chains; the wage laborer is bound to his owner by invisible threads. The appearance of independence is maintained by a constant change in the person of the individual employer, and by the legal fiction of a contract" (CI 719/599). However, Althusser also ascribes a great deal of importance to the critique of the fiction of a "purely technical division of labor"; that is, the idea that the division and organization of tasks in the labor process follows a purely technical, rather than social and political, function (*Sur la reproduction*, 62). This aspect of Althusser's critique, along with his critique of the surveillance internal to the labor process, would seem to apply to the dense technological and social relations of real subsumption.

92. Deleuze and Guattari use the term *resonance* [*résonance*] to describe the way in which the state overcodes all the different social structures and apparatuses (*A Thousand Plateaus*, 211).

93. Alliez and Feher, "The Luster of Capital," 345.

94. In different ways Althusser, Deleuze, and Guattari insist on this distinction between the generic condition of "subjection/subjectification" as a component of the capitalist production of subjectivity; that is, a general element of individuation and consent opposed to "machinic enslavement, and the specific "ideology" that is actualized within the generic condition.

95. Warren Montag has insisted on this ultimately Spinozist point of the power of the multitude, offering an important corrective to all of those who understand the critique of subjectivity to be tantamount to nihilism ("The Soul Is the Prison of the Body: Althusser and Foucault, 1970–1975," 77).

96. Althusser, *Sur la reproduction*, 229. Michael Hardt has demonstrated how the tension between the unification and dispersion of the different social institutions—the institutions of civil society—has played itself out in the history of writing on civil society. On one side of this history is Antonio Gramsci, who saw in the plurality of institutions the possible material grounds for a contestation of state power, while on the other side is Michel Foucault, who on the contrary understood the plurality of institutions to be undermined by the singular strategy of "statization" ("The Withering Away of Civil Society," 29).

97. Of course as we have seen in the previous section, consumption is also production—it produces new subjectivities, new ways of living. Thus it might be more accurate to indicate a conflict between two different logics of production. Hardt and Negri argue that the various countercultural movements of the 1960s can be understood as the emergence of a new regime of production (Hardt and Negri, *Empire*, 274).

98. Warren Montag, "Beyond Force and Consent: Althusser, Spinoza, Hobbes," 105.

99. "Object," 104/280.

100. Thus as Althusser argues as much as terms such as *survivals, residual, underdevelopment,* and, in this case, *archaisms* function to indicate the complexity of temporal change within any mode or production, they do so against an assumption of an overall direction of progress (ibid., 105/281).

101. Of course I have argued all along that production in Marx cannot be simply limited to the production of things. Here I am referring to Balibar's remarks (cited above) that locate in the concept of reproduction an innovation of the concept of production, a production not of things but of relations. Thus, although I have argued that production for Marx is always the production of relations and subjectivities, there is a historical difference in how production acts on subjectivity and social relations. The detour through reproduction highlights this transformation of the production of social relations from formal to real subsumption.

102. Deleuze, "Postscript on Control Societies," 181.

103. Lazzarato, "Immaterial Labor," 143.

104. Hardt and Negri, *Empire*, 367

105. By definition a "form of life" is one in which bare living cannot be separated from its particular way of being lived, in that what is at stake in a form of life is living itself (Giorgio Agamben, "Form of Life," 151).

106. Althusser, "Ideology and Ideological State Apparatuses," 156.

107. Lazzarato, "Immaterial Labor," 136.

108. Ibid., 135.

109. Here I am following Deleuze in using the term *control* to designate a contemporary mutation in strategies of power. Although discipline worked with spatially demarcated areas—prison, factory, home—control operates in relation to processes that have neither spatial nor temporal limits, monitoring, continuous assessment, and observation (Deleuze, "Postscript on Control Societies," 179).

110. Antonella Corsani, Maurizio Lazzarato, and Antonio Negri, *Le Bassin de Travail Immatériel dans la Métropole Parisienne*, 72.

111. Alliez and Feher, "The Luster of Capital," 349. In Deleuze and Guattari's terms, which Alliez and Feher are drawing from, "It could be said that a small amount of subjectification took us away from machinic enslavement, but a large amount brings us back to it" (*A Thousand Plateaus*, 458).

112. Hardt and Negri, *Empire*, 56.

113. Giorgio Agamben, *The Coming Community*, 80.

114. Negri, *The Politics of Subversion*, 118.

115. Marazzi, *La place de chaussettes*, 55.

CONCLUSION

1. Étienne Balibar, *The Philosophy of Marx*, 121.

2. Karl Marx and Frederick Engels, *The German Ideology*, 57.

3. Antonio Negri, "The Specter's Smile," 12.

4. Fredric Jameson has argued that the question of "organization," of the formation of political structures capable of resisting capital, now takes on a more fundamental dimension because it is no longer a question of what direction or form "the party" should take but of the very form of political organization itself (*Brecht and Method*, 113). A similar idea of a return to "first principles," to the idea of organization at its most basic and even ontological level, underlies Michael Hardt and Antonio Negri's concept of the "multitude" (*Empire*).

BIBLIOGRAPHY

Adorno, Theodor W. *Negative Dialectics.* Translated by E. B. Ashton. New York: Continuum, 1992.

Agamben, Giorgio. *The Coming Community.* Translated by Michael Hardt. Minneapolis: University of Minnesota Press, 1993.

———. "Form of Life," translated by Cesare Casarino. In *Radical Thought in Italy: A Potential Politics,* edited by Paolo Virno and Michael Hardt. Minneapolis: University of Minnesota Press, 1996.

———. *Homor Sacer: Sovereign Power and Bare Life.* Translated by Daniel Heller-Roazen. Stanford, Calif.: Stanford University Press, 1998.

Aglietta, Michel. *A Theory of Capitalist Regulation: The U.S. Experience.* Translated by David Fernbach. London: New Left Books, 1979.

Albiac, Gabriel. "Spinoza/Marx: le sujet construit." In *Architectures de la raison: Mélanges offerts à Alexandre Matheron.* Edited by Pierre-Francois Moreau. Saint Cloud, France: ENS Editions Fontenay, 1996. 11–17.

Alliez, Eric, and Michel Feher. "The Luster of Capital." Translated by Alyson Waters. *Zone* 1 and 2 (1986): 314–359.

Althusser, Louis. *For Marx.* Translated by Ben Brewster. London: New Left, 1969. Originally published as *Pour Marx.* Paris: François Maspero, 1966.

———. "From *Capital* to Marx's Philosophy," in Louis Althusser and Étienne Balibar, *Reading Capital,* translated by Ben Brewster. London: New Left Books, 1970. Originally published as "Du 'Capital' à la philosophie de Marx." In Louis Althusser, Étienne Balibar, Roger Establet, Pierre Macherey, and Jacques Rancière, *Lire le Capital.* Paris: Editions Découverte, 1965.

———. "The Object of *Capital,*" in Louis Althusser and Étienne Balibar, *Reading Capital,* translated by Ben Brewster. London: New Left Books, 1970. Originally published as "L'objet du 'Capital.'" In Louis Althusser and Étienne Balibar, *Lire le Capital.* Paris: Editions Découverte, 1965.

————. "Ideology and Ideological State Apparatuses: Notes Towards an Investigation," translated by Ben Brewster. In *Lenin and Philosophy*. New York: Monthly Review, 1971.

————. "The Crisis of Marxism," translated by Graham Locke. Edited by Patrick Camiller and Jon Rothschid. In *Power and Opposition in Post Revolutionary Societies*. London: Ink Links, 1979. 225–238.

————. "Is It Simple to Be a Marxist in Philosophy?" translated by Graham Locke. In *Philosophy and the Spontaneous Philosophy of the Scientists*. Edited by Grebury Elliot. New York: Verso, 1990. 203–240.

————. "Le courant souterrain du matérialisme de la rencontre." In *Écrits philosophiques et politiques,* vol. 1. Paris: Stock/IMEC, 1994.

————. "Marx dans se limites." In *Écrits philosophiques et politiques,* vol. 1. Paris: Stock/IMEC, 1994.

————. *Sur la reproduction*. Paris: Presses Universitaires de France, 1995.

Althusser, Louis, Étienne Balibar, Roger Establet, Pierre Macherey, and Jacques Rancière. *Lire le Capital*. Paris: Quadridge/Press Universitaires de France, 1996.

Anderson, Perry. *Lineages of the Absolutist State*. New York: Verso, 1974.

Arendt, Hannah. *The Human Condition*. Chicago: University of Chicago Press, 1958.

————. *On Revolution*. New York: Viking, 1963.

Balibar, Étienne. "The Basic Concepts of Historical Materialism," translated by Ben Brewster. In Louis Althusser and Étienne Balibar, *Reading Capital*. London: New Left, 1970. 199–308. Originally published as "Sur les concepts fondamentaux du matérialisme historique." In Louis Althusser, Étienne Balibar, Roger Establet, Pierre Macherey, and Jacques Rancière. *Lire le Capital* , Paris: Editions la Découverte, 1965.

————. "Sur la dialectique historique: quelques remarques critiques à propos de *Lire le Capital*." In *Cinq études du matérialisme historique*. Paris: François Maspero, 1974.

————. "Plus-values et classes sociales: contribution à la critique l'économie politique." In *Cinq études du matérialisme historique*. Paris: François Maspero, 1974.

————. "Appareil." In *Dictionnaire critique du Marxisme*, edited by Georges Labica and Gérard Bensussan. Paris: Presses Universitaires de France, 1982.

————. "Sur le concept marxiste de la 'division du travail manuel et du travail intellectuel' et la lutte de classes." In *L'intellectuel: l'intelligentsia et les manuels*, edited by Jean Belkhir, Paris: Éditions Anthropos, 1983. 97–117.

————. "Marx, the Joker in the Pack (or the Included Middle)," translated by David Watson. *Economy and Society* 14, no. 1 (1985): 1–27.

————. "The Notion of Class Politics in Marx," translated by Dominique Parent Ruccio and Frank R. Annunziato. *Rethinking Marxism* 1, no. 3 (1988): 18–51.

————. "Class Racism," translated by Chris Turner. In Étienne Balibar and Immanuel Wallerstein, *Race, Nation, Class: Ambiguous Identities*. London: Verso, 1991. 204–216.

———. "From Class Struggle to Classless Struggle?" translated by Chris Turner. In Étienne Balibar and Immanuel Wallerstein, *Race, Nation, Class: Ambiguous Identities*. London: Verso, 1991. 153–184.

———. "Foucault and Marx: The Question of Nominalism," translated by Timothy J. Armstrong. In *Michel Foucault: Philosopher*. Edited by Timothy Armstrong. New York: Routledge, 1992. 38–57.

———. "The Non-Contemporaneity of Althusser." In *The Althusserian Legacy*, edited by E. Ann Kaplan and Michael Sprinker. London: Verso, 1993. 1–16. Originally published as "Le non-contemporain." In *Écrits pour Althusser*. Paris: Editions la Découverte. 1991. 91–118.

———. "Althusser's Object," translated by Margaret Cohen and Bruce Robbins. *Social Text* 3 (Summer 1994): 157–188.

———. *Masses, Classes, Ideas: Studies on Politics and Philosophy before and after Marx*. Translated by James Swenson. New York: Routledge, 1994.

———. "The Infinite Contradiction," translated by Jean-Marc Poisson with Jacques Lezra. In *Depositions: Althusser, Balibar, Macherey, and the Labor of Reading. Yale French Studies* 88 (1995): 142–165.

———. *The Philosophy of Marx*. Translated by Chris Turner. New York: Verso, 1995. Originally published as *La philosophie de Marx*. Paris: Éditions la Découverte, 1993.

———. "Structural Causality, Overdetermination, and Antagonism." In *Postmodern Materialism and the Future of Marxist Theory*, edited by Antonio Callari and David F. Ruccio. Hanover, N.H.: Wesleyan, 1996.

———. *La Crainte des masses: Politique et philosophie avant et après Marx*. Paris: Galilée 1997.

———. *Spinoza: From Individuality to Transindividuality*. Rijnsburg, Netherlands: Eburon Delft, 1997.

———. "Conjectures and Conjunctures." *Radical Philosophy* 97 (1999): 31–41.

Barrett, Michèle. *Women's Oppression Today: The Marxist/Feminist Encounter*. New York: Verso, 1988.

Baudrillard, Jean. *The Mirror of Production*. Translated by Mark Poster. St. Louis: Telos, 1975.

Benjamin, Walter. "The Critique of Violence," translated by Edmund Jephcott. In *Reflections: Essays, Aphorisms, Autobiographical Writings*, edited by Peter Demetz. New York: Schocken, 1978. 277–301.

Butler, Judith. "Merely Cultural." *New Left Review* 227 (1998): 33–44.

Butler, Judith, Ernesto Laclau, and Slavoj Žižek. *Contingency, Hegemony, Universality: Contemporary Dialogues on the Left*. New York: Verso, 2000.

Colleti, Lucio. "Bernstein and the Marxism of the Second International," translated by John Merrington and Judith White. In *From Rousseau to Lenin: Studies in Ideology and Society*. New York. Monthly Review, 1972.

Corsani, Antonella, Maurizio Lazzarato, and Antonio Negri. *Le Bassin de Travail Immatériel (BTI) dans la Métropole Parisienne.* Paris: Éditions l'Harmattan, 1996.

Dalla Costa, Mariarosa. "Women and the Subversion of Community." In *The Power of Women and the Subversion of Community.* Bristol, England: Falling Wall, 1972.

De Angelis, Massimo. "Marx and Primitive Accumulation: The Continuous Character of Capital's 'Enclosures.'" *The Commoner* 2 (September 2001).

Deleule, Didier and François Guéry. *Le corps productif.* Paris: Mame. 1973.

Deleuze, Gilles. *Foucault.* Translated by Sean Hand. Minneapolis: University of Minnesota Press, 1988. Originally published as *Foucault.* Paris: Éditions de Minuit, 1986.

———. "Postscript on Control Societies," translated by Martin Joughin. In *Negotiations: 1972–1990.* New York: Columbia, 1995.

———. *Negotiations: 1972–1990.* Translations by Martin Joughin. New York: Columbia, 1995.

———. "Desire and Pleasure," translated by Daniel W. Smith. In *Foucault and His Interlocutors,* edited by Arnold I. Davidson. Chicago: University of Chicago Press, 1997.

Deleuze, Gilles, and Félix Guattari. *Anti-Oedipus: Capitalism and Schizophrenia.* Translated by Robert Hurley, Mark Seem, and Helen R. Lane. Minneapolis: University of Minnesota Press, 1983. Originally published as *l'Anti-Œdipe: Capitalisme et Schizophrénie.* Paris: Éditions de Minuit, 1972.

———. "Balance Sheet Program for Desiring Machines," translated by Mark Seem. *Semiotexte* 2, no. 3 (1977): 117–136. Originally published as *L'Anti-Œdipe: Capitalisme et Schizophrénie.* Paris: Editions de Minuit, 1972.

———. *A Thousand Plateaus.* Translated by Brian Massumi. Minneapolis: University of Minnesota Press, 1987. Originally published as *Mille Plateaux.* Paris: Éditions de Minuit, 1980.

Derrida, Jacques. *Specters of Marx: The State of Debt, the Work of Mourning, and the New International.* Translated by Peggy Kamuf. New York: Routledge, 1994.

Dyer-Witherford, Nick. *Cyber-Marx: Cycles of Struggle in High-Technology Capitalism.* Urbana: University of Chicago Press, 1999.

Engels, Frederick. *The Origin of Family, Private Property, and the State.* New York: Pathfinder, 1972.

Fortunati, Leopoldina. *The Arcane of Reproduction: Housework, Prostitution, Labor, and Capital.* Translated by Hilary Creek. New York: Autonomedia, 1995.

Foucault, Michel. *The Order of Things: An Archaeology of the Human Sciences.* New York: Vintage, 1970.

———. *Discipline and Punish: The Birth of the Prison.* Translated by Alan Sheridan. New York: Vintage, 1977. Originally published as *Surveiller et Punir: Naissance de la prison.* Paris: Éditions Gallimard, 1975.

———. *The History of Sexuality.* Vol. 1, *An Introduction.* Translated by Robert Hurley. New York: Vintage, 1978. Originally published as *Histoire de la sexualité 1: le volonté de savoir.* Paris: Éditions Gallimard, 1976.

———. *Power/Knowledge: Selected Interviews and Other Writings, 1972–1977.* Edited by Colin Gordon. New York: Pantheon, 1980.

———. "The Subject and Power." Afterword to *Michel Foucault: Beyond Structuralism and Hermeneutics,* by Hubert L. Dreyfus and Paul Rabinow. Chicago: University of Chicago Press, 1982.

———. "Governmentality," translated by Colin Gordon. In *The Foucault Effect: Studies in Governmentality.* Edited by Graham Burchell, Colin Gordon, and Peter Miller. Chicago: University of Chicago Press, 1991. 87–105.

———. "Questions of Method," translated by Colin Gordon. In *The Foucault Effect: Studies in Governmentality.* Edited by Graham Burchell, Colin Gordon, and Peter Miller. Chicago: University of Chicago Press, 1991. 73–87.

———. "La vérité et les formes juridiques." In *Dits et Écrits Tome II: 1970–1975.* Edited by Daniel Defert and François Ewald. Paris: Éditions Gallimard, 1994.

———. "La naissance de la médecine sociale." In *Dits et Écrits Tome III: 1976–1979.* Edited by Daniel Defert and François Ewald. Paris: Éditions Gallimard, 1994.

———. "Les mailles du pouvoir." In *Dits et Ecrits Tome IV: 1980–1988.* Edited by Daniel Defert and François Ewald. Paris: Éditions Gallimard, 1994.

———. *"Il Faut Défendre la Société" Cours au Collège de France 1976.* Paris: Éditions Gallimard, 1997.

———. "The Punitive Society." In *The Essential Works of Michel Foucault,* Vol. 1: *Ethics,* edited by P. Rabinow. New York: New Press, 1997. 23–39.

Gane, Mike. "On the ISAs Episode," in *Economy and Society,* 12 (November 4, 1983): 431–467.

Godelier, Maurice. "La notion de 'mode de production asiatique' et les schemas marxistes d'evolution des societes." Paris: Centre d'Études et de Researches Marxistes, 1964.

Gorz, André. *Critique of Economic Reason.* Translated by Gillian Handyside and Chris Turner. New York: Verso, 1988.

Granel, Gérard. "L'ontologie marxiste de 1844 et la question de la 'coupure.'" In *L'endurance de la pensée.* Paris: Plon, 1968.

Guattari, Félix. *Molecular Revolution: Psychiatry and Politics.* Translated by Rosemary Sheed. New York: Penguin, 1984.

———. "Regimes, Pathways, Subjects," translated by Brian Massumi. In *The Guattari Reader,* edited by Gary Genesko. London: Blackwell, 1996. 95–105.

Haraway, Donna J. *Simians, Cyborgs, and Women: The Reinvention of Nature.* New York: Routledge, 1991.

Hardt, Michael. "The Withering Away of Civil Society." In *Deleuze and Guattari: New Mappings in Politics, Philosophy, and Culture,* edited by Eleanor Kaufman and Kevin Jon Heller. Minneapolis: University of Minnesota Press, 1998. 23–39.

———. "Affective Labor." *Boundary 2,* 26 no. 2 (1999). 89–100.

Hardt, Michael, and Antonio Negri. *The Labor of Dionysus: A Critique of the State Form.* Minneapolis: University of Minnesota Press, 1994.

———. *Empire.* Cambridge: Harvard University Press, 2000.

Hartmann, Heidi. "The Unhappy Marriage of Marxism and Feminism: Towards a More Progressive Union." In *Women and Revolution: A Discussion of the Unhappy Marriage of Marxism and Feminism,* edited by Lydia Sargent. Boston: South End Press, 1981. 1–41.

Hegel, G. W. F. *Phenomenology of Spirit.* Translated by A. V. Miller. Oxford: Oxford University Press, 1977.

———. *System of Ethical Life and First Philosophy of Spirit.* Edited and translated by H. S. Harris and T. M. Knox. Albany: State University of New York Press, 1979.

———. *Elements of the Philosophy of Right.* Translated by H. S. Nisbet. Cambridge: Cambridge University Press, 1991.

Henry, Michel. *Marx: A Philosophy of Human Reality.* Translated by Kathleen McLaughlin. Bloomington: Indiana University Press, 1983.

Hindess, Barry, and Paul Hirst. *Pre-Capitalist Modes of Production.* New York: Routledge, 1975.

Jameson, Fredric. *The Political Unconscious: Narrative as a Socially Symbolic Act.* Ithaca: Cornell University Press, 1980.

———. *Late Marxism: Adorno, or the Persistence of the Dialectic.* New York: Verso, 1990.

———. *Postmodernism: Or, the Cultural Logic of Late Capitalism.* Durham, N.C.: Duke University Press, 1991.

———. "Marxism and Dualism in Deleuze." *South Atlantic Quarterly* 96, no. 3 (1997): 393–416.

———. *Brecht and Method.* New York: Verso, 1998.

———. *The Cultural Turn: Selected Writings on the Postmodern.* New York: Verso, 1998.

Keenan, Thomas. *Fables of Responsibility: Aberrations and Predicaments in Ethics and Politics.* Stanford, Calif.: Stanford University Press, 1997.

Laclau, Ernesto, and Chantal Mouffee. *Hegemony and Socialist Strategy: Towards a Radical Democratic Politics.* New York: Verso, 1985.

Lazzarato, Maurizio. "Le 'cycle' de la production immatérielle." *Futur Antérieur* 35–36 (1992): 111–120.

———. "Immaterial Labor," translated by Paul Colilli and Ed Emory. In *Radical Thought in Italy: A Potential Politics,* edited by Michael Hardt and Paolo Virno. Minneapolis: University of Minnesota Press, 1996. 133–147.

———. "Du biopouvoir à la biopolitique." *Multitudes* 1 (2000): 45–57.

Lazzarato, Maurizio, and Antonio Negri. "Travail immatériel et subjectivité." Translated by Giselle Donnard. *Futur Antérieur* 6 (1991): 86–99.

————. "Annexe 2: Du service a la relation de service. Recherche exploratoire." In *Le Bassin de Travail Immatériel (BTI) dans la Métropole Parisienne.* Edited by Antonella Corsani, Maurizio Lazzarato, and Antonio Negri, Paris: Éditions l'Harmattan, 1996. 197–260.

Lebowitz, Michael A. *Beyond Capital: Marx's Political Economy of the Working Class.* New York: St. Martin's, 1992.

Lecourt, Dominique. *The Mediocracy: French Philosophy since the Mid-1970s.* Translated by Gregory Elliot. New York: Verso, 2001

Lefort, Claude. "Marx: From One Vision of History to Another," translated by John B. Thompson. In *The Political Forms of Modern Society: Bureaucracy, Democracy, Totalitarianism,* edited by John B. Thompson. Cambridge: MIT Press, 1992. 139–180.

Lukács, Georg. *History and Class Consciousness: Studies in Marxist Dialectics.* Translated by Rodney Livingstone. Cambridge: MIT Press, 1971.

Mandel, Ernest. *Late Capitalism.* Translated by Joris De Bres. New York: Verso, 1975.

Marazzi, Christian. *La place de chaussettes: le tournant linguistique de l'économie et ses conséquences politiques.* Paris: Editions de l'Éclat, 1997.

Marx, Karl. *The Eighteenth Brumaire of Louis Bonaparte.* New York: International, 1963.

————. *The Poverty of Philosophy.* New York: International, 1963.

————. *The Economic and Philosophic Manuscripts of 1844.* Translated by Dirk Struik. New York: International, 1964. Also published as Karl Marx Friedrich Engels, *Gesamtausgabe Band 2.* Berlin: Dietz Verlag, 1982.

————. *A Contribution to the Critique of Political Economy.* Translated by S. W. Ryasanskaya. New York: International, 1970. Also published as *Zur Kritik der Politishen Ökonomie.* Berlin: Dietz Verlag, 1958.

————. *Critique of Hegel's "Philosophy of Right."* Translated by Annette Jolin and Joseph O'Malley. Cambridge: Cambridge University Press, 1970.

————. *Grundrisse: Foundations of the Critique of Political Economy.* Translated by Martin Nicolaus. New York: Penguin, 1973. Also published as Karl Marx Friedrich Engels, *Werke Band 42.* Berlin: Dietz Verlag, 1988.

————. *Capital: A Critique of Political Economy, Volume I.* Translated by Ben Fowkes. New York: Penguin, 1977. Also published as Karl Marx and Friedrich Engels, *Werke Band 23.* Berlin: Dietz Verlag, 1988.

————. "Results of the Immediate Process of Production." In *Capital: A Critique of Political Economy, Volume I.* Translated by Ben Fowkes. New York: Penguin, 1977. 949–1085. Also published as Karl Marx and Friedrich Engels, *Gesamtausgabe Band 4.* Berlin: Dietz Verlag, 1988.

————. *Capital: A Critique of Political Economy, Volume II.* Translated by David Fernbach. New York: Penguin, 1978.

————. *Capital: A Critique of Political Economy, Volume III.* Translated by David Fernbach. New York: Penguin, 1981.

Marx, Karl, and Frederick Engels. *Selected Correspondence.* Edited by S. W. Ryanzkaya and translated by I. Lasker. Moscow: Progress, 1955.

————. *The German Ideology.* Edited and translated by C. J. Arthur. New York: International, 1970.

Massumi, Brian. *A User's Guide to Capitalism and Schizophrenia: Deviations from Deleuze and Guattari.* Cambridge: MIT Press, 1992.

Montag, Warren. "The Soul Is the Prison of the Body: Althusser and Foucault, 1970–1975." In *Depositions: Althusser, Balibar, Macherey, and the Labor of Reading. Yale French Studies* 88 (1995): 53–77.

————. "Beyond Force and Consent: Althusser, Spinoza, Hobbes." In *Postmodern Materialism and the Future of Marxist Theory,* edited by Antonio Callari and David F. Ruccio. Hanover, N.H.: Wesleyan University Press, 1996.

————. "Althusser's Nominalism: Structure and Singularity (1962–6)." *Rethinking Marxism* 10, no. 3 (Fall 1998): 64–73.

Negri, Antonio. *The Politics of Subversion: A Manifesto for the Twenty-First Century.* Translated by James Newell. Oxford: Polity, 1989.

————. *Marx Beyond Marx: Lessons on the* Grundrisse. Translated by Harry Cleaver, Ryan Cleaver and Maurizio Viano. New York: Autonomedia, 1991.

————. "Marx et le travail: le chemin de la désutopie." *Futur Antérieur* 35–36 (1992): 189–206.

————. "Notes on the Evolution of the Thought of the Later Althusser," translated by Olga Vasile. In *Postmodern Materialism and the Future of Marxist Theory,* edited by Antonio Callari and David F. Ruccio, Hanover, N.H.: Wesleyan University Press, 1996. 51–68.

————. "Twenty Theses on Marx: Interpretation of the Class Situation Today," translated by Michael Hardt. In *Marxism Beyond Marxism,* edited by Saree Makdisi, Cesare Casarino and Rebecca E. Karl. New York: Routledge, 1996. 49–180.

————. *Insurgencies: Constituent Power and the Modern State.* Translated by Maurizia Boscagli. Minneapolis: University of Minnesota Press, 1999.

————. "The Specter's Smile," translated by Patricia Dailey and Costantino Costantini. In *Ghostly Demarcations: A Symposium on Jacques Derrida's Specters of Marx,* edited by Michael Sprinker, New York: Verso, 1999. 5–18.

Pashukanis, Eugenii. *Law and Marxism: A General Theory.* Translated by Christopher Arthur. London: Ink Links, 1978.

Perelman, Michael. *The Invention of Capitalism. Classical Political Economy and the Secret History of Primitive Accumulation.* Durham, N.C.: Duke University Press, 2000.

Postone, Moishe. *Time, Labor, and Social Domination: A Reinterpretation of Marx's Critical Theory.* Cambridge: Cambridge University Press, 1996.

Rancière, Jacques. "The Concept of 'Critique' and the 'Critique of Political Economy': From the Manuscripts of 1844 to Capital," translated by Ben Brewster. In *Ideology,*

Method, and Marx, edited by Ali Rattansi. New York: Routledge, 1989. 74–181. Originally published as "Le concept de critique et la critique de l'économie politique des 'Manusrits de 1844' au 'Capital.'" In Louis Althusser, Étienne Balibar, Roger Establet, Pierre Macherey, and Jacques Rancière, *Lire le Capital.* Paris: Editions Découverte, 1965.

Readings, Bill. *The University in Ruins.* Cambridge, Mass.: Harvard University Press, 1996.

Ricardo, David. *Principles of Political Economy and Taxation.* Amherst, N.Y.: Prometheus Books, 1996.

Rosdolsky, Roman. *The Making of Marx's "Capital."* Translated by Peter Burgess. London: Pluto, 1977.

Rubin, Gayle. "The Traffic in Women: Notes on the 'Political Economy' of Sex." In *Women, Class, and the Feminist Imagination: A Socialist–Feminist Reader,* edited by Karen V. Hansen and Ilene J. Philipson. Philadelphia: Temple University Press, 1990. 74–113.

Sahlins, Marshall. *Culture and Practical Reason.* Chicago: University of Chicago Press, 1976.

Schmidt, Alfred. *The Concept of Nature in Marx.* Translated by Ben Fowkes. London: New Left Books, 1971.

Seltzer, Mark. "Serial Killers (1)." *Differences: A Journal of Feminist Cultural Studies* 5, no. 1 (1993): 92–108.

Sohn-Rethel, Alfred. *Intellectual and Manual Labor: A Critique of Epistemology.* Atlantic Highlands, N. J.: Humanities Press, 1978.

Spivak, Gayatri Chakravorty. "Scattered Speculations on the Question of Value." In *In Other Worlds: Essays in Cultural Politics.* New York: Routledge, 1988.

Sprinker, Michael. *Imaginary Relations: Aesthetics and Ideology in the Theory of Historical Materialism.* New York: Verso, 1987.

Thompson, E. P. *The Making of the English Working Class.* New York: Vintage, 1966.

Tronti, Mario. *Ouvriers et Capital.* Translated by Yann Moulier-Boutang. Paris: Cibles, 1977.

Vincent, Jean-Marie. *Abstract Labor: A Critique.* Translated by Jim Cohen. New York: St. Martin's, 1991.

Virno, Paolo. "The Ambivalence of Disenchantment," translated by Michael Turits. In *Radical Thought in Italy: A Potential Politics,* edited by Michael Hardt and Paolo Virno. Minneapolis: University of Minnesota Press, 1996. 13–36.

———. "Notes on the General Intellect," translated by Cesare Casarino. In *Marxism Beyond Marxism,* edited by Saree Makdisi, Cesare Casarino, and Rebecca E. Karl. New York: Routledge, 1996. 265–273.

Weeks, Kathi. *Constituting Feminist Subjects.* Ithaca, N.Y.: Cornell University Press, 1998.

Wittfogel, Karl. *Oriental Despotism: A Comparative Study of Total Power.* New Haven, Conn.: Yale University Press, 1964.

Young, Iris. "Beyond the Unhappy Marriage: A Critique of the Dual Systems Theory," in *Women and Revolution: A Discussion of the Unhappy Marriage of Marxism and Feminism.* Edited by Lydia Sargent. Boston: South End, 1981. 43–71.

Žižek, Slavoj. *The Sublime Object of Ideology.* New York: Verso, 1989.

INDEX

Absolute Surplus Value, 91, 96, 105, 111

Abstract; As quantity, 76; Materiality of the, 62, 66, 70, 72, 105, 149, 150; subjective activity, 89; subjective potential, 10, 66, 91, 135–136

Abstraction, 23, 62, 64–65; History of, 68. *See also* real abstractions

Abstract labor, 17, 56, 66, 72; Antagonistic dimension of, 80, 150; as alienation, 78; Definition of, 83–4; in Hegel, 67, 76; and disciplinary power, 67, 9, 148; and humanity, 72, 134, 150, 156; and living labor, 80, 90, 97, 181n. 80; as norm, 75, 134, 136; in Ricardo, 66–67, 76; as unconscious presupposition of commodity production, 70, 74; and value, 73, 83, 119

Adorno, Theodor, 167n. 26

Affective labor, 128

Agamben, Giorgio, 150, 180n. 73, 195n. 77, 198n. 105

Aglietta, Michel, 195n. 78

Alienation, 36, 77–78, 154

Alliez, Eric and Michel Feher, 143, 149, 183n. 112

Althusser, Louis, 4, 5, 8, 12, 29–35, 39–42, 49, 53, 74, 85, 101, 112, 133, 137, 141, 142, 145,146, 148, 153, 157, 167n. 28, 167n. 29, 168n. 32, 168n. 39, 170n. 56, 171n. 66, 173n. 83, 173n. 86, 182n. 93, 194n. 68, 194n. 70, 196n. 86, 196n. 91, 197n. 94, 197n. 100. *See also* immanent causality, overdetermination, problematic, and symptomatic reading

Antagonism, 13, 97, 113, 124; Condensation of, 98, 144; Displacement of, 98, 144, 191n. 31; and fixed capital, 132–133;

History of, 158; in Foucault, 89; in Marx, 89, 184n. 11; and real abstractions, 134

Antagonistic: constitution of the capitalist mode of production, 97, 98, 112; logic, 17, 80, 89, 91, 118, 144, 151

Anthropological: Schema of labor, 11, 114, 115, 119, 129, 159; Foundation of classical political economy, 20, 46, 49–50, 130, 173n. 83

Anthropology: Marx's research on, 47; Philosophical, 77, 79

Apparatus (*dispositif*), 87–88, 136, 142, 147

Archaisms, 137, 144–145

Arendt, Hannah, 294n. 73

Asiatic Mode of Production, 38, 40, 55; Critique of, 172n. 70; Despot in, 40, 43, 46, 55, Relation to Capitalism, 43, 144, 154, 157; Reproduction in, 45

Autonomist hypothesis, 13–15, 194n. 67

Autonomist Marxism, 13

Axiom, 70–1, 136, 192n. 57, 193n. 63

Balibar, Etienne, 4, 9, 21, 24, 43–44, 57, 87, 94, 97–98, 106, 154, 163n. 12, 170n. 62, 171n. 67, 175n. 7, 175n. 9, 177n. 36, 183n. 107, 184n. 116, 185n. 121, 185n. 124, 194n. 71, 195n. 79, 196n. 89. *See also* economic, political, and mode of subjection

Base (and superstructure), 4, 56, 101, 142

Belief, 41, 55, 56, 70–1

Benjamin, Walter, 166n. 23

Biopolitical production, 147

Bio-power: and Capitalism, 139–140, 146–147; and disciplinary power, 195n. 80; Foucault's definition of, 140–141, 146; Hardt and Negri's definition of, 146–147

Body: Fragmented by machinery, 119, 189n. 19; Inorganic, 77; as organizing principle of production, 116; Social, 116
Butler, Judith, 3, 174n. 96.

Capitalism: Development of at the time of Marx's writing, 126; Mercantile, 58, 108, 140;Utopian dimension of, 134. *See also* capitalist mode of production
Capitalist mode of production, 31, 41, 66; Cooperation in the, 101; defined as an ensemble of relations, 23; Development of the, 91, 103, 107, 135; Differential temporality of the, 145; Power in the, 85; Presuppositions of, 21, 22, 24–25, 38–39, 61, 66, 82, 105–106; and primitive accumulation, 26, 29; Subjectivity and, 60, 62, 86, 99, 102,123, 149, 153, 156, 159
Capitalist valorization, 135, 149
City: and immaterial labor, 130
Civil Society, 67, 197n. 96
Class, 25–26, 50, 59, 64, 94
Class struggle, 56, 59, 138, 154
Classical political economy, *see* Political Economy
Code, 40, 54–55, 58, 106, 156, 170n. 54, 173n. 92, 190n. 21; differentiated from axiom, 70, 71, 136; and precapitalist modes of production, 174n. 94, 182n. 96.
Collectivity, 143, 144, 154–155
Colletti, Lucio, 177n. 30
Colonization, 27, 106, 133
Commodity, 27, 32, 68, 97; Labor as, 35
Commodity Fetishism, 42–44, 69–70, 74, 168n. 32; as an element of the society effect, 71
Commodity form, 34, 74, 75, 139, 168n. 32
Communism, 79, 155, 187n. 3, 188n. 9
Concrete Labor, 33, 68
Conscious organs (*bewußte Organe)*, 117, 124, 131
Consumption, 49, 70, 122, 123; And production of subjectivity, 148; Productive dimension of, 50, 130
Contingency, 39, 109, 112
Control, 93, 100, 114, 137, 141
Cooperation, 13, 36, 91, 101, 104, 143, 155
Cynicism, 134, 160, 192n. 57

Dalla Costa, Mariarosa, 128, 142
Darstellung (Presentation), 30–33, 122, 167n. 28, 169n. 48

Debord, Guy, 150
Deleuze, Gilles, 88, 90, 146, 185n. 125, 186n. 134, 189n. 15, 198n. 109
Deleuze, Gilles and Félix Guattari, 6, 27–28, 39, 41–42, 53–55, 66, 71, 82, 99, 136, 137, 144, 164n. 17, 170n. 54, 173n. 92, 174n. 94, 178n. 41, 182n. 96, 184n. 117, 188n. 12, 189n. 15, 192n. 57, 193n. 63, 197n. 94, 198n. 111. *See also* axiom, code, and social machine
Derrida, Jacques, 154, 163n. 2, 187n. 2
Deterritorialization, 66, 118, 176n. 18
Dialectic, 30, 58
Differential temporality, 145, 157
Disciplinary power, 85–86, 93, 97, 140
Discipline, 67–68, 95
Distribution, 49–51
Division of labor: and ideology, 94; Sexual, 47–48; Social, 59, 79, 116, 146; Technical, 100, 101, 115, 116, 196n. 86
Division of mental and manual labor, 64, 93, 94, 95, 97, 100, 148
Dyer-Witherford, Nick, 192n. 5

Economism, 29, 37, 50, 160
Economy, 29; as ahistorical, 50, 60; determinate role of 43–44, 106; "Short circuit" of politics and, 87, 106, 107, 141, 183n. 107
Engels, Frederick, 47, 55, 95, 169n. 46
England: Luddites in, 131, 186n. 135; Marx on the struggle over the working day in, 96, 97
Ensemble of social relations, 23–24, 25, 92
Exchange value, 33, 68, 71, 75, 105, 120
Exploitation, 28, 47, 62, 67, 73, 84, 89, 91, 97, 98, 99, 106, 120, 128, 134, 146
Expressive causality, 34, 53, 74

Factory, 84, 88, 122, 141, 159, 191n. 29
Family, 47–48, 73, 128
Feminism, 73; Marxist, 73, 172n. 77, 172n. 78
Feuerbach, Ludwig, 23, 78
Fixed capital, 80, 120; Machinery as, 132; and reification, 132: Subjectivity as, 123–124, 132–133
Forces of production: and relations of production, 52, 114, 173n. 86
Form, 40, 44, 149
Form of life, 62, 81, 134, 147, 198n. 105
Formal Subsumption, 10, 61, 105–109, 133; and the production of subjectivity, 136, 137, 148–149; Transition from, 108, 137, 148
Fortunati, Leopoldina, 73, 126, 142

Foucault, Michel, 2, 6–7, 28, 67, 85–90, 95, 140, 164n. 14, 164n. 16, 166n. 15, 176n. 15, 182n. 96, 182n. 99, 183n. 102, 184n. 116, 184n. 117, 184n. 120, 195n. 80. 196n. 83. *See also* bio-power and disciplinary power
Fourier, Charles, 123, 124
Free-time, 123–124

Gender, 73, 172n. 76
General Intellect, 119–120, 133, 190n. 23; as immeasurable, 121; As real abstraction, 134, 150
Gramsci, Antonio, 3, 33, 197n. 96
Granel, Gérard, 180n. 65

Handicrafts, 115; Anthropological limit of, 116
Haraway, Donna, 131
Hardt, Michael, 197n. 96.
Hardt, Michael and Antonio Negri, 180n. 81, 190n. 29, 192n. 54
Hartmann, Heidi, 73
Hegel, G.W.F., 3, 30, 59, 62, 65–67, 76, 176n. 20, 177n. 22
Henry, Michel, 179n. 59
Hindess, Barry and Hirst, Paul, 188n. 6
History, 5, 19, 21, 75; Capitalist as subject of, 166n. 16; Foucault's philosophy of, 86; Hegel's philosophy of, 47, 63; and genealogy, 57; of ideas, 64; Marx's philosophy of, 6, 8, 25, 56, 86, 113, 158, 161; and nature, 138; Periods in, 26, 113; and the Production of subjectivity, 156, 158; Proletariat as subject of, 24; of technology, 52
Housework, 48, 73, 82, 138, 139, 191n. 34

Ideology, 20–21, 40, 42, 63, 99, 100, 143; and contract, 100, 144; of the market, 182n. 94 Materiality of, 63–64, 94; and power, 83; and production of subjectivity, 148 and reproduction, 137; Spontaneous, 83, 144, 155, 182n. 93; and wage, 99, 156
Immanence, 50, 51, 53, 77, 78; of the production of subjectivity to the mode of production, 56, 90, 135
Immanent Causality, 8–10, 31–32, 60, 88–89, 164n. 14, 167n. 31. *See also* Structural causality
Immaterial labor, 127–139; Communication and, 146, 148, 151; Consumption and, 130, 148
Inorganic nature, 45

Jameson, Fredric, 11, 167n. 26, 176n. 18, 182n. 94, 198n. 4

Kant, Immanuel, 69
Keenan, Thomas, 178n. 46
Knowledge: and machinery, 94, 119, 188n. 11; and production of subjectivity, 146, 147; as productive force, 118, 120, 121; and transformation of labor, 119; Transformation of in the transition from handicrafts to large scale industry, 117, 119

Labor: Anthropological schema of, 11, 114, 115, 119, 122, 124; as concrete essence of humanity,77, 183n. 102; as object of criticism, 76–77; Ontology of, 160 Productive, 125–6, 138; as subject of criticisim, 76–77. *See also* abstract labor, concrete labor, immaterial labor, and living labor
Labor power, 67, 71; Collective, 92, 97, 149
Laclau, Ernesto, 3; and Chantal Mouffe, 168n. 41
Lazzarato, Maurizio, 61, 127, 146, 148, 190n. 28
Lebowitz, Michael, 181n. 88
Lefort, Claude, 37, 57, 116
Lifestyle, 2, 127, 131
Living Labor, 17, 76; and abstract labor, 77, 79, 80, 90, 97, 181n. 80; as critical strategy, 77, 155; Definition of, 80–82, 91; mystification of, 110, 132; Political problem of, 84; In real subsumption, 120–122, 132, 146; and subjectivity, 79, 90, 144; Rhetorical meaning of, 80; Transformation of, 113, 117
Lukács, Georg, 132, 148, 168n. 168, 179n. 57

Machinery, 114, 121; and abstract labor, 95; De-skilling of labor and, 94–95, 119, 129, effects of on the anthropological schema of labor, 115–117; Political aspects of, 131–132; Surveillance and, 100, 114
Mandel, Ernest, 195n. 76
Manufacture, 93, 94, 116
Marazzi, Christian, 191n. 34, 191n. 37
Marx, Karl, 3, 5–7,37–38,41, 61; critique of "so-called primitive accumulation," 20–22, 144 on cooperation, 13, 91; and determinism, 184n. 120; on hoarding, 22, 54; on the basic schema of labor, 114; on power, 84–85, 86–7, 103, 105; redefinition of materialism, 78–79; theory of primitive accumulation, 16, 22–29; "1857 Introduction," 30–31, 48–51, 64–68, 122;

Marx, Karl (cont.),Capital: Volume I, 20, 29, 32–33, 34–35,42, 68–72, 73, 83, 91, 92, 97, 103, 111, 114–115, 119, 137, 138, 158, 186n. 135; Capital: Volume II, 195n. 79; The Communist Manifesto, 10, 56, 73, 118, 158; A Contribution to the Critique of Political Economy, 33, 48; Critique of Hegel's 'Philosophy of Right, 63; The Economic and Philosophical Manuscripts of 1844, 74, 79, 123–4, 165n. 10, The Eighteenth Brumaire of Louis Bonaparte, 165n. 4; "Fragment on Machines," 118, 122, 190n. 22; Grundrisse, 24, 29, 37–38, 48–49, 76, 77, 79, 88, 89, 106, 110, 120, 123–4, 138; The Poverty of Philosophy, 170n. 56; "Pre-Capitalist Economic Formations," 16–17, 37–43, 55, 102, 135, 158; "Results of the Immediate Process of Production," 103–110, 145, 179n. 58; Theses on Feuerbach, 3–4, 23, 79
Marx, Karl and Engels, Frederick: The German Ideology, 5, 42, 46, 55, 63–64, 89, 93–4, 118, 138, 154
Marxism, 3, 6, 33, 46, 113, 164n. 17, 195n. 80; as dogmatic, 158; Polemics in, 52, 169n. 46
Mass intellectuality, 103, 146
Massumi, Brian, 193n. 61
Materialism, 10, Marx's redefinition of, 79
Materiality: and effectivity, 175n. 4; of ideology, 63–64, 94; of power, 86, 107; of social relations, 160
May 1968, 137
Mode of Production: 3–6, 20, 37, 40–41, 84, 95; and apparatus (dispositif), 87; Expansive sense of, 88, 117; Feudal, 24, 58, 81, 86, 106, 126; Limited sense of, 88, 115; and power, 86, 87; Precapitalist, 57, 60, 62, 116, 135; Presuppositions of, 21, 40–41, 57, 61; and the production of subjectivity, 55, 135. See also capitalist mode of production
Mode of subjection, 10, 90, 101, 136, 146
Modernity, 134, 145, 157
Money, 38–39, 58, 71, 99; As real abstraction, 134; as simultaneously abstract and material, 70
Montag, Warren, 167n. 31, 185n. 120, 197n. 95
Morris, William, 186n. 147
Mystification, 43, 108–9; immanent to the capitalist mode of production, 113, 132, 157

Need, 46, 80, 90, 99; Creation of new, 48, 81, 82, 123–124; and economy, 49–50
Negri, Antonio, 13, 19, 28, 36, 57–59, 61, 81, 88, 97, 100, 113, 122, 151, 159, 169n. 48, 172n. 80, 181n. 88, 186n. 143, 187n. 1, 194n. 68. See also antagonism, autonomist hypothesis, and multitude

Overdetermination, 88, 141, 146, 194n. 70, 196n. 86

Perelman, Michael, 169n. 43
Plato, 117
Political Economy, 19–20, 49–51, 62, 64–65,66, 77, 87
Political imaginary, 160
Political: Organization of the,160, 198n. 4; "Short-circuit" of the economic and the, 87, 107, 141, 183n. 107
Population, 64–65, 140
Post-Marxism, 3, 28
Postone, Moishe, 76, 178n. 44, 190n. 24
Post-structuralism, 6, 8, 164n. 17
Primitive Accumulation, 16, 22–29, 40, 58, 84, 121, 139; Social, 128
Problematic, 5, 33–34, 37–38, 74, 138, 140, 155
Production, 2; Cultural, 125–7; Deleuze and Guattari on, 53–54; Foucault on, 85–86,164n. 16; in classical political economy, 49; in pre-capitalist modes of production, 46; Ontology of, 55, 60, 77, 122, 130, 159, 196n. 89; of production, 51, 74,125; Relation of consumption and, 50–52, 82, 143; of social relations, 110, 126. See also mode of production, production of subjectivity
Production of subjectivity, 7, 36; and commodity production, 72; in the capitalist mode of production, 60, 62, 86, 99, 102,123, 149, 153, 156, 159; as fixed capital, 123–124, 145; in Foucault, 89; and history, 58; and ideology, 54; of labor, 75; and material production, 89, 115; and the mode of production, 36, 54, 62, 107, 135
Proletarianization, 92–93, 97, 118, 128, 145, 184n. 114

Rancière, Jacques, 180n. 70
Readings, Bill, 137
Real abstractions, 65, 149; Definition of, 175n. 10; of formal subsumption, 134, 136, 150; of real subsumption, 134
Real subsumption, 10, 18, 102, 104, 107, 112; Actually existing, 126, 193n. 64; Contradiction of, 118, 151; and relative surplus value, 111; and subjectivity, 124, 137,

148; as transformation of social relations, 129, 147

Reification, 41, 132

Relations of production, 115

Relative surplus value, 96, 111, 139

Representation: of the capitalist mode of production, 30–31, 167n. 26, 167n. 28; of the difference between capitalism and precapitalism, 55

Reproduction, 39; of biological existence, 47, 55, 81, 137–138, 140; and biopower, 141; Concept of, 138, 194n. 71, 195n. 79; and formal subsumption, 136, 142; of a mode of production 41, 135, 141; in precapitalist modes of production, 45–48, 123, 135, 139; and production, 58, 81, 128, 196n. 89, 197n. 101; of relations of production, 54; and self-valorization, 82

Reserve army of labor, 139

Reterritorialization, 71, 82

Ricardo, David, 63, 66–67, 76

Rubin, Gayle, 172n. 76, 181n. 87

Self-valorization, 80–82, 83

Service, 125–126

Smith, Adam 63, 65

Social factory, 122, 159

Social formation, 57, 108

Sociality, 80, 92, 121; of cooperation, 122, 143; and ideology, 143

Social machine, 54, 95–96

Social relations, 20, 52; and mode of production, 55, 106, 108, 110–112; Productive force of, 121; and real subsumption, 113, 114

Socialization, 93, 101, 118–119, 128, 145, 184n. 114

Society; anthropomorphic presentation of, 50

Society effect (l'effet de societè), 41–45, 55, 71, 104, 110, 142, 144, 160, 170n. 56, 188n. 12

Socius, see society effect

Sohn-Rethel, Alfred, 70, 175n. 10

Species-being (Gattungswesen), 59, 78, 92, 180n. 69

Specifically capitalist mode of production, See real subsumption

Spivak, Gayatri, 180n. 62

Stalin, 33, 168n. 33

State, 140; Marx's critique of the, 94

Structuralism, 90, 98, 163n. 12, 167n. 26

Structural Causality, 31, 44, 55. See also immanent causality

Subjection, 15, 64, 89, 90, 99, 104, 106, 143, 156; Social, 99

Subjectification, 15, 138, 142–143, 156

Subjectivity, 2, 41, 50; in the Asiatic mode of production, 59; Biological basis of, 74, 137, 148; and class, 59; in Foucault, 89–90; in Marx, 89–90; materiality of, 10, 20, 79; in Post-structuralism, 7; Primitive accumulation and, 36; and reproduction of relations of production, 41; and social relations, 25; Worker, 101. See also mode of subjection, production of subjectivity, subjection, subjectification

Surplus value, 33, 63, 80, 83, 93, 95, 106, 111, 145. See also absolute and relative surplus value

Symptomatic reading, 12–14, 32, 76, 85, 91

Technology: in capitalism, 96, 117, 118; History of, 52, 95, 97, 115, 129; politics of, 94, 114, 118, 131–132

Thompson, E.P., 188n. 10

Transversal, 86, 95

Tronti, Mario, 13, 65–68, 77, 97, 98, 101, 176n. 20

Use value, 33, 46–47, 68, 116, 135

Utopia, 79, 160

Value, 122; and abstract labor, 71, 73; Cartographies of, 131; Labor theory of, 62, 66, 69; as measure, 120, 131

Violence, 24, 27–28, 84, 153

Virno, Paolo, 103, 120, 131, 133

Virtuoso, 119

Wage, 81, 82, 99, 121, 139, 150, 181n. 88, 188n. 5

Wage labor, 73, 82, 150

Wealth, 32, 48, 56, 62, 66

Workers, 21, 81; Temporary, 149

Working Class, 36, 80, 97, 99, 140, 180n. 81; Of immaterial labor, 161

Working day, 105, 112; As constraint to capital, 111; Struggle over, 96–98, 112

Žižek, Slavoj, 173n. 85